DUST OF A DISTANT MESA

ONE BOY'S YEARLONG UNEXPECTED PATH TO
BRAVERY

DALE B. SIMS

ILLUMIFY MEDIA GLOBAL
Littleton, Colorado

Published by
Illumify Media Global
www.IllumifyMedia.com
"Write. Publish. Market. *SELL!*"

Library of Congress Control Number: 2020902659

Paperback ISBN: 978-1-949021-94-3
eBook ISBN: 978-1-949021-95-0

Cover design by Debbie Lewis

Printed in the United States of America

CONTENTS

CONTENTS

To the wonderful people of the Navajo and Pueblo Nations, who saved my life and set my feet on a path that was different from the one my family had trod

And to my lovely wife, Debbie, whose unconditional love for her unusual and unkempt husband allowed him to follow that path

This book is a memoir of the time my family spent in New Mexico from the fall of 1962 to the fall of 1963. According to the *American Heritage Dictionary, Second College Edition,* one definition of memoir is "An account of the personal experiences of an author." I have told the story in the way that I remembered it. My mother told me recently that she doesn't remember much about that time, but she was certainly glad to leave New Mexico. My dad's health is very poor these days. I suspect that he does not have long to live. I am not sure what he remembers or what he would admit to remembering. My brothers were under the age of five, so they have no memory of that time. My sister, who would have clearly remembered many of those things, died in 2000. Although I was only seven and eight at the time I clearly remember the events. They are forever burned into my memory.

I did not go back to New Mexico to research the book or try to connect with anyone mentioned in the book. In all of those years between then and now I have not kept contact with any of those people.

Yet there are some things which I cannot remember. The names I couldn't remember I made up.

I think it is important to remember that this happened a long time ago in another place and time.

Dale B. Sims

Grand Prairie, Texas

ONE

LOOKING BACK

LATE NOVEMBER 2019

I t usually happens when I am out hunting. I am walking through areas of brush and trees. I am camouflaged, wearing good boots and a broad-brimmed hat on my head. I have my pack on my back and my rifle slung over my shoulder. I walk silently through the leaf- and twig-strewn ground among the trees. I walk a few feet before stopping to look around. The air is fresh and the sky is clear. I can smell trees and grass and dirt and rotting leaves. I slowly swivel my head to the right and then to the left before taking a few more steps. I watch the ground, making sure that I don't step on a twig or shuffle my feet through a pile of leaves. Then I hear his voice. It is soft and has the strange cadence of the Navajo and Pueblo. It always comes from behind me and to the right for some reason.

"What do you see when you look down, Young White?" the silent voice asks.

Looking down I see deer tracks impressed on the bare ground.

"How old are they? Are they made by a buck or a doe?" asks my silent friend.

1

I kneel and study the tracks. The imprint of the dew claws is deep and the front hoof is splayed. It is not from an animal that was running. The sides have weathered a little bit, but not much. It looks like a big buck came walking by here in the last day or so. I look around, slowly moving my head from side to side to take in my surroundings.

The voice comes from a very distant past and place. It carries over the years and I am glad for the company of the spirit that speaks to me. "See that log over there? Sit on that log and wait. You will see the buck soon enough. This is a regular path for him. Be patient, Young White."

I go over to the log and sit down. It is good to rest after walking for a couple of hours. I cautiously lean my rifle against the log and quietly slip off my pack. I lift my water bottle and take a drink. My log seat is about fifteen yards inside the tree line. In front of me is a small field. I sit quietly and listen to the wind rattle the tree branches. I hear the small birds chirping to each other and flitting from one bush to another. The sun is directly behind me making the shadows of the trees lengthen, and stripe the field. The sun feels good on my back as I doze off for a few minutes.

It is during times like these that I feel the presence of my friend even though he has been gone for decades. As I have done many times in the past I thank God for my friend. An old hymn, "Man of Sorrows," comes to mind. Surely God understood my friend because he was also a man full of sorrow. All he wanted was peace.

I hear the voice again. "What do you see, Young White?"

I look out over the field and see movement. It is a young buck, large but not yet in his prime. I slowly reach for my rifle.

"Do you need the meat from this buck?"

I had shot a doe earlier in the day and the carcass had already been field dressed.

"Do you need his hide?"

I study the beast in the field and watch his muscles ripple as he walks along browsing on the grass.

"Are his antlers bigger than those already on the wall at your house?"

I shrug and continue to watch the buck as he feeds on the grass in the field. I know why these questions are asked. I first heard them, or questions very like them, when I was just a boy.

I hear a soft grunt. Did that come from the imagined spirit beside me or from the buck?

"Just watch him and learn by the watching," the voice says, ending our silent conversation. My friend always tried to teach me. I was a stupid student, slow to understand. Then again, I was very young in those far-off years in the middle of the last century.

I sit for an hour watching the field. The buck is joined by several does. They are grazing in peace, and I rejoice in their easy grace. They take turns lifting their heads to scan their surroundings with sight and scent. The shadows lengthen. The air grows noticeably cooler. For a while I can still see the deer moving in the field, but just barely. Finally, the dark swallows their forms and it is time for me to return to camp by the light from my flashlight. There will be fire and food at the camp. My fellow hunters will be there and we will tell stories about our adventures.

Life itself is an adventure. As we travel that path we learn about friendship, faith, bravery, redemption, and death. People come into our lives and leave their mark on us. Some marks create scars. Some marks are so subtle that they can only be seen through introspection and reflection. Every mark is important and there for a purpose.

I think it is time for me to tell this story about a friend. The events of this story happened over half a century ago, but they refuse to vacate my memories. I have hesitated to tell the story. Are my memories clear and true? I think so. . . I hope so. Time and experience color our memories. The edges become fuzzy and our mind glosses over some things and sharpens others. It is not always clear what is true and what is simply wishful. The events of that story from long ago were part of the forces that shaped me into the man that I became. The one-way linearity of time prevents me from physically going back. Still, in my mind I can visit that distant place, and now I am inviting others to visit as well. Remember that it happened long ago.

TWO

MOVING TO NAVAJO COUNTRY

LATE AUGUST 1962

I was listening to my second grade teacher as she explained about verbs and nouns. I knew how to read before I left kindergarten. In the first grade I had read two books all by myself. Even though I intuitively knew some things about language, the information regarding verbs and nouns was new and interesting.

"A proper noun, such as someone's name or the name of a planet, will always be capitalized," she patiently explained as she wrote some examples on the chalkboard.

Suddenly the door to the room opened, and a woman, whom I recognized as someone who worked in the school office, walked in. She marched over to my teacher and whispered something in her ear. She showed her a paper and their heads bowed together as they read it. My teacher nodded and the other lady went to stand over by the door.

"This will only take a minute, class," my teacher told us. She turned to a boy in the third row. "Allen, please collect all of your personal things from inside your desk, leave your books, and follow Mrs. Wilhite."

Allen stared around at all of us with his mouth open. He looked surprised and shocked. Quietly he gathered all of his papers and rulers and pencils and erasers from his desk. He awkwardly held them in his arms and dutifully walked out the door following Mrs. Wilhite. As the door slammed behind them the sound and reverberation made us jump in our seats. Our teacher sighed and then mustered a slight smile as she turned to face us.

"I know that you are all wondering about this. Let me see if I can explain it in a way that you can understand." She crossed her arms over her breasts and tapped her foot a few times while she stared up at the ceiling. "Allen didn't do well in his studies in the first grade," she told us slowly. "His mother and father requested that he be sent back to first grade so that he could completely understand some things. This happens sometimes. It is not a bad thing. It is a helpful thing and I think that Allen will do quite well in first grade this time around."

I raised my hand and my teacher caught the movement out of the corner of her eye as she turned back to write on the board. "Yes, Dale. Do you have a question?"

"I was just wondering if they can really do that. Doesn't Allen get a choice? How do they know he didn't learn all of the things?"

The teacher smiled in a condescending manner and pointed her finger at me. "His parents made the decision and that is all there is to it. Do you understand?"

I nodded and bent my head so that she couldn't see my eyes. It scared me that someone else could decide just how smart you were. I had found first grade to be a big bore and I certainly didn't want to go back there. I made up my mind to try just as hard as I could to stay in second grade. I determined that I was never going to go back to first grade.

Two days later I was writing down some figures on a math worksheet when the classroom door opened and in walked Mrs. Wilhite. Every eye followed her as she made her way to the front of the room. She whispered something to my teacher that I strained to hear. My teacher nodded her head and then looked directly at me! They whispered a few more words among themselves before Mrs. Wilhite went to stand by the classroom door.

"Dale," my teacher's voice rang out clear in the silent room. "Gather all of your personal things from your desk. Leave your books, please. When you have everything, please follow Mrs. Wilhite."

I was shocked. It didn't seem fair. I looked around the room at the faces of all of my classmates. Some quickly bent their heads to look at their desktop. Others had a smirk on their face, and I could tell that they were glad something was happening to me and not to them. I quickly gathered up my Big Chief writing tablet, pencils, erasers, and other small items. I felt numb all over, but I forced my feet to walk over to Mrs. Wilhite and follow her out the door. Out in the hallway she slowed down a bit to walk beside me. She placed her hand on my shoulder and smiled, which I found to be quite comforting. When we got to the door of the office she opened it for me and ushered me inside. I looked around and to my surprise I saw my mother talking with the principal. I could tell that they were just finishing their conversation. Mom turned and smiled at me. The principal kind of gave me a wave.

"I am glad that you were one of our students, Dale," he said warmly. "I am sure that you will do well in your next school."

Mom came over and took my hand to lead me outside. I was very confused. Why did the principal say something about a new school? Why was Mom at the school to pick me up? My mother did not drive, but occasionally she would persuade a neighbor to take her places. I expected to see one of the neighbors outside, but I received another shock. My dad was leaning against the family car waiting for us. The car was pulled up right in front of the school and behind it was attached a U-Haul trailer. As I got closer I saw that my sister and two brothers were also in the car. Mom took my school things and carefully stacked them on the floor between her feet.

"What's going on?" I asked. "Where are we going?"

Dad opened the back door. "Get in and shut up," he growled. He thumped my head hard and gave me a rough shove with his large hand.

I slid into the back seat rubbing my head and pushing my sister and two brothers toward the other side of the large seat. Dad walked around to his side and started up the car, cautiously pulling away from the curb. He kept looking anxiously in the rearview mirror. He muttered to himself and Mom put a soothing hand on his arm. Soon I noticed that we were not following the usual route to our house.

"Where are we going?" I asked. "This doesn't seem to be the way to the house."

Dad looked at me in the mirror with squinted eyes. Mom turned around and smiled at me. "We are going on a trip, kind of an adventure. When we get out of town we will stop for just a few minutes and your dad will tell you more about it."

It seemed to me that we were driving toward the edge of town. The houses thinned out, and soon we only saw farms and open country. As we got farther and farther from the city Dad began to relax. I could see his shoulders lose their hunched up look and when I looked at his eyes in the mirror I noticed that they had stopped their constant roaming. Now he just concentrated on driving us down the road. Whatever he was worried about or expected to see never materialized.

We drove for hours. The steady hum of the road and the heat of the day caused all of us in the back seat to fall asleep. I dreamed about how I had seen my dad baptized by my uncle, the Baptist pastor. I dreamed about how Dad moved us to Texas so he could attend seminary and study to be a preacher himself. I dreamed about hearing the Sunday sermon last year when the preacher's words made so much sense to me. I had listened closely and then made my own decision to allow God to direct the path of my life. A few Sundays later I was baptized. When I came up out of the water it was as if I could hear all of heaven singing. A great peace had come over me. Sometimes my mother would bend down to look me in the eye.

"I see in your eyes the peace that passes all understanding," she would say with a smile. She was a true Christian who wore her joy for all to see. She was a good woman and to me she was a saint. Life was good in my dreams and I wanted to stay there in dreamland.

The car began to slow down and the change in speed woke me up. I looked out the window. It was getting dark outside. We were stopping at a gas station. Dad opened his door and bounced out in order to gas up the car. Mom got out and walked around to the other side to get my youngest brother, Paul. He was only two and still enjoyed having Mom hold him.

"Everyone out for a potty stop," she said in a cheery voice. I opened the door and looked around to see if I could figure out where we were. My sister, Linda, yawned beside me as she jostled our brother, Roger, to get him to wake up. I was seven, Linda was five and a half, and Roger was four. As I looked around I noticed that the landscape was mostly sand and brush. The stars were just starting to become visible as the sun was settling in the west.

Dad's rough hand grabbed the back of my neck and jerked me out of the car. "Get out of the car and go to the bathroom. What are you waiting for?" he asked in a vexed voice. "Take your brother with you. Don't take too long."

I held Roger's hand and together we stumbled to the bathroom. It stunk, and Roger said as much in a whining voice. He had red hair and blue eyes. My hair wasn't quite as red, and my eyes were a bluish green color. Our faces were spotted with a myriad of freckles that seemed to be the mark of our clan. Dad pointed out to me many times that I was my brother's keeper, directly responsible for making sure that Roger and Paul were safe and well-behaved. When he finished his business I helped Roger pull up his pants and get them buttoned and zipped up. While he stood and whined about the stench in the bathroom I relieved myself.

We washed our hands and quickly ran out into the clean outdoor air.

Next to the gas station was an old wooden picnic table with benches. Dad had pulled the car over and parked it by the table. He was standing, smoking a cigarette and staring out at the setting sun. Mom and Linda were at the table working on something. Mom looked around and saw us walking toward her. She waved us over and turned around again to help Linda. They were pulling sandwiches and fruit out of a paper grocery bag. Roger and I plunked ourselves down on a bench next to Paul who was busy trying to reach a bug that was in the middle of the table. He looked at me and pointed to the table top.

"Bug," he said loudly. "Want bug," he piped in his high-pitched baby voice.

I reached out and grabbed it before it could crawl away. Turning to Paul, I opened my hand and showed it to him. Quick as a monkey he grabbed it, and before I could stop him he shoved it into his mouth. I heard the crunch of the bug's shell as Paul crushed it with his teeth.

"Paul ate a bug," Roger said loudly. He pointed and laughed. Linda made a face and turned her back as if she couldn't bear to watch.

Mom turned quickly and grabbed Paul by his lower jaw. She pulled his mouth open.

"Spit it out right now!" she commanded. She swept her finger through his mouth, but it came out empty. "Where is that bug?" she demanded.

Paul grinned up at her. "I eat bug," he said with pride as if he had accomplished something good.

Dad had walked over when he heard Mom's voice. "Where did he get that bug?" he asked.

"Dale gave it to him," Roger said happily. I started to protest, but before I could say anything Dad grabbed my arm and pulled me off the bench. Keeping hold of my arm he leaned down and put his face right in front of mine.

"You are the oldest," he hissed at me. I could smell his smoker's breath. "How many times do I have to tell you that you must watch over your brothers and sister?" He spun me around and struck my bottom four or five times with his hand. It hurt, but I was used to his spankings, and I knew better than to cry out. That would just make him pour it on even more. My tears were more from righteous indignation than from physical pain. I was punished without anyone hearing my side of the story. It was unjust.

He released my arm and shoved me back to the table. "Sit there, and stay out of trouble," he commanded. Mom stroked his arm and whispered something in his ear. Together they walked a little way from the table and began to talk softly. I know they didn't want us kids to hear what they were saying, but I had really good hearing, and I heard it all.

Mom, whispering: "You act like you are worried about something."

Dad, speaking in a low voice and looking back down the road we had been traveling on: "Those men may come after us. We only have enough money to make this trip and start over. If those guys show up I don't know what we will do. I don't know how we can pay them and then have enough money to live on."

Mom, stroking Dad's hair: "The rent and all of the bills are due on the first of the month. That is ten days away. They won't start looking until a few days after that." Dad nodded, and they kissed. "The principal assumed that we were moving back to Kansas, and I didn't tell him any different." Dad nodded again. "Why don't we go over to the table and eat a little bit? Then you can tell the kids where we are going."

They held hands and walked back to the table. I could see that some of the tension was gone from Dad. I was shocked, but I tried not to show it. Mom began to serve out the sandwiches and fruit. She had a large plastic jug that held water which she poured in plastic cups and handed around to us. We hungrily munched on our food while we looked at the surrounding landscape. Finally Dad broke the silence.

"We are moving to New Mexico," he declared. He spoke as if he were addressing an army about to march on the enemy. He stared out into the desert while he spoke to us. "I decided to go there to help an old missionary couple who work on a Navajo Indian reservation. They have worked there a long time, and now that they are old they can't do everything they want to do."

"What kind of things will you help them with?" I asked. Dad turned and glowered at me, which made me cringe. Then his look softened, and he gave out a loud sigh.

"I know that they are having trouble with an old well pump. I suppose I will help with that and other things like that. Sometimes I will preach. Most of those Indians are still just savages, and they need God." He looked off into the distance and took another bite of his sandwich. "I have found a small apartment that we can afford, and that is where we will live," Dad said almost as an afterthought, seemingly without reference to anything else he had just been speaking about.

Mom was wiping Paul's face after he had spilled things all down the front of his shirt. He was happily oblivious to the mess he had made. She turned with the wash rag in her hand to speak to Dad.

"Where is this apartment exactly?" she asked, as if this was news to her as well as to us.

Dad took another bite of his sandwich before answering. "It's in a village right on the edge of the reservation."

"Oh," Mom said in a little voice. There were a lot of unspoken things behind that "Oh." I heard some disappointment and perhaps a little fear. Maybe Dad didn't hear it because he just kept eating his sandwich and looking off into the distance. It sounded to me as if they had not talked things out between themselves.

"What else did you arrange when you made the trip out there last month?" she asked.

I knew Dad had been away from the house for a few days, but I didn't know where he had gone. Another question was answered, another mystery solved.

Dad nodded. "I got a job working for the Johnson sawmill. I will work during the day with the logs that they bring down from the mountain. I can work some nights as a guard to make extra money. Occasionally a bear or a wolf will come down out of the mountains and roam around the mill yard. I'll have to get a gun to make some noise and scare them away."

Mom cast a frightened look his way. "It sounds dangerous," she said biting her lip nervously.

Dad ignored her remark. "There is a small Baptist church in town. I spoke with the pastor there, and he said that they could pay a little bit every week if I would help with the youth and with some staff things."

Mom still looked doubtful. She walked over to Dad and put her arm around him in a hug. "What about your smoking? Won't the church object to that?"

Dad got up and squared his shoulders. He reached into his shirt pocket and pulled out his pack of cigarettes. We all watched with our eyes as big as saucers and our mouths hanging open as he crumpled the pack and dumped it in the trash can by the table.

"I am going to give up smoking starting right now," he proclaimed.

Mom smiled real big. I knew she was happy that he had given up that habit. "Isn't this wonderful, children?" she gushed. I agreed. I had always hated the stench that got into our hair and clothes and never seemed to leave. Dad didn't say anything, but I saw a muscle in his jaw twitch. Perhaps he was already sorry that he had made such a rash resolution.

Mom and Linda went to the bathroom while I helped Dad

clean up the table. When they returned we all loaded back into the car.

"We are going to drive through the night," Dad said, turning in his seat to face us. "I can't go very fast pulling this trailer. I'm afraid the car might overheat. You kids go to sleep, and when you wake up we will be close to the reservation."

He turned back around, settled himself into his seat, started the car, and smoothly rolled out onto the highway. The sun was down, and the air was cool as it streamed in from the open windows. The little kids went to sleep fairly quickly, but I was too excited to sleep just yet. I watched the scenery as the miles and hours rolled by. I finally fell asleep around midnight and dreamed of wild Indians.

"Wake up, children!" Mom said in a loud and cheerful voice. "Look out the window."

We all woke up slowly, rubbing our eyes and yawning. The early morning sun was illuminating the flat desert. I looked out the window and saw an old buckboard wagon being pulled by a pony alongside the road. Riding on the wagon was an Indian family. They wore shirts that were faded by the sun and jeans that were patched. They looked like regular people to me. Their skin was darker than mine, and their hair was jet black. I was disappointed that they weren't wearing buckskin and feathers. I didn't see a single tomahawk or spear. They had some bundles of cloth and what looked like some large plastic water bottles on the wagon. The people turned to look at us, and I stared back at them. I turned in my seat and watched them until they disappeared from sight. I wondered if all Indians looked that way.

Eventually the flat desert gave way to a land that was dotted with mesas. In the distance I could see a mountain range, green with pines trees. After a bit more driving we entered a small, dusty town. It had the usual gas station and small grocery store. There seemed to be only one main road that went through the town. We went past the Baptist church and a large Catholic church with a wrought-iron fence and gates that enclosed a courtyard. There were other buildings and businesses, but I couldn't tell what they were just from looking out the car window. Soon we came to a crossroads. Dad maneuvered the car and trailer into a drive that seemed to service two large houses. On my left was a large, two story adobe house painted a light brown. There was a tall tree in the fenced in front yard. The house had a deep front porch with wide concrete steps. On my right was a house painted white that seemed trim and in good shape. When I craned my neck I could see that the drive went on to the back of the houses and ended at a place where the land dropped steeply away to a canyon with a small creek at its bottom. On the other side of the creek, a long way off, were some small shacks that appeared to be made of tin and old lumber.

"We are home," Dad pronounced. We all looked around in bewilderment. Which home was ours?

Dad motioned toward the large brown house. "That house has been divided into four apartments, two downstairs and two upstairs. We have the apartment downstairs that is closest to the driveway."

None of us moved to get out of the car. Even Dad just sat there as if the finality of his decision had finally hit him. I pointed to the shacks across the creek. "What are those?"

Dad moved his hand over his shirt pocket, and I realized that he was looking for his cigarettes which he had thrown away. He ran his hand through his hair, and I saw the muscle in his jaw jump.

"Those are called the Colonia. Poor Mexicans live there. Try to stay away from them," he replied as we continued to stare at the shacks. I wanted to ask why, but I caught him looking at me in the rearview mirror, and something in that look kept me quiet.

Finally Mom opened her car door. "Well, let's see what our new place is like," she said with a smile. We all piled out and stretched our legs. Mom picked up Paul and watched as Dad unlocked the apartment door. He walked in without hesitation. Mom was fussing with Paul and didn't look up until she was in the doorway. I was right behind her and almost ran into her because she had stopped as soon as she crossed the threshold. I heard her draw a deep breath, hold it for a few seconds, and then let out a long sigh. I twisted my neck to look around her. The scene was bleak, and I understood her reaction.

The door opened into a kitchen/dining area. The floor was covered in a dingy linoleum that was worn down from foot traffic and curling on the edges. The walls and ceiling were whitewashed adobe. There was an old refrigerator and a grimy cook stove. The kitchen sink faucet dripped water that was tinged red from rust, and there was a large red stain in the sink. A fine layer of sand dust covered everything. There was a smell emanating from somewhere in the kitchen, and Roger let out a loud "Phew!" Just at that moment my mother began to scream. She pointed at the back of the kitchen, and her hand was shaking.

"A rat!" she hollered. "A giant rat! Right over there!" Dad came running into the room just in time to see the creature scuttle under the refrigerator.

"It was a mouse, not a rat," he said in an annoyed voice. "We can get rid of that problem easily."

Mom's back straightened, and I could tell she was trying to get ahold of herself. She hugged Paul tighter. I reached up and grabbed her free hand. She looked at me and smiled. One step at a time we made our slow way together into the kitchen. Linda and Roger held hands and crept in behind us. To our left was an opening into a living room. We went into the room and just gawked at our living space. There was a front door that opened out onto the porch. Mom opened it up to let in some fresh air and get rid of the odor. Dad had found an old broom and was busy trying to flush the mouse out from under the refrigerator. Mom pulled me along with her to explore further. Off the back of the living room was a large hallway that went to the right. We saw that there were two bedrooms opening off the hallway. One was small. The other was larger, and the only bathroom was accessible by walking through the large bedroom. The bathroom had a sink, toilet, and bathtub—all of which were stained with rust just like the kitchen sink. The bad smell permeated the whole apartment. Mom stood looking at everything as if she could not comprehend the situation. Finally she turned and gave us a wan smile.

"Everything will be OK," she said in a quiet voice. It sounded as if she was trying to convince herself as well as us.

Dad came into the room and gave her a hug. "I will get the cleaning supplies out of the trailer and help you with this," he told her in a cheerful voice.

"First, I think we need to get something to eat," Mom said with a forced smile. "It is almost noon, and I am sure the kids are hungry."

I could tell that Dad hadn't thought about food. He scratched his head in a bewildered way as Paul began to cry. He took Paul out of Mom's arms and bounced him up and down a few times to quiet him. When he gave Paul back to Mom he looked down at me and kind of jerked his chin in the direction of the door.

"Dale, you come with me. We'll get out those cleaning supplies and then go buy something to eat." I let go of Mom's hand and followed him out to the trailer.

Dad opened the trailer door and found the cleaning supplies in a box. He lifted out two boxes and gave me one to take inside. I ran the box into the kitchen and hurried back for another. Mom began to unload the supplies and gave me instructions to look for other things that she needed. Soon there was a small pile on the kitchen floor. Mom told Linda to watch Roger and Paul while she began to dust and clean. Dad and I carried in box after box. He carried the heavy boxes, and I carried the light stuff. Together we carried in the furniture and clothes and all of our belongings. It didn't take long because we didn't have much.

"I'm going to take Dale with me to get some food. After lunch we will make a trip into Albuquerque to turn in the trailer," Dad

17

yelled to Mom. She was up to her elbows in soap suds and just nodded to us as she went back to work.

We found a small store in town where we bought bread, cheese, lunchmeat, and milk. After we delivered that to the house, Dad and I drove off to deliver the rented U-Haul trailer to Albuquerque. We had dropped the food off at the apartment without stopping to eat. I was hungry, but I didn't say anything. I figured that I could go without food if Dad could go without food. On the way into the big city Dad began to talk to me about the desert and the Indians and his expectations for me.

"When you go to school you will be one of a few white kids," he said looking down and sideways at me as he drove. "In order to get by you will have to fit in. You must act like an Indian and learn to think like them. Do you understand me?"

I nodded in the affirmative, but I didn't say anything. I was tired and hungry. I dozed off and dreamed of Indians doing a war dance around my family. I must have slept through the rest of the trip because the next thing I knew we were back at the apartment, and Dad was shaking me.

"Wake up! We are back," Dad said in a tired voice. I rubbed my eyes and slipped out of the car. I forced my feet to drag me up the steps to the kitchen door. Dad opened the door, and we both saw the mouse scoot across the floor again and disappear under the refrigerator. Dad looked around at me.

"That's going to be your responsibility," he said. "You will set out some mouse traps every night before you go to bed, and every morning you will empty them and reset them."

I nodded. It seemed like a gruesome job, and I didn't know if I could do it.

Dad yelled to Mom as we walked in. "We're home! Where are you?"

Mom appeared as if by magic, a finger to her lips.

"Quiet!" she hissed. "I just got Paul settled in his crib. I put Linda in the small bedroom." Mom hugged me and seeing how

tired I was she propelled me across the room with her hand on my back.

In the large hallway between the two bedrooms were Paul's crib and an old roll-away bed. Mom had put the crib together and folded down the bed. There were pillows and a sheet and blankets. Roger was already asleep on the bed, but there was plenty of room for me. I took off my shoes and clothes and climbed under the covers. My eyes were closed, but I heard Dad say to Mom that he was going to set up some mouse traps before going to bed. My stomach rumbled, and I remembered that I hadn't eaten anything that day. I was more tired than hungry. It was the last thing I heard or thought about before drifting off to sleep in that new and strange place.

THREE

STRANGER THINGS

"Why aren't you children in school?" the lady asked. She looked at us over glasses that were perched on the end of her nose. She was leaving her apartment, the one next to ours. "It is Friday, and school starts in an hour."

I had made up a rule that I liked to use when dealing with adults who asked questions. When the question could be answered with a "yes" or "no" I would say "yes, ma'am" or "no, ma'am," "yes, sir" or "no, sir." If it was a question that required an easy answer I gave the answer and smiled. If the answer required an explanation I just shut up and let another adult answer the question. My mom was close by when the lady asked this question. She had Linda and me helping her clean off the front porch. I looked up at Mom, expecting her to answer for me.

"Hi. I'm Marliene Sims," my mom said with a smile and a handshake. "We just moved in yesterday. I thought I would let the kids get used to their new home and rest up today before taking them to school on Monday."

The lady looked down at us over her glasses and cleared her throat. "I am Mrs. Woodley. I teach first grade at the school." She shifted her purse to her other arm and looked down. "My husband died last year."

Mom reached over and touched her gently on the shoulder. "I'm so sorry to hear that. I'll be praying for you."

Mrs. Woodley just gave a small nod and continued to keep her head bowed as if in deep thought. Finally, she raised her head and stared directly at Linda.

"What grade are you in?" she asked in a quiet voice. Mom answered before Linda could say anything.

"She is almost six, and she was supposed to start first grade this year, but things have been so unsettled that we just couldn't get her in. Now I am afraid that she will be behind." Mom reached over and pulled Linda close to her, smoothing her hair as she talked.

Mrs. Woodley gave a tight smile. "I can give her lessons and catch her up, but she will have to work hard. Lessons start this evening. We will work together every evening after supper and every morning before school." She didn't ask if we wanted to do that. She just spoke as if it were an order that had to be obeyed. I looked at Mom, expecting to hear a protest and was surprised when Mom slowly nodded her head in assent.

"She will be there, Mrs. Woodley. Thank you," Mom said quietly.

Mrs. Woodley looked us over again before turning her back on us and marching down the porch steps to her car. We watched her start the car, back up into the street, and pull forward out into traffic with authority. Mom let out a deep sigh.

"She seems like a nice lady," Mom said with a smile. Linda looked at me and rolled her eyes. I shrugged and went back to my job of scrubbing the concrete surface of the porch right in front of the door. There was a dark stain there that seemed to resist all efforts to lighten it up or make it disappear. I hoped that I wouldn't have to work on this all day because I was already tired.

Dad had awakened me early that morning. The sun was just coming up as I stumbled into the bathroom. When I finished I quickly pulled on the clothes that I had been wearing for the last two days. The rest of the family was still asleep. Dad handed me a piece of toast that had butter, cinnamon, and sugar on it. I devoured the toast quickly. He poured a small glass of milk for me, which I eagerly guzzled down. Dad looked impatiently out of the kitchen window as I finished my breakfast.

"Can I have another piece of toast?" I asked. I was starving, having gone to bed without any food the day before.

"No," he replied. "You have some work to do." I noticed that he was drawing on a piece of paper. I stood beside him and looked it over. I immediately recognized the floor plan of our apartment. Dad had placed "X" marks at six different locations. He pointed at one of the spots he had marked.

"I put out six mouse traps last night. That will be your job every night from now on. Right now we will go around and check those traps. I'll show you what to do."

He reached down and picked up a threadbare old pillowcase. I picked up the map and walked with him from place to place. Every trap had a mouse in it. Dad would pick up the mouse by the tail and throw both mouse and trap into the pillowcase. We walked out of the house and around to the back where the land dropped steeply away to a shallow arroyo with a small creek at its bottom. Dad upended the pillowcase and dumped the mice out onto the dusty ground. Two of the mice were still alive, their hind quarters caught and paralyzed by the trap. They tried to drag themselves away from us with their front paws while making pathetic little squeaking sounds. Dad searched the ground around us and found an old brick stuck in the ground. He grunted as he pulled it free from the dirt. He quickly dusted it off and just as quickly dashed it against one of the mice that was trying to drag the trap away from us. Blood splashed on the ground, and the eyes of the mouse bugged out. He died with his mouth open. I turned away and promptly vomited up whatever food I had in my belly.

"Don't be a sissy, son," Dad growled at me. I was still having the dry heaves because there wasn't enough left in me to vomit out. Dad grabbed my arm and spun me around to face him. "Listen to me. Mice carry diseases. They eat our food and poop and piss in our house. It's the mice that make the house smell bad. Do you want a mouse nibbling on your brother's toes?"

I shook my head, but it didn't remove my nausea to know why I had to kill those poor creatures. Dad handed me the brick.

"Now, you have to kill the other mouse. It won't live because of what the trap did to it. You will be putting the mouse out of its misery and helping the family at the same time."

I took a deep breath and hit the mouse hard. The brick bounced on the tiny mouse body and rolled off to one side. The mouse stopped moving, and blood trickled out of its mouth. I cried even though I knew that Dad had spoken the truth. Dad dried my eyes with the sleeve of his shirt. He showed me how to take the mice out of the trap without hurting my fingers. He gathered three mice by their tails and told me to do the same. I gingerly picked up three mice by their tails. Together we walked to the edge of the canyon. Dad swung his arm out wide and threw the mice down the steeply sloping arroyo wall. Their bodies twisted and tumbled down toward the creek. I did the same with my three mice.

"Before the day is over there will be a cat or dog or hawk or snake that will eat them. Just remember to throw them as far down the canyon as possible every morning, and stay away from them during the day." Dad turned his head slightly, and I could tell he was listening to something. "Hear that kind of dry rattling sound?" he asked. "That's a rattlesnake. Be real careful out here. There are snakes everywhere." He looked thoughtfully across the arroyo at the shacks of the Colonia. "I don't know how those poor slobs over there live like that," he said with disgust and then spit on the ground.

We stood listening to the snakes for a moment before turning back to trudge up to the house. We picked up the pillowcase and mouse traps. The sour taste of vomit was still in my mouth, and the tears still dropped from my eyes. I didn't say anything to Dad because I was sure he would criticize me again. I just kept my gaze on the ground and followed him to the house.

When we entered the kitchen I saw that Mom was cooking eggs and making toast. In spite of my nausea I heard my stomach rumble. The smell of cooking food made me hungry again. I noticed that Linda and Roger were seated at our small table, and Paul was strapped into his high chair. They were sipping from small glasses of milk. Dad walked over and kissed Mom.

"I'm going to make the rounds today. I'll drive out to the Johnsons' sawmill and then over to the church. The pastor and his family live right there on the church property. I want to meet with the Roberts and see what I can do to help them." I saw Dad fumble with his shirt pocket again trying to find the cigarettes he had vowed to give up. Mom patted him on the arm, and he gave a low growl. Mom laughed lightly and turned back to her cooking.

"Are the Roberts the missionary couple you said you were going to help on the reservation?" she asked. He nodded as Mom grabbed a plate and put a spoonful of eggs and two pieces of toast on it. Dad took it and walked to the table where he quickly wolfed down the food. He washed it all down with a big mug of coffee.

Mom gave me a plate with eggs and toast on it. "Dale, give that one to Roger, and come back for Linda's." Dutifully I walked over and plunked the plate down in front of my brother. As I turned to leave Dad gave me his empty plate.

"Don't forget to run some water on that," he commanded. I did as I was told, and when I finished Mom handed me another plate.

"This is for your sister," she said. She smiled down at me. "You are such a good son. I know I can always count on you." I took the plate and put it down in front of my sister.

Dad pushed his chair away from the table and walked over to kiss Mom goodbye. "I should be back this afternoon." He turned toward me and fixed me with an earnest stare. "Do what your mom tells you to do. Help her with the house and your brothers and sister."

"Yes, sir," I replied. He turned his back on me and hurried out the door. Mom put eggs and toast on another plate for herself and sat down next to Paul's highchair. She gave Paul a piece of toast, and she sipped at her coffee.

I looked at them eating and heard my stomach rumble again. Quietly I got a plate down from the cabinet and put what was left of the eggs on it and grabbed the last piece of toast. I poured some milk into a small glass. Making my way to the chair that Dad had just vacated I sat down and began to eat. Mom looked at me over her coffee mug.

"Are you hungry? Didn't you already eat something this morning?" she asked me.

"I threw up outside. Now I'm hungry again," I mumbled through a mouthful of toast. A look of concern quickly covered Mom's face. She reached over and put her hand on my forehead.

"Are you sick?" she asked. I shook my head in the negative. "Why did you throw up?" she asked. I shrugged and looked at Linda and Roger as they munched on their toast. I wasn't going to tell them about the mice while they were eating. Linda made a face at me.

"You are disgusting," she said. She made a face and stuck out her tongue. Roger laughed and pretended to throw up.

"Quit that, you two," Mom commanded. She watched me for a few minutes but seemed to be relieved when I finished all of my food and drank all of my milk. She shrugged and gave Paul another piece of toast.

After breakfast Mom let Roger and Paul play together in the living room while she took Linda and me out to the front porch to help her clean it. That is when we met Mrs. Woodley. An hour after she had left I was still scrubbing the concrete surface of the porch right in front of the door. I just couldn't get that stain to disappear. Mom came over to have a look. She bent over with her hands on her hips and made a small sound.

"I just don't think we are going to get rid of that stain," Mom said. We looked at each other, and suddenly she smiled at me. "Why don't you take a break? Go explore for a little bit. Don't go far, and come back in time for lunch."

I stood up and gave Mom a hug before racing down the steps. I could hear Linda whining and asking if she could go with me. I swung through the gate and picked up speed as I loped down the side of the main road that ran through town. I wanted to get as far away as I could as quickly as I could in order to discourage Mom from letting Linda tag along. I ran past a large Catholic church, a gas station, and some small run-down looking buildings before coming to a grocery store. It was small but looked modern and well stocked. I stopped in front of the large windows and watched a man stocking the shelves. It looked clean and cool in there. The man ignored me, and I soon lost interest. Since I didn't have any money I saw no reason to go inside. I walked around the corner of the store to the back where I could see the arroyo. I slowly followed its rim back toward my house. I found a long stick to carry in case I ran across a snake. Eventually I found myself in back of our new apartment at the exact spot where Dad and I had thrown the dead mice down the arroyo wall. There was no sign of the dead mice which affirmed Dad's remarks about wild animals eating them. I looked over toward the shacks on the other side of the creek. A movement caught my eye, and I turned in time to see part of the wall of one shack swing open like a door. The shacks were made of old tin metal roofing and pieces of lumber. The door seemed to just be a large piece of metal roofing that was hinged to the wall. Two children stumbled out of the shack, a boy and a girl. They each grabbed a stick from a group of sticks that were leaning against their shack. They walked to the edge of the creek and helped each other jump across it to my side. They looked around, and it seemed as if they were discussing something. The boy happened to glance up, and I could tell from the way he pointed up in my direction that he had seen me. The girl's gaze followed his pointing hand she shielded her eyes with her hand to see me better. I waved at them, and they waved back. They walked to their left for a few steps and then began to climb up out of the arroyo with the boy in the lead. I looked closely and noticed for the first time a narrow footpath that came up a shallower slope of the arroyo. I walked over to the head of the path and got there at the same time as they did. We stood there for a minute just looking each other over. Their skin was brown, and their hair was thick and dark. The girl was shorter than the boy, and they were both very thin. Their jeans and shirts were patched but clean. They had leather sandals on their feet. When they smiled their teeth seemed very white against the brown of their skin. The girl was missing a front tooth, and I figured she was about the same age as my sister Linda. I stuck out my hand to shake with them.

"I'm Dale Sims," I said with a smile as I shook the boy's hand. I don't know why, but I expected his skin to feel different from mine, and I was surprised that it didn't.

"My name is Miguel, and this is my sister Maria," the boy said quietly. His eyes looked a little sad and serious at the same time. His sister didn't offer to shake my hand so I let it swing down to my side.

"We just moved into that house," I told them, pointing with my thumb at the building behind us.

Miguel nodded. "I saw you throw those mice bodies down the hill this morning." Miguel had an accent, but his English was very understandable. There was a large boulder close by, and Miguel motioned toward it with his stick. We all walked over to it and sat on the relatively flat top.

"Why aren't you in school?" I asked.

"The nuns let us out today because of the holiday," Maria said. I must have had a very blank look on my face because she added "You know, the washing of Our Lady."

28

"What nuns?" I asked.

Miguel laughed. "The nuns at the school at the church," and he pointed in the direction of the large Catholic church. I could just see one corner of it from my angle.

"There's a school at that church?" I asked, trying to get my thoughts in order.

Miguel made a low sound of disgust. "You don't know much, do you?"

The fact that they knew things I didn't made me view them with a little more respectability. I hated to admit that I didn't know something, but my curiosity was aroused.

"Who is Our Lady?" I asked. Both kids hooted and laughed loudly. Miguel said something to Maria in a language I didn't understand. She laughed again and shook her head as if my ignorance was beyond belief.

"You know, Our Lady is Mary, the mother of God," Maria said with a smile.

"You mean Mary from the Bible? The mother of Jesus," I asked. "I thought she died a long, long time ago." My remark made them laugh again.

Miguel put his hand on my shoulder. "I think you are not Catholic, yes?"

"I'm a Baptist," I told him warily. "I'm not sure what difference it makes."

Miguel shook his head sadly. He said something to Maria who looked sideways at me and also shook her head sadly. "In my church we have a statue of Mary. During this month we have a holiday to remember how sad she was when her son died. So we wash her statue to show her that we love her. It makes her more willing to take our prayers to her son so that he will answer them. After we wash the statue we take it out of the church and parade it up and down the street so that people will honor her."

"Does it work?" I asked.

Miguel shrugged and then smiled.

"If you have enough faith it works. At least that is what the nuns tell us," he said in a sincere voice.

"What's a nun?" I asked.

Maria just stared at me with her mouth open. She said something to Miguel who shrugged again.

"A nun is a holy woman who serves the church," he told me in a reverent tone.

"Sometimes they are strict," said Maria. "But they only hit us when we deserve it. They are the teachers in our school."

I didn't know what to say to that, but I knew that I wanted to see a nun. I decided to change the topic while I thought things over.

"My dad doesn't know how you live like that over there," I said and pointed with my stick toward the shacks on the other side of the creek.

"It was worse than this in the place we came from," Miguel said looking at the ground. "No place to call our home, no food, no work. My dad found a job here and brought us all here to live." I decided not to comment so Miguel continued. "There were men looking for my dad to get some money from him. We ran away from them and came to here."

I was astounded. "It was the same with us," I said. "My dad took us away from some men who wanted our money."

Miguel nodded his head wisely.

I had a hundred questions running through my mind about Miguel and his family. I hesitated to ask because I didn't want to be rude. As I was considering how to bring up certain subjects I heard a gradually increasing noise behind us. It was the sound of many feet shuffling along the road and many voices saying words that I could not understand. I turned to look, and so did Miguel and Maria. I watched in astonishment as a colorful river of humanity flowed down the road. Miguel pointed with his chin.

"Those are the Indians. This happens every Friday after the Indian agent gives out the head money," he said with disgust in his voice.

"What is head money?" I asked. Miguel gave a huge sigh and said something to his sister that made her laugh.

"You don't know much, do you?" he asked.

I shrugged. What could I say? Everything was new to me in this place.

Miguel ran his hand through his hair. "Everybody who is a member of a tribe is listed on a head roll. If your name is on the roll then you get money from the government. The agent works for the government and hands out the money."

"So these people are going to get their head money?" I asked.

"No! Those people already have their head money. Now they are going to spend it." Miguel spit on the ground just like my dad had done when he spoke of Miguel's family.

I looked at the group again with new eyes. I saw children and adults. I saw young people and old people. They were talking among themselves in low voices and in a language I could not understand.

"Are they going to the store?" I asked.

"Follow us, and I will show you where they go," Miguel said.

Miguel led off with Maria beside him, and I followed. We walked alongside the long line of Indians who were talking quietly among themselves. They were colorful and exotic. It was hard not to stare at them. I looked ahead and saw that the line ended at the door of one of the old run-down looking buildings I had seen earlier. A man came out and held up four fingers. The first four people in the line shuffled into the building, and the man closed the door behind them. Sitting on the dusty ground outside of the building were children of all ages. The older children made sure that the younger children didn't stray too far. Miguel tugged on my shirt and said, "Follow me." He led me to the back of the building where there was another door. Miguel and Maria stood soberly looking at the door so I stood beside them. I didn't understand what they were waiting for, and I soon got bored. I heard a sound over to my right. The sound came from a stand of trees. Before I could determine the source of the sound the back door of the building opened, and three people lurched out. The man who I had seen at the front was supporting two Indians who could barely walk. They staggered over to the stand of trees, and the Indians kind of flopped to the ground. I looked closer and discovered that the ground under the trees was littered with bodies. I suddenly realized that the sound which had caught my attention was groaning and snoring sounds coming from the drunk Indians lying on the ground.

We strolled over to look at the sight of so many Indians passed out on the ground.

"Drunks!" Miguel said with a sneer. He spit on the ground, and Maria did the same. They looked at me expectantly, but I refused to spit. Miguel shrugged and led us back toward my apartment house.

"What was that all about?" I asked.

Miguel looked at me out of the corner of his eye to see if I was kidding him. "Can't you see? The Indians go into that bar to get drunk. Once they get drunk the man who runs the bar helps them find a place to sleep under the trees. Then he lets more people come in to get drunk."

We walked up the porch steps, and I could see that my mother was on her knees scrubbing away on the stain in front of the door. She stopped and straightened up to look at us.

"Hi, Mom," I said with a smile. "These are my new friends, Miguel and Maria. They live in the Colonia back of the house." Mom kind of nodded to them. Miguel pointed at the stain.

"You won't get that stain out of there. You can work as hard as you want to, but it won't come out," he said with absolute conviction.

"Why not?" Mom asked.

"That is a blood stain," Miguel told her. "A man came here one night and screamed at the man who used to live here. He said that he wanted his money. The man in the house stabbed him, and he died." Miguel pointed at the stain. "He died right here." Miguel touched his forehead, his left chest and then his right, before touching his belly, making the sign of the cross. Maria did the same.

Mom looked at the stain openmouthed. "You're telling me that a man died on this very spot?" she asked incredulously.

Miguel nodded sadly. "The man who killed him tried to run away, but they caught him. Now he is in prison."

Maria craned her neck to look past Mom so that she could see the inside of the house. "They say this house is haunted by the ghost of the man who died. They say that his ghost walks this place at night."

Mom's mouth closed to a tight line. "Who says that? Who says this house is haunted?"

Maria shrugged. "Everybody says that. I only tell you what everybody says."

Mom looked behind her into the living room where Linda and Roger were playing with Paul. She turned and looked at us with a big smile.

"I know how to take care of this," she declared. "Bow your heads, and we will just ask God to get rid of the ghost."

Miguel and Maria looked at each in astonishment and then bowed their heads. I did the same, and Mom began to pray.

"O, great and mighty God. You are the creator of all things in heaven and earth. You know and see all things. You know that on this very spot a man lost his life. I pray that you give his spirit rest and cause it to leave this house forever. I humbly ask you to put your mighty arms of protection around this house and all who live in it. Keep us safe, and hold us in your hands forever. I pray in the name of Jesus. Amen."

Miguel and Maria crossed themselves and smiled in relief. Mom patted them on their heads. "Where have you kids been?" she asked.

Quickly I told her about the Indians and the bar and the children. Mom walked to the front of the porch in order to see the crowd better. I stood beside her and pointed to the building. I also told her about the drunk Indians lying in the shade of the trees out in back of the bar. She watched for a little bit before turning to Miguel.

"Those children stay out there all day until their parents sober up?" she asked quietly.

Miguel gave a shrug and nodded his head.

"Dale, you come with me," she said quietly.

We went into the kitchen, and Mom set a box up on the kitchen table. She placed a gallon of milk in one corner and gently laid two loaves of bread and a plastic cup beside it. She motioned for me to pick up the box and follow her. She marched out of the house and across the street to the children. As I followed in her wake it seemed to me that I was walking through a mist of righteousness and disapproval that trailed behind her. She found a gap in the line of adult Indians and pushed through it to the other side where the children were playing. I looked back at the house just in time to see Miguel and Maria hurrying off the porch to disappear around a corner of the house. Mom stopped and placed a hand on my shoulder to pull me up closer to her. We walked together until we stood in front of a group of curious children. Mom smiled at them and told me to put the box on the ground. She opened a bag of bread and began to hand out slices to every child that came her way until all of the bread was gone. I heard a low murmur among the adults, and one Indian woman began to screech at some of the children who backed off from us and refused to take any bread. Mom didn't pay any attention. She took the plastic cup, filled it with milk, and passed it to a child. When that was finished she refilled it and handed it to another child. This time there were several Indian women yelling at the children. Mom quietly ignored them, handing out milk until it was all gone. She picked up the box and took my hand.

"Let's go home," she said with a satisfied smile. She took my hand and led me through the line of Indians. I noticed that they were all looking back down the line at something coming down the road toward us. Mom and I stepped out into the street to have a closer look. It was an astonishing sight.

A man in a brown robe was walking down the street holding in front of him a large cross with a small statue of Jesus on it. I had never seen anything like it before, but I knew the story of Jesus's death on the cross so I figured that was what I was looking at. The man in the brown robe was chanting something in a kind of sing-song in a language that I didn't understand. Ten men followed behind him holding on their shoulders a platform made of poles of wood. On the platform was a statue of a woman with heavily painted features. A large group of people followed. I saw Miguel and Maria walking in the crowd of people with their heads bowed and their hands pressed together as if in prayer. I decided this was the statue of Mary that they had told me about earlier. Some of the Indians in the line behind us knelt on the ground and crossed themselves. Others just stood there watching with stony faces. My mother put her hands on her hips and let out a long sigh. When the procession got a little closer she raised her right hand and pointed at the statue.

"That is nothing but idolatry!" she said in a very loud voice. "I don't worship idols. I only worship God Himself!"

The man in the brown robe acted unperturbed. His step never faltered, and he kept up his chanting kind of singing. As he came up beside us he stepped away from the procession and stood between us and the statue. He lifted the cross he was carrying just a little bit higher. Mom smiled at him.

"Just because you are holding a cross doesn't make you a Christian," she said loudly. "You need to give your heart to Jesus, and stop worshipping idols. You are leading these people astray, and you should feel ashamed of yourself."

He didn't stop his chanting. The cross he was holding never wavered. He turned his eyes toward heaven as if he were praying, as if we were beneath his notice. When the procession was finally past us he turned and kind of trotted back to the front of the group so he could continue leading them.

Mom had a disgusted look on her face as she watched them walk toward the other end of town. She shook her head and walked across the street to our apartment. I followed a little behind her. I watched her walk with her head held high and her back straight. It was all a little bewildering to me. I wasn't sure if I should say or do anything, so I just kept quiet and followed Mom into the apartment. I noticed that she sidestepped the stain in front of the door.

That afternoon I sat on the porch and thought about all of the strange things I had learned. Mice carried disease. A man had been killed on our front porch, and Mom had asked God to protect us from ghosts. I saw some Indians who were drunk and had helped Mom feed some Indian kids. Miguel told me about nuns, and I still didn't exactly know what they were. I saw a parade of idol worshippers, and Mom yelled at them.

Supper was on the table when Dad came home that evening. He walked in through the kitchen door and kissed Mom. My attention was drawn to a holster and pistol that he had in his hand. He opened a cabinet door and placed them on the top shelf. Then he pulled a box out of his pocket and put that up there as well. When he was seated at the table Dad glared around at all of us.

"I don't ever want to catch you fooling around with the gun," he growled. "Especially you," and he pointed at me. I hung my head and moved some food around on my plate.

Mom began to chatter on about all of the things she had seen and done that day. When she told Dad about Miguel and Maria he reached over and thumped me hard on the head.

"I told you to stay away from the Colonia," he said angrily.

"I didn't go there," I protested. "They came up the hill to see me."

Dad thumped me again, and Roger laughed. "Don't backtalk me, boy," he said in a low voice. I hung my head again and ate some more food. Mom continued dispensing news in her cheerful way.

Dad nodded in a knowing way when she told him about the stain caused by the blood of the murdered man.

"His name was Verne Woodley," Dad said. He took another bite and chewed it slowly. "His widow lives in that apartment next door. I got this apartment cheap because everyone says this is a haunted place, and nobody wanted to live here."

Mom told him about her prayer asking God to ban the ghost which led right into her telling him about the parade of idol worshippers. Dad laughed when Mom told him what she said to the priest.

Mom eventually ran out of gossip, and Dad finally told us about his day. He had checked in at the saw mill and bought a gun and some bullets off a guy that worked there. He went by the reservation and met Mr. and Mrs. Roberts. He had gone by the church and met the pastor, Mr. Gray. They had worked out a deal where Dad acted as a kind of associate pastor. He would also create the bulletins every week for the service.

"Dale, you'll go with me to the reservation tomorrow," Dad said. "We will spend most of the day there." There was no discussion, and I nodded to show that I had heard the command.

I helped Mom clean up the kitchen after supper. Linda went next door to Mrs. Woodley's apartment. I read a book to Roger and Paul. Mom and Dad sat at the table and discussed a few things in quiet, hushed tones. We didn't have a television or a telephone, and from the snippets of conversation I overheard it didn't seem that we would ever have those things.

When Linda came back from Mrs. Woodley's she was very excited about the new things she was learning. Mom made us all take baths in the rusty bathtub. The tub got filled up one time, and we all took turns taking a dip in it. We had two towels—one for the adults and one for the kids. I always took my bath first because the water was fresher and cleaner, and the towel was drier. When I finished my bath I put on the fresh underwear that Mom had laid out for me. Linda was the only one who had pajamas. Dad felt that the boys should only wear undershorts to bed. I learned to sleep nearly naked in every kind of weather.

Dad had prepared the rollaway bed in the hallway outside of Linda's room. I crawled onto the bed and pulled the covers up to my chin.

"What do you think you are doing?" Dad growled at me. "You haven't done your job yet. No sleep until the work is done, understand?"

I nodded and followed him over to where he had laid out the mousetraps. He showed me how to bait them with peanut butter and directed me to put them in the spots he had shown me earlier in the day. I carefully set them out and then ran back to bed. By then Linda had crawled into her bed. Dad went into her room, and I heard him talking to her about her dolls. Linda had dozens of dolls that people had given to her as gifts. I heard Dad tell her that he would build a shelf on the wall for all of the dolls so that she could see them.

Mom brought Roger and Paul over to the bed. Paul went into the crib, which was fast becoming too small for him. Roger dove into the rollaway and under the covers. Mom kissed us all. She stood where we could all see her, and she sang a song to us.

"Good night, my God is watching o'er you

Good night, His mercies go before you

Good night, and I'll be waiting for you

So, Good night, may God bless you"

Dad took her by the hand and led her to their bedroom. They turned off all of the lights and left us to sleep in darkness.

"Do you think the ghost will bother us?" Roger whispered to me.

"Mom prayed the ghost away," I said.

"What if the ghost comes back?" Roger asked in quavering voice.

My brother annoyed me. I was very tired, and all I wanted to do was sleep. "The ghost will only look for people who make noise or move around a lot in their sleep," I whispered to him.

He grew very quiet, and soon I heard his deep and even breathing as he fell asleep. I slept well that night, but I was occasionally awakened by the snap of a mousetrap. I knew what I had to do in the morning with the mice bodies, and I wanted the night to last a long time. What I had to do in the morning bothered me a lot more than a ghost.

FOUR

APPEARANCES

I heard Dad and Mom moving around in the kitchen, and soon I smelled the morning coffee that they loved to drink. Mom had laid out clothes for me. It was good to trade in my smelly clothes of the last two days for something clean. After a visit to the bathroom I grabbed the old pillowcase we had used yesterday and went about collecting the dead mice in their traps. I slipped quietly out of the kitchen door and dealt with the mice in the way that Dad had showed me the day before. As I threw the bodies down the arroyo I did a quick calculation in my head. Twelve mice in two days seemed like a lot to me. As I collected all of the traps I wondered just how long I would have to do this before we had trapped out all of the mice. I turned to leave and saw a man standing in front of the house next door. He was thin and had dark hair and dark eyes. He was watching me with his arms crossed over his chest and a look of disapproval on his face.

"Hey!" I said as I waved at him. That word "hey" was kind of a universal greeting that I had picked up somewhere. The man grunted and pointed at the arroyo.

"Don't you 'hey' me, boy," he said in a low voice. "When you speak to another person you should say something civil such as 'Good morning.'" His eyes seemed to bore into me so I simply nodded that I understood. He grunted. "Why are you throwing dead mice down there?" he asked in a commanding voice. I looked around to see if there were any supporting adults to help. Mom and Dad were in the kitchen, and it didn't seem quite right to ignore the man.

"I'm just doing wh-what my dad told me to d-do," I stammered out. I found it hard to get all the words out when I was concerned or under pressure. The man grunted again. I wondered if he had a problem because he sure seemed to grunt a lot.

"Tell your dad that when you do that it attracts snakes. They like mice," he said with a sour look.

I thought for a moment before replying. "If the snakes like m-m-mice so much maybe it's g-good to get them out of the house. If we don't get r-rid of them maybe the snakes will f-follow them inside."

The man squinted up at the sky. He scuffed the ground with his shoe and took a deep breath. "Maybe you have something there," he said. He stroked his chin as if he was in deep thought. "See that metal box over there?" He pointed with his chin toward a square metal box that sat right next to his house. "That is my trash box. You can drop the dead mice in there, and I will haul them off."

"Thank you!" I said with true appreciation. "My name is Dale Sims." I held out my hand the man shook it.

"I am Mr. Garza," he told me. "You can use the trash box whenever you like."

I instinctively liked Mr. Garza. He seemed to be upfront and honest with me.

I walked into the kitchen just in time to sit at the table for breakfast. Dad was finishing his morning coffee. He looked at me in a way that worried me.

"How many mice did we have in the traps?" he asked. I thought it was interesting that he made the assumption that there were mice in traps.

"We caught six," I replied. "Just like yesterday."

Dad nodded slightly. "Just don't forget to set those traps out every night and empty them every morning." He turned to look at Mom who was washing the morning dishes in the sink. "I'm taking Dale, and we are going to the reservation. I don't know when we will be back."

Mom came over and kissed us goodbye. "Would you stop at the store and bring home a couple of loaves of bread?" she asked. "I gave away most of our bread yesterday."

"Can we go too? Can we go? Please let us go too?" Linda and Roger begged.

Dad gave a little sigh and got up to go out. He motioned for me to follow him. "I'm only taking Dale with me today," he told them. "You little ones stay here with your mom." We walked out to the car, and I noticed Dad fumbling with his shirt pocket again. He seemed to do that a lot when food was involved, especially after he had eaten something. Dad growled as he started up the car and backed out into the street.

"What's a reservation?" I asked.

Dad never took his eyes off the road as he answered. "Ever since the Christian white man got to this country we've had to fight against the dirty, thieving, killer Indians. They would attack and kill and scalp people. Since the Indians declared war on us we fought back. When we won we were kind to them and gave them big parcels of land to settle on and to call their own. That big parcel of land is called a reservation because the land is reserved only for the Indians. We tried to teach them how to farm and read and become civilized. They are mostly still heathens and savages. I don't think they are very smart. Those people need Jesus."

"Are they still dirty, thieving killers?" I asked.

"Some still are," Dad said with a grimace. "Mostly they are just ignorant, dirty savages."

We turned off of the asphalt and onto a dirt road. A cloud of dust followed us as we bounced along. We seemed to drive quite a ways before we came to a large gate. There was a sign hanging on the open gate that read "Navajo Reservation. Approval needed to enter." Dad ignored the sign and drove right onto the reservation.

"Do we have approval?" I asked.

"Sure," Dad replied. "The Roberts have invited us to help them at Tinian Mission."

I looked out my window at a world of dust, sage brush, and large mountainous things. Dad told me that each mountainous thing was called a mesa, which comes from the Spanish word for table. The landscape was so unusual that I felt like I was in another world. As we drove along I kept wondering when we would see the Navajo town and the Tinian Mission. Soon I saw a scattering of very modern looking houses spread out along the road. Dad pulled the car off the road and pointed out the window at some of the houses.

"I want you to see the way these Indians prefer to live," he said with disgust in his voice. We looked at the houses in silence for a few minutes. Each house had all of the windows busted out. The doors had been removed and were lying on the ground by the house. The doorways had been covered by blankets. A few skinny horses nuzzled the ground for the scarce wisps of grass that cropped up here and there. I saw old rusty cars, refrigerators, trash, and broken furniture strewn around the outside of the house. Colorful clothes flapped on a clothesline in back of the house.

"These people need our help so that they can learn to live like modern people," Dad told me. His sincerity was unquestioned. I knew that he wanted to help the Navajo. It made me want to help them as well.

Dad pulled the car back onto the road and sped off toward Tinian Mission. Soon we came to a place where there were many houses made out of mud and logs. There was one house that was made completely from wood and looked more like a regular house.

Nailed to the outside of the house was a sign that read Tinian Mission. Dad parked the car up next to the building. He fixed me with a hard look.

"Don't say anything, and don't do anything to get in trouble here. Remember that we are here to help God," he said in a low and earnest voice. I nodded, but I wasn't sure why Dad thought I would cause trouble.

We left the car and walked together into the mission building. The first thing I saw were some Indian men sitting on metal folding chairs. Dad ignored them as he walked through another doorway into the next room. I stopped and stared at them. They stared back at me with a stony gaze. Finally I waved and smiled. "Hey," I said quietly. One man looked at the others and said something. They all chuckled. He held up his hand and said, "How." That surprised me, and I didn't know what to think of it. All of the men were still chuckling as if there was some joke I was missing.

"Does your 'How' mean 'Hey' as in 'Hello' or 'How' as in a question?" I asked. One man actually laughed out loud. The man who said 'How' groaned and turned to talk to the others. Before I could get a good answer I felt fingers tugging hard on my ear. I looked up to see Dad with a scowl on his face.

"Didn't I tell you to stay out of trouble?" he hissed at me. "You follow me until I tell you otherwise."

I rubbed my sore ear and followed him into the other room where an older couple was smiling at us as we walked in. Dad introduced them as the Roberts, and I shook hands with them. They were very nice but quickly turned their attention to Dad and the water well they wanted his help with. Mr. Roberts laid some papers on the table and spread them out so that we could see them better.

"Jim, this is a map of the reservation provided to us by the Bureau of Indian Affairs," he told Dad. "You can see these marks that show the location of all of the wells. There are two close to where we are right now, but only one of them works. There is another one about three miles away." He pulled another paper on top of the map. "This is the well that we need to work on. You can see that it is drilled deep and uses a wind mill to power it."

Dad studied the drawings and asked Mr. Roberts a question. I didn't understand all of the technical things, and I soon became very bored. I walked over to a window and looked out onto the dusty grounds and buildings surrounding us. I saw boys and girls walking around. I saw sheep and goats wandering from place to place. I felt a presence beside me and turned to see Mrs. Roberts standing there. She smiled at me and pointed out of the window.

"See those buildings? They are traditional Navajo buildings made out of mud and logs. They are called a hogan," she said in a quiet voice. "There are not as many of those left as there used to be. Many of the Indians have moved into modern houses along the road."

I looked at the nearest hogan and studied it. There was a window in it and one door with a blanket covering it. Mrs. Roberts pointed to another hogan. "Do you see any differences between the hogans?" she asked.

I studied the dwellings for a minute before answering. "Yes. One has a window, and the other doesn't. One has more logs on it than the other one."

"Good," Mrs. Roberts said. "Whenever you go to visit a family you must stand back from the entrance and throw a few pebbles against the side of the door. If the people inside want you to come in then they will pull back the blanket and motion you to come inside. You must be patient. Sometimes they are not ready for a visitor. If the blanket is not pulled back after a few minutes then you should just assume they are not interested and go away."

Mrs. Roberts turned to the men who were deep in discussion about the problem of the well. "I think we should let Dale go out and meet some of the Navajo," she suggested.

Dad looked at me in a doubtful way. "That boy finds trouble wherever he goes," he told them.

Mr. Roberts laughed. "He can't get into much trouble here," he said lightly. "Let him go on, but tell him to stay close by."

Dad nodded and jerked his thumb toward the door. "Go ahead," he said. "Just stay close, and stay out of trouble. If you hear me call your name you better come running. Hear me, boy?"

"Yes, sir," I said.

Dad glowered at me as I sidled past him to the door. When I got to the next room I noticed that all of the Indian men were gone. I opened the outer door and walked into a world that was very different from the one I was used to.

The first thing I noticed was the smell of bread baking. I stood and sniffed for a while until I figured out where the smell came from. I noticed some Navajo women standing close to something that looked like a miniature igloo built out of mud or stucco. Smoke drifted out of a hole in the top of it. The smell coming from the oven was of pine wood burning and bread baking. While I was considering the oven I smelled something else that wasn't nearly as pleasant. About a dozen goats were walking past me making all kinds of noise. I backed up a bit just to get away from the smell. I looked in the direction from which they came, and I saw a sight that I still remember vividly to this day.

A young Navajo man dressed in a red shirt and blue jeans was staked out on the ground, his arms and legs spread out. His hair was cut short, and his head lay in the dust.

Two older men sat on a log close by watching him. Another man who was partially naked held some feathers and gourds in his hands and seemed to be dancing and singing around the man on the ground. He had on a covering made of skins and feathers that fell over his face. He was painted white and red and black. A woman stood close by, and occasionally she would give the man on the ground a drink from a gourd.

I walked over and stood close to the men on the log so that I could see things better. The painted man reached into a bowl and grabbed something which he sprinkled on the man tied to the ground. I watched in silence until my legs got tired.

"Can I sit here and watch?" I asked one of the older men on the log. He turned quickly and looked angrily at me.

"Get out of here!" he commanded. "There is no place for you here."

Suddenly the young man on the ground shouted out. "Let him stay," he said loudly. "There is something about him. I see something in his eyes."

The older men on the log stared at him. Finally one of them gave a slight shrug and moved over to make room for me to sit beside him. Gratefully I sat down. One of the older men leaned forward to speak to the man on the ground.

"What do you see in his eyes?" he asked the young man. "Is there something wrong with his eyes?"

The man on the ground shook his head. Sweat drenched his shirt, and the dust covered his dark face. "No! I see something else there." He looked in my direction. "Come closer, Young White."

I left the log and slowly crept up close to the man. I bent down so that I could look him in the face. He stared intently into my eyes.

"Sometimes my mom looks into my eyes and says that she sees the peace that passes all understanding," I said.

"That's it!" he exclaimed loudly. "Yes, that is it! Your eyes are the color of water, and I see the peace of the water. Peace, peace, God's peace flowing over me like billows of love."

He seemed to be crazy, and it scared me. I backed up and sat back down on the log.

"Praise God from whom all blessings flow!" he shouted out. His ravings and ramblings went on and on. The man who was dancing and singing and shaking gourds got just a little bit louder and threw some more stuff on the young man on the ground. I turned to one of the older men sitting next to me.

"Is he crazy?" I asked.

The man shook his head slightly. "Not really," he said, still looking at the young man.

"Why did you tie him up?" I asked.

"Because he asked me to," the man told me. "He has a sickness, and he asked me to help him break it." I looked in wonder at the dusty young man who was still raving in a loud voice.

"Why did he ask you?" I said to the man next to me.

He looked at me, and I thought he was angry. Finally he shrugged and said something to the other man on the log. They spoke for a minute or two, and then they looked at me. The other man stood and stretched his back. He motioned for me to follow him.

"You come with me, Young White," he said quietly. Instinctively I trusted the man although I couldn't explain why. I left the log and followed him to a nearby hogan. He sat with his back to the side of the building and patted the ground beside him. Obediently I sat with him in the shade and watched the crazy man writhe and holler on the ground.

"I know you are only a boy, Young White," the man said. "I know that you have many questions. I can answer some of them because I have more patience than my brother," and he motioned with his chin toward the man who remained on the log. "You can ask any question, but I may not answer all of them. If you listen I think you will come to understand a little bit."

"I want to understand," I told him in all sincerity. "Why are you and your brother helping him?"

"First, because he asked us to help. Second, because he is our nephew. Third, because he was in the military, just like us."

"My dad was in the Navy," I said with pride. "He was stationed at Pearl Harbor."

"We were all in the Marines," the man told me. "My brother and I fought in the Big War," he said. He looked out over the sage brush as if he was thinking of a place far away. "We were on an island in the Pacific called Tinian. We were Code Talkers. God found us in that place, or maybe we found Him. I am not sure which." He picked up a pebble from the ground and shook it in his fist for a few minutes. "We want all of our people to know about God so we started this mission. We asked for help from the whites, and they sent us the Roberts."

I thought that over for a little bit. Dad had told me that all of the Indians were dirty thieves who needed God. I didn't know what a Code Talker was, but I knew this man and his brother were already Christians, and they even started a mission. It bothered me that Dad was wrong. I decided to tell him when I got the chance.

"Who is that man singing and dancing around your nephew?" I asked. I watched as he threw some more stuff on the crazy man.

"He is a medicine man. He is singing the old songs of the Enemy and the Blessing. He has been trained in things that I don't know about," the man replied without looking at me.

I thought quietly for a minute before replying. "That doesn't seem to be very Christian to me," I said looking at him to see his response.

He shrugged and kept his eyes focused on a point far away and over the tops of the sage brush. "He is praying to God in his own way, asking God to look down and help the people who need help. He will continue to pray and to dance and to shake the gourds for many hours in order to draw God's attention to the problem." He looked at me with an inscrutable gaze. "I went to a Christian church in Nevada once where a woman had painted her face with white and red and blue. She had sparkly things on her clothes, danced around on the stage, and spoke things that I couldn't understand. People said 'Praise Jesus' and raised their hands and gave money to the woman. Is that so much different from this?"

I didn't know what to say about that so I just kept my mouth shut. He stayed quiet for a few minutes as well, but I could tell he was thinking about something. Finally he cleared his throat softly.

"Sometimes what we see and do is not based on the way things really are," he told me. "I was there yesterday when your mother gave away bread and milk, and you helped her."

"We were helping just like Jesus told us to do," I said with some pride.

"What you did was wrong," the man told me quietly. I was shocked because I was so sure that what we did was right. "Did you hear some women yelling at their children?" he asked me. I nodded, and he continued on. "The women were telling their children to not drink from the cup or eat the white bread."

"Why would they do that?" I asked. I still didn't understand why anyone would be upset with us.

"The women didn't want their children sharing a cup to drink the milk. Some kids have tuberculosis and worms and illness, and their moms were afraid they would give it to their children when they drank out of the same cup. Also, the white bread doesn't move through the body very well, and kids can get bloated."

I was shocked! I thought we were doing good things, and now I saw that perhaps we shouldn't have done anything. I was very confused. How was I supposed to understand all of this?

"Did you see the parade of the idol down the street?" I asked him. He nodded. "Did my mom do wrong by yelling at the priest?"

He chuckled quietly. "No, that was funny. I liked it." He picked up another pebble from the ground and shook it in his fist with the first one. I could hear them hitting together in his fist, and the sound was kind of soothing. "Did you see some people kneeling when the parade went by? Well, those people are not Christians. They do that for a reason."

He got up and stretched his back, a small groan escaping his lips. "Get up, Young White, and I will show you the reason. Come with me."

Together we walked along the dusty road toward the other end of the village of hogans. We walked so far that I could no longer hear the chanting and singing of the medicine man or the raving of the man staked to the ground. After about ten minutes of walking we came to a large circle of twenty hogans. The man stopped and pointed to them.

"Right there is the reason, Young White. Tell me what you see," he motioned with his hand toward the circle. I looked closely, but I wasn't sure of what he meant.

"I see that all of the houses are arranged in a circle. I see small gardens with flowers and vegetables growing in them." I hesitated. "I'm not sure what it is that you want me to see," I told him.

"What is in the middle of the circle, Young White?" he asked while looking intently at me.

I sighed and looked again. In the middle of the circle was a windmill. At the base of the mill I saw a woman filling a jug from a spigot. When the jug was full she turned off the spigot by pushing down on a handle. I watched her walk past a small wooden building that had a cross on it.

"There is a well here, and I think that is a church over there," I pointed to the small building with the cross on it. The man quickly pushed my pointing hand back down to my side.

"It is rude to point," he said quietly. "You are right. There is a well here that works all the time, and that building is not a church. It is a Catholic chapel. The priest comes to give Mass here twice a month. He brings a man with him to do maintenance on the well." We stood looking at the well and the chapel.

"I still don't understand," I told him. He nodded and walked over to a bench that was sitting over against one wall of the chapel. I followed him, and we sat together for a few silent moments.

"I call this 'Catholic Town.' The people who live here go to the Catholic church in town every week. They kneel when the priest goes by them. They confess and ask him to bless them. They pay him to come out here to say Mass twice a month. In return they get to build their houses next to the well. If your house is next to the well you have water for drinking, for washing, and for growing plants." He watched a woman water her garden and made a small noise at the back of his throat.

"But there is another well in town. I know because I saw the plans for it. My dad talked with Mr. Roberts about fixing it," I said excitedly.

"Yes," he said agreeably. "But the priest gets men to go at night and break the other well so that only the Catholic well works all the time. Only Catholics can use this well. If you really need to use it you can pay big money for the water, but Catholics use it for free. Most people just hitch up a horse to a buckboard wagon and drive out three miles to the next well for water rather than pay for Catholic water." He made the small noise again and pursed his lips. "Nobody really trusts the priest."

We watched silently as other people came to get water from the well. A few came over and spoke to us. When they spoke to me they only said a few words in English, but they spoke to the man who was with me in their own Navajo language. Some of them would squat down on their haunches to speak with him. We sat there for about an hour quietly observing Catholic Town. I was thinking about what the man said and what I had seen.

"I saw some houses out on the road when we drove into the reservation," I told him. "Windows were broken out, and doors were torn off. I saw refrigerators and things out in the yard. It looked really junky."

The man just watched a woman hanging out clothes to dry. I waited for a response, but he didn't seem ready to give one.

"Why do people live like that?" I asked. "My dad says that they aren't civilized."

The man looked at me with a stony gaze. I thought he might be angry, but he soon turned back to watching the woman hang up her clothes.

"The windows were busted out because the new houses smelled bad. It is better to smell the sagebrush and feel the wind than to be in a place without air moving around. Sometimes a man or woman gets drunk and breaks out a window for no reason," he said, still looking away from me. "A white man door means to keep people out and keep people in. We want privacy, but we like the blankets. It is what we are used to, and it is more friendly than a wood door."

"What about all of the junk scattered around?" I asked.

The man threw a pebble at a pile of goat manure. "When things break and don't work the Bureau gives us a new one, but they don't take away the old one. Some people tried to bury the old things, but the Bureau told us that we couldn't. The Elders asked the Bureau to haul off the old things, but they told us that there was no money to do that."

Finally the man got up and stretched his back. I took it as a signal to get up as well. Together we walked back toward his nephew who was still staked out on the ground.

"I have to go to the bathroom," I told my companion. He looked at me with a slight smile.

"We don't have bathrooms here," he said quietly. I was astounded.

"Where do people go if they have to pee?" I asked with some urgency, looking around in desperation.

He pointed his chin toward a very small building off to the left. "That is an outhouse. We go there," he said. "Have you ever used an outhouse?" I had used one at a farm once. I nodded in the affirmative as I began to dance a rather nervous jig. "I will take you there," he said with a chuckle.

We quickly walked over to the building, and I opened the door. A terrible smell assaulted my nose. Flies buzzed around landing on my hair and face. I saw a wooden bench against the back wall that had a hole in it. I noticed a crust of something that I could only guess was poop. I was desperate so I took a deep breath and held it while I did my business. As soon as I finished I burst out of the building and gasped for sweet clean air. The man laughed out loud and clapped me on the shoulder. "You will get used to it soon, Young White," he said with a smile.

We walked back to the log where his brother still sat watching

DUST OF A DISTANT MESA

the medicine man who was still chanting and dancing and shaking his gourds. The man sat next to his brother, and I sat next to him. Now that I knew the medicine man was asking God to pay attention to the problems here on earth I wasn't nervous about watching.

"My mom asked God to get rid of a ghost," I said by way of conversation. The two men looked at me with interest and surprise. "A man was killed right at our front door, and his ghost haunted our place, but Mom prayed, and God made the ghost leave."

The two brothers talked together quietly for a few minutes. They seemed to be upset about something. They refused to look at me, and I saw them move a little bit away from me. I decided to change the subject by asking about something that bothered me.

"Why does everyone call me 'Young White'?" I asked. "My name is Dale."

The brother farthest from me looked at me with renewed interest. "We Indians like to name people after some physical thing we see in a person. What do you think we should call you? I wanted to call you 'Skinny Butt' or 'Spotted Face,' but my nephew called you 'Young White' because you are young and white. That is what we will call you now."

"When you put it that way I think 'Young White' will be just fine," I said with a smile. I liked the fact that I had a name chosen by the Indians. "What is your name? What is the name of your nephew?" I asked.

The men looked at me soberly. They talked together for a few minutes before the man I had been with all morning turned and answered.

"It is not polite to ask one of the People for their name. Because you are young I will let it pass. I can tell you the Christian name of my brother and me. I am Andrew. People call me Andy. My brother is Amos." He stopped and looked at his nephew who had raised his head off of the ground and was listening intently. He pointed at him with his chin. "He would have to agree to tell you his name. I can't tell you myself."

The man staked out on the ground said something to the medicine man who paused in his chanting before replying. There was a conversation in Navajo that seemed to last for a long time. Finally both men looked at me. The man on the ground spoke to me in a harsh voice.

"I will tell you, Young White, but this man must purify you a little bit first. The name I will tell you is not my real name. It is more like a nickname. Do you understand?" he asked.

I nodded and watched with apprehension as the medicine man approached.

"Stand up and walk over there," Andy told me indicating a spot a little ways from the log. I walked over there and waited. "Don't move while the medicine man purifies you."

I stood still as a tree while the medicine man walked around me chanting. He threw some kind of powder on me. He took a feather out of a bag that he carried, and he moved it up and down on my body, just barely brushing me with it. Finally, he shook the gourds over me for a few minutes. I didn't feel any different, but it was an interesting experience. The medicine man finished and walked back to resume his chants around the man on the ground. I followed him from a discreet distance.

I stopped and went down on my haunches like I had seen Indians do before so that I was closer to the man on the ground. He raised his head to look at me.

"You can call me Yas," he said. "It means 'snow' in our language." He put his head back on the ground as if the effort to speak was getting to be too great for him. His mother came carrying her gourd and tilted it to give him a drink.

I watched silently for a moment before going to sit back on the log. I thought that it was strange that a man would have the name Snow, but I figured there had to be a reason. The brothers and I sat silently on the log for quite a while. Everything was so different and strange to me. Although I had a hundred questions I was afraid to ask them because I felt that I had made enough mistakes for one day. Now that I was purified I figured I had better stay that way for a while.

Right about the time that my stomach rumbled I saw two women come around the side of the hogans. The woman in the lead carried something in one hand that was covered by a cloth and in the other she had a small kettle with a spoon sticking out of it. The other woman carried some gourd bowls. They came to us and stopped in front of Amos. He lifted the cloth and pulled two flat, round pieces of bread off the pile. The lady with the bowls handed him one, and he filled it with beans from the kettle. It smelled great. Andy did the same as Amos.

Then the ladies stood in front of me. Andy said something to them, and the lady with the bowls gave a soft grunt and handed me a bowl. The other lady handed me two pieces of bread and dipped out some beans for me from her kettle. She smiled and said, "You will like this, Young White. It is fry bread and beans with just a little chili."

I started to eat, but Andy and Amos bowed their heads to pray. I did the same. We all prayed silently, and I looked up when I heard a sigh from one of the brothers. I don't know why, but I was a bit surprised to see them pray when just a few feet from us a medicine man was dancing and chanting.

I smiled and watched as the women served Yas's mother. She in turn helped Yas eat by tearing off small chunks of the bread and using it as a scoop for the beans. She carefully placed it in his mouth, waiting patiently while he chewed it. He ate until he was full and then turned his head away from his mother. She sat back and ate the rest herself. I heard Yas give a long drawn out sigh, and then he began to rave again.

"Sweet manna from heaven!" he yelled out. "Jesus feed me 'til I want no more! Christ will gird himself and serve us with sweet manna all around!"

I ate my food as I had seen Andy and Amos eat theirs. They had torn off a bit of bread and used it as a scoop for the beans. I did the same and promptly burned the roof of my mouth. I was hungry, but I waited a few minutes for things to cool down before starting to eat again.

When I finished Andy took my bowl and stacked it with his. We sat quietly while our food settled and watched as Yas alternated between resting and raving. Soon he was resting more than raving.

Andy looked over at me, and I could tell he was thinking about something. After a few minutes he asked me a question.

"Young White, are you a Christian?" he asked with all sincerity. He watched my eyes as I answered.

"Yes, I am. I gave my heart to Jesus, and He guides me every day," I said with a smile.

He nodded in a thoughtful manner. "Does God hold you in His hand?" he asked quietly.

"What does that mean?" I asked. I was confused by the question.

"Does God keep you safe from harm? That is what I am asking."

I thought about that for a few minutes before replying. "I think He does. I heard that every person gets a guardian angel. I know that God loves me and knows everything about me. I think He protects me." I tried to answer confidently, but the fact that he asked the question made me reflect on what it means to be guarded from harm.

Andy nodded again, and we returned to watching Yas thrash around on the ground.

The quiet waiting put me to sleep as well. I barely remember someone picking me up and sitting me against a building in the shade. I slept soundly until I felt something tugging on my shoe. At first I thought it was a goat, and I kicked out to shoo it away. I opened my eyes just a slit and saw my dad standing in front of me. His hands were on his hips, and he didn't look pleased to see me sleeping. He kicked my foot, and I realized that was what I felt earlier. I jumped to my feet and dusted off my bottom.

"Where have you been?" he asked me. "I called your name, and you didn't come when I called."

I started to tell him about Catholic Town, but he held up his hand to silence me. Yas had begun to rave again, and Dad had turned toward the sound.

"What are they doing to that poor man?" he said between clenched teeth. He walked quickly over to the log where Andy and Amos were sitting. I trotted behind trying to explain about Yas, but Dad didn't seem to be listening. He stopped in back of the log and spoke angrily to the men.

"Why are you torturing that poor man?" Dad asked, and he pointed at Yas who was raving on about rocks and trees and skies and seas. "In the name of Jesus I command you to release him and set him free."

Andy stood up and faced Dad. "My name is Andy," he said and held out his hand. Dad didn't shake so he let it fall back to his side. He pointed toward his brother with his chin. "This is my brother, Amos," he said. Amos lifted his hand a little bit.

Dad turned red in the face. He seemed very angry. "Do you think this is funny?" he asked the brothers. "I said to let that man go."

Andy looked at Dad for a moment before replying. "In the name of Jesus I am going to say 'No.' That man will stay right there."

Dad bunched his fists, and for a minute I thought there might be a fight. Finally Dad said, "Let's go, boy." He grabbed my shoulder and wheeled me around. He marched stiff legged and straight backed over to the car. I just had time to hop in before he started it up, threw it into gear and drove off quickly.

"I'm going to report them to the Sheriff," he said angrily. I heard him muttering other things that sounded like threats.

"Dad," I began. "Andy and Amos are the uncles of the man on the ground whose name is Yas. They staked him to the ground because he asked them to do it. They are just trying to. . ."

"Shut up!" My dad rounded on me, and his anger seemed to fill the car. "Didn't I tell you that all Indians are dirty, lying thieves? You can't trust an Indian—ever!" he exclaimed. "What part of that don't you understand?"

Dad drove on, and I heard him say something about having a stupid son. It hurt my feelings, but I kept it to myself.

"Why are you so angry?" I asked. He jammed on the brakes, and the car came to a shuddering stop. Dad leaned over and got his face very close to mine.

"Amos and Andy are two black Negro comedians on television. Those men were putting on an act for you. I don't know what their real Indian names are, but they certainly knew you were an idiot who would believe anything. That other guy, Yas? Well that's the way Negroes say 'yes.' You don't know anything." Dad straightened up and started the car back onto the road. "Dale, you have to be smarter in the future. I can't believe how stupid and gullible you are."

We rode in silence back to the house. I thought over everything he told me. It didn't seem to me that the men were lying.

Supper was on the table when we walked in the door. Mom kissed Dad, and we all sat down to eat. Mom asked questions, and I just told her about the bread and beans. I described the hogans to Linda and Roger. I kept the rest to myself.

That night I set out the mouse traps before going to bed. Roger crawled in on his side, and Mom put Paul in his crib. Linda jumped into her bed and asked Mom to sing to us before the lights went out.

I went to sleep thinking about God watching over us, and I fell asleep wondering what it meant when Andy asked if God held me in His hands. I hoped He did. I counted on it.

FIVE

THE HAND OF GOD

I woke up excited about the day ahead. It was Sunday, and we were going to a new church. I took it for granted that we would join the church because Dad was going to be doing some work for them. I knew that it was important for us to be on time and to be on our best behavior.

I gathered the mice traps quickly and ran outside to deposit the dead bodies into Mr. Garza's metal trash box. I ran back in and took my place at the breakfast table. Dad and Mom were drinking coffee and talking to each other in low tones. Mom was never happier than on Sunday when we were in church. I figured it was the one time each week when she was absolutely sure of her faith and how to live it out.

Mom hummed a hymn as she walked around the kitchen preparing and serving our breakfast of toast and eggs. We waited until the food was on the table before Dad prayed and asked the Lord to bless it. As I dug into my eggs I noticed that Paul was throwing some of his food on the floor and that he had spilled some milk on himself. Mom had just lowered herself into a chair to eat so I hopped up to help with Paul.

As I picked up the eggs and wiped Paul's shirt and face I felt that I was being watched. I looked over at Dad and noticed that he was watching me over his coffee mug.

"Your hair is a mess," he said. "As soon as you finish eating I will take care of that."

I didn't usually pay much attention to how I looked. I wasn't sure what he meant by my hair being a mess. I ran a hand over my red-brown hair and felt some hairs on the crown of my head standing up. I ran my hand over the hairs several times to see if I could press them down, but they just kept springing back up.

After breakfast Dad took Roger and me into the bathroom. I saw my Sunday clothes laid out, ready to be put on, but Dad led us right past them. He stood me in front of him so that I could see myself in the mirror. Dad took out a comb and a brush and a bottle of something with writing on the cover. I read the word "Vitalis" and I wondered what it was for. Dad unscrewed the lid and promptly doused my head with a generous portion of liquid. My eyes began to burn, and tears streamed down my cheeks. My scalp felt as if it was on fire. The smell of the stuff took my breath away, and I found myself gasping, sobbing, and dancing from foot to foot desperately trying to escape the torture.

"Hold still!" Dad growled at me. He spanked me hard on the bottom, and I made a valiant effort to follow his orders. He attacked my hair with the brush, and then he scored my scalp with the comb while trying to make a straight part in my hair. The burning liquid forced its way into my skin and caused my head to ache from ear to ear. Finally Dad gave a grunt of satisfaction and pushed me out of the bathroom.

"Get dressed, and don't mess up your hair," he barked at me. I could hear Roger crying as he was being doused with the fiery liquid and I had the greatest sympathy for him at that moment. I squirmed into my clothes, trying hard not to move any hairs out of place.

Mom came out of Linda's room holding her by the hand.

"Doesn't she look lovely?" Mom asked with a big smile. I thought she looked fine, but I couldn't understand what all the fuss was about.

"Did you put any Vitalis on her hair?" I asked. Mom laid her hand on Linda's head, running it over her smooth hair.

"Linda doesn't need anything like that," Mom replied. "Her hair is already perfect."

Linda stuck her tongue out at me, and I turned my back on her. I decided that I would just ignore her. Roger came up behind me crying softly. I helped him into his clothes, and he calmed down. If I could have found the inventor of Vitalis at that moment I would have held him down and doused him with the fiery liquid just so he would know how it felt. I was sure that he didn't use it himself or he never would have marketed the stuff.

Mom took Paul out of his crib and made sure that he was ready to go to church. He was drooling quite a bit. Mom said it was because he was teething. She handed him to me.

"Dale, hold your brother just a minute while I go to the bathroom," she said with a smile. I took the drooler and tried to hold him out away from me. He promptly reached up and started to play with my hair. I put him on the ground and ran over to a mirror that Mom had hung on the wall. Frantically I tried to fix my hair, but the effect was ruined, and I just couldn't get it right. I looked over to check on Paul, and to my horror I saw him eating dirt from a plant Mom had on the floor. He had dirt on his face and all down the front of his drool-drenched outfit. I reached down to stop him just as Dad came into the room.

"Dale!" he yelled. "Why aren't you watching your brother? And just look at your hair. What is the matter with you?" Dad smacked me hard on the bottom for the second time that morning. "Come with me, and I will get your hair fixed again."

Mom swooped in and took charge of Paul. I heard her talking and cooing to him as Dad tortured me again with Vitalis. I tried to stand still and not cry, but tears rolled down my cheeks anyway. As

I walked over to the back door trying to hide my distress Mom came up and gave me a large Tootsie Roll. She smiled at me and said, "This is for later." I was always grateful for Mom's little kindnesses. I put the Tootsie Roll in a pants pocket for whenever "later" came around.

Finally, it seemed that we were all ready for church. We drove up to the church, and the first thing I saw was a lady standing in front of the church with dark hair piled up high on her head and very red lipstick on her lips. She was holding a camera, and she waved at us as if she knew who we were and was expecting us. She seemed to be really excited because she was shuffling her feet in kind of a dancing motion. Dad turned to Mom and said, "That is Jewel Gray, the preacher's wife."

Mom cocked an eyebrow and tried to smile, but I could tell that Mrs. Gray wasn't making a good impression on her. Mom helped all of us kids out of the car before taking Dad by the hand. Together we walked up to the church. Mrs. Gray was saying things such as "Goodness gracious" and "Lord have mercy." She lurched forward and shook Dad and Mom by the hand.

"You must be Marliene," she said, turning a bright smile on Mom. "Brother Gray and I have already met Jim, and we just couldn't wait to meet you and your sweet children."

I could tell that Mom was trying to be gracious and friendly, but it sounded kind of forced to me. "Thank you, Jewel. It is so nice to be here. I hope we will like it," Mom said with a slight smile.

"Just call me Sister Gray," Mrs. Gray said. "You know we are all just brothers and sisters in Christ." Mom was holding Paul in her arms, and Sister Gray put her face close to Paul's. "You are sweet enough to eat," she cooed.

I didn't like anyone who even joked about eating my brother. She had big teeth, and I could just imagine her taking a bite out of Paul's chubby leg. Sister Gray turned her attention to Linda and stroked her hair. "You are just precious beyond words," she said as she continued to stroke her hair. Something in the way she stroked

Linda's hair bothered me. I didn't know why, but it just made me uncomfortable. Linda, though, preened and kind of twirled around as if to say, "Why, yes! I am special, aren't I?" It was enough to make a person gag.

Sister Gray's eyes happened to light on Roger. He had some kind of skin ailment that made his eyes crust up at the edges. His nose was always running, and snot ran in a continual river down his face. She bent down to see his face better.

"Is he all right?" she asked in a concerned voice. "We don't have a doctor here in town, but there is a good veterinarian who could look at him." Roger ran his tongue over his upper lip and sucked in some snot. Sister Gray gasped loudly.

"What's a veterinarian?" I asked.

Sister Gray turned her head slightly to get a better look at me. I caught her eye and knew immediately that she didn't like me, and I decided that I didn't like her.

"You must be the oldest," she said. She looked me up and down. "You sure are a scrawny little thing, aren't you now?"

I just looked at her in a way that I hoped showed how much I distrusted her. She gave a little laugh and kind of waved her hand. "A veterinarian is usually called a vet. They are just animal doctors is all," she said with a slight tilt of her head. I was not happy that she suggested that Roger go to see an animal doctor. I noticed that Sister Gray kept her distance from me and didn't have anything nice to say about me, which suited me just fine.

Sister Gray straightened up and held her camera up for us to see. "I want to take a picture of you all in your best clothes on this first day here," she said brightly. She arranged us together on the front steps of the church and took a picture. I still have a copy of that picture in my house. Every time I see it I am taken back in my memories to that day. I still see Sister Gray focusing her camera on us. I still hear Mom urging us to smile and stand still for the photo. I still remember the morning sun making me squint as I tried to obey Mom and muster up a smile.

After we took the picture Sister Gray led us into the church. The first thing I noticed was that the inside of the church was covered from top to bottom in pine paneling. The sanctuary smelled pleasantly of wax polish. The pews were made from the same pine and were made to be serviceable, not comfortable. I saw a few people in the church, and I figured that the rest would show up later. Sister Gray introduced us to everyone, but I couldn't keep all of the names straight.

Every man we met wore boots and bolo ties. Some wore western-style cowboy hats, which they took off their heads and held in their hands as they were introduced to us. The women were pleasant, and a few had turquoise and silver jewelry on their arms. They were plain, hard-working people who were friendly and outgoing. As we were making the rounds a short bald headed man trotted up and clapped Dad on the back.

"It is good to see you, Jim," he said with a hearty laugh. He turned to Mom and took her hand. "Hi. I'm Brother Gray, the preacher here. I think you have already met Jewel."

Mom nodded her head. "Yes. She has been introducing us to the other church members."

Brother Gray turned to Sister Gray and gave her a look that made her lower her head. "Sister Gray," he said in a quiet voice, "I don't see our children sitting in the pew. Perhaps they need their mother to get them out here."

Sister Gray murmured something I couldn't hear and quickly disappeared through a door at the front of the sanctuary. Brother Gray watched her go and then turned to face Mom.

"I don't know if Jim told you, but we live here at the church. We have a regular house with three bedrooms and two bathrooms attached to the sanctuary. You all are invited to have lunch with us today, and we can even visit a bit after the evening service," he said with a smile.

"Thank you!" Mom replied with a smile. "It is so nice of you to invite us for lunch."

Bother Gray ignored us children and immediately left to talk to the church members who were starting to file in. Dad went with him, and I heard him talking to some of the other men. I took the opportunity to look the church over again.

There was no place for a choir, but there was a large baptistery with a painted mural of rocks and water on the back wall. Some of the old casement windows had been cranked open to let out the morning heat and let in the cool breeze. There was a pine pulpit for the preacher to stand behind, and the front pews went right up to the pulpit.

I was looking at the baptistery trying to figure out how people got in and out of it when I heard a door open. I watched as four boys and a girl walked into the sanctuary followed by Sister Gray. The girl and two of the boys were teenagers. The other two boys looked to be about my age.

Sister Gray brought them over and introduced them to us. I only caught the names of the younger boys—John and Wesley. It turned out that John was one year older than me, and Wesley was one year younger. They didn't smile, and they didn't shake hands with us. The Gray children acted as if they would rather be anywhere than in a church service.

"We always have a Sunday school before church. I teach the children. We go to a room off to the side of the sanctuary," Sister Gray told Mom, and she indicated a door off to the left. She smiled, and I thought once again that she had big teeth and a smile that was just this side of wicked. I didn't want to have her as a Sunday school teacher, but when you are just a kid you don't get to make many choices.

Sister Gray pointed to the door and watched as John and Wesley obediently went inside. I held Roger and Linda by the hand as I led them into the sparsely furnished room. I saw a number of metal chairs set up around the perimeter and a small table and chair positioned opposite the door. John and Wesley were already seated to the left of the table. I steered us over to the right so that we could sit facing them. The boys just sat hunched over with their heads hanging down. We stared at them as they stared at the floor. They straightened up quickly when Sister Gray came into the room. Their eyes were already glazed over, and they seemed to be staring off into space.

"Good morning, children!" Sister Gray said with enthusiasm.

"Good morning," Linda, Roger, and I replied in unison. John and Wesley looked at us as if we were idiots for saying anything.

Sister Gray sat behind the table and fussed around with some papers she had brought in with her. She smiled brightly at us.

"Today we are going to learn about the disciples of Jesus," she said slowly. She talked as if we were stupid. I tried to listen respectfully, but it was difficult.

"There were only twelve disciples, and these people left everything to follow Jesus," she said with conviction.

I thought about that while she rattled on about leaving everything and following Jesus. I was sure that there were more than twelve disciples, but I was also sure that there were twelve apostles.

"Can anyone tell me their names? You know, the names of the twelve men who followed Jesus," she said, looking down at her paper.

I raised my hand she looked at me in surprise. "Dale, do you think you know their names?"

"I have a question," I said. "I am sure that there were more than twelve disciples. I think you are talking about the twelve apostles."

Sister Gray's eyes narrowed, and her mouth became a hard thin line. "Are you saying that I, the preacher's wife, don't know what I am talking about? You're just a runty little kid, and I am the preacher's wife."

John and Wesley had their mouths hanging open, and their heads swiveled from their mom to me and back. I swallowed hard, and I could feel the warmth as a blush rose to my face.

"All I am saying, Sister Gray, is that there were all of these other people like Mary, and Martha, and Lazarus who were disciples." I stopped to see if my logic had any effect on her. She just looked at me as if I was a dog to be pitied. "I think the men who you are talking about are called the apostles. I know some of their names, but I don't remember all of them."

Her eyes bore into mine. "OK. So what do you remember, Mr. Smarty Pants?"

I looked up to a corner of the room and recited what I could from memory. "There was Andrew and Peter, James and John." I paused to think about the other names. "There was Judas and Matthew and Simon. I think I remember a guy called Doubting Thomas." I looked at her and shrugged. "That's all I've got," I said. "Sorry, but I can't remember the rest."

John started laughing so hard that he choked, and Wesley had to slap him on the back. When he caught his breath he said, "You dummy. You forgot Mark and Luke and Paul and Barnabas."

Sister Gray turned on him quickly. "You mind your tongue," she told him in an angry voice making John wince and shrink back in his chair. She struggled to regain her composure by looking down at the table and shuffling papers again.

Linda leaned over and whispered "Why don't you just shut up? You are such a showoff."

After a minute or two Sister Gray seemed to calm down. She looked up with a grim smile and said, "Let's continue on. There is a really good song about the apostles, and I think we can sing it together." She hummed a little tune and then began to sing.

"You get a line and I'll get a pole, honey.

You get a line and I'll get a pole, babe.

You get a line and I'll get a pole,

We'll go down to the crawdad hole,

Honey, baby mine"

She smiled at us. "Why don't we all sing this song together?"

I raised my hand and waited for her to acknowledge me. She tilted her head slightly and stared at me as if I were an unruly dog.

"Sister Gray, I don't think that song has anything to do with the apostles or the disciples. I don't think it sounds very biblical," I said with all sincerity.

"Didn't Jesus say that he was going to make them fishers of men? Weren't some of those men fishermen?" she asked through gritted teeth. "I have been fishing all my life! Don't you tell me what songs we sing and don't sing," she said with a straight back and righteous, burning eyes. "Now let's sing that song."

So we sang the song three or four times. There were some other verses that I have forgotten, but I haven't forgotten the animosity of Sister Gray toward me. It was a real thing that hung in the air and had caused the hair on my arms and neck to stand up. I knew that it wouldn't ever go away, and I was concerned.

When we finished singing Sister Gray began to talk about the disciples and apostles. Her voice droned on and on, and I just stopped paying attention. I could tell that John and Wesley had developed a method of coping with the boredom by simply staring out into space. Roger and Linda seemed to be listening, but I just didn't know how much longer I could take it. I put a hand in my pocket and felt the Tootsie Roll that I had placed in there earlier. I blessed Mom for it and started to pull it out of my pocket when a thought crossed my mind.

I know that the one place the devil should be uncomfortable is in church, but I swear that he preys on those in the congregation who are bored or angry or just plain stupid. The thought that crossed my mind came straight from the devil himself. It grew in my imagination, and soon a plan was fully formed.

I unwrapped the Tootsie Roll as slowly and quietly as I could with one hand while it was still in my pocket. When Sister Gray looked down at her papers I pulled the Tootsie Roll out of my pocket and put it behind my back. I put my other hand back there as well and quickly and quietly rubbed the candy between my hands. I could tell that it was taking shape, and I just hoped that nobody noticed anything unusual until I was finished. Finally I had the shape just the way I wanted it. I waited for a diversion, and

Wesley provided it. The poor boy fell asleep and slipped out of his chair. His head hit the floor with a heavy thud, and the chair fell over backward. While Sister Gray was hounding him back into his chair and threatening him with fire and brimstone I threw the Tootsie Roll on the floor not far from where Sister Gray was sitting. Nobody noticed, and I waited for the perfect time to spring my trap.

When Sister Gray finished with Wesley she sat back down and began to drone on again as if nothing had happened. I let her go on for a minute or two before pointing to the Tootsie Roll on the floor.

"What is that?" I asked with the most innocent look I could muster. Sister Gray stopped speaking and craned her neck for a better look. John, Wesley, Linda, and Roger just stared at the dark object lying there. I went forward and picked it up, holding it so that everyone could see it. I held it to my nose and pretended to smell it. I wrinkled up my nose.

"This is dog poop!" I exclaimed. Then I took a bite of it and chewed lustily.

"Lord God Almighty! God have mercy!" Sister Gray shrieked. Her face went white with a slight greenish shade. I tore off a bit of the Tootsie Roll and gave it to Roger. He chewed it and grinned, showing teeth covered with the brown candy mixed with snot.

Sister Gray promptly leaned over a small trash can and threw up everything that she had in her stomach. It was a smelly stream of liquid and bits of food. When her stomach emptied out she began to have the dry heaves, retching over and over again.

I grabbed Linda and Roger by the hand and scooted out of there. We made our way over to Mom and Dad who were sitting in a pew listening to an older man read from the Bible. We sat next to them, and they seemed surprised to see us.

I saw John and Wesley run out of the Sunday school room and whisper something in the ear of their oldest brother. His eyebrows shot up, and he promptly left the pew. He went over to his father and bent down to whisper in his ear. Just then Sister Gray staggered out of the Sunday school room. She looked around with bleary eyes and finally focused in on me.

She pointed a shaking finger at me.

"That boy," she gasped between retches. "He is full of the devil, and God needs to get His hands on him."

Everyone looked at me, and I just shrugged as if I didn't know what she was talking about. Dad reached over and grabbed my ear.

"What have you done now?" he hissed at me.

"I just ate some of my Tootsie Roll," I said in all innocence. I held up the stub of it that was left.

Dad took it, smelled it, and took a bite. Sister Gray shrieked again and ran to a door that I assumed led to their living quarters. A shocked gasp rose from the audience. The Gray family disappeared one at a time following Sister Gray through the door.

I glanced around just in time to see Linda whispering in Mom's ear. Mom's head was bowed as she listened but suddenly lifted. Her eyes flashed toward me, and I knew that this was not going to end well. Mom leaned over and whispered in Dad's ear. His eyes were locked on me the whole time, and I saw his face grow angrier and darker.

Dad leaned down so that his face was right in mine.

"You are going to sit here quietly for the rest of the service. You won't say or do anything, do you understand me? I will deal with this when we get home." It was a death threat, pure and simple. I prayed and asked God to forgive me for giving in to temptation. I asked Him to have mercy on my soul.

Brother Gray came back into the sanctuary and walked to the front. The man who had been reading the Bible closed the cover of the Holy Book and yielded the pulpit to the preacher. Brother Gray cleared his throat and mustered up a smile.

"Well, we certainly have had some excitement this morning," he said in a comforting voice. "Sister Gray will be just fine. The children are caring for her. Now, being the godly woman that she is, she asked that we continue our services today."

Everyone murmured their approval, and I could see people nodding their heads. The congregation was full of people who expected to be able to soldier on in spite of pain or hardship. The cows must be milked, the crops must be harvested, the wood must be chopped, the buildings must be repaired regardless of how sick or hurt you might personally be.

Brother Gray beamed a smile over all of us. "I believe that we will now have some singing, and I will preach a shorter sermon so that I can help attend to Sister Gray."

That met with more murmurs of approval. There was a buzz of whispering, and I got the impression that everyone was glad that the sermon would be shorter.

Brother Gray turned to look at our family. "Today we have a special family with us. This is Jim and Marliene Sims. Why don't you stand so that we can see you better?"

We all stood, and Dad rested his hand on my shoulder as a reminder. Everyone offered an "Amen." There was no clapping in those very reserved days of a time gone past.

"Jim, why don't you come up here and help lead us in the music?" Brother Gray asked.

Dad quickly walked up to the front. He said a few words about how happy we were to be in New Mexico and how he hoped that we would make good friends here as we served the Lord. He opened the hymnbook and called out a page number. We sang a hymn called the doxology. It sounded familiar to me, and I was sure that I had heard some of the words spoken recently.

Dad sang in a strong tenor voice, and the people in the congregation seemed to respond well. There was an old lady who banged around on a piano that seemed to be in tune sometimes and other times not so much. The people in the congregation started out a little rusty, but their voices got stronger and richer as we continued on through the song. After we finished that song Dad led us in another song before turning the service back over to Brother Gray.

Dad sat next to me and indicated that I should put up my

hymnbook. The front of the book flew open, and I saw these words: "Edited by Walter Hines Sims." I pointed it out to Mom, and she shook her head.

"I don't think he is any relation of ours," she whispered. "I don't know of any well-educated people named Sims."

Brother Gray began to preach. He read some Scripture condemning women who wore jewelry and rich clothing. He railed about the use of lipstick and fingernail polish. He expounded on the loose morals of short skirts and being quick to follow the way of the world. He flung his arms about and paced back and forth in a very energetic way. Soon he was sweating and wiping his brow with a red handkerchief which he had produced from his back pocket.

While he was preaching away I heard something behind me. It was a clicking sound that seemed to be timed to the pastor's words.

"God hates those loose women who flaunt their bodies!"

Click.

"God is pleased with modesty and pureness."

Click.

Then I heard Brother Gray say "God calls us all to be people who set an example of holiness for the rest of those sinners. God grabs the sinners in His hands and throws them into the fiery pit. They are descending even now into the depths of hell!"

I heard a loud "AMEN!" coming from the same location as the clicks I had been hearing. I just couldn't help myself. I was compelled to turn and look.

There at the back of the sanctuary sat a man with a neat mustache. He held something in his hand that was silver and shiny. It took me a second to recognize it as fingernail clippers. That explained the clicks I had heard. He had been trimming his fingernails. He was looking up at the ceiling of the church with a kind of rapturous look on his face. I was about to turn back around, but I wasn't fast enough for Dad who thumped me hard on the head. I turned around quickly and sat like a statue until Brother Gray wound down his sermon. He gave a traditional Baptist invitation to anyone who wanted to be saved or join the church.

Dad grabbed my arm and forced me to stand up and walk with him. Mom carried Paul and the little kids followed suit as we walked up to the front of the sanctuary. Brother Gray shook all of our hands, and Dad told him that we were joining the church. Brother Gray motioned for the piano player to quit her playing. Quickly he lined us up at the front to the sanctuary.

"Brothers and sisters, we have a precious family joining our fellowship today. Brother Jim Sims will be helping us around the church. He works over at Brother Johnson's sawmill. He is also going to help the Roberts out on the reservation."

Brother Gray stopped and turned to Dad. "Watch your step among them injuns," he warned in a friendly way. He turned back to the congregation. "We need to vote them in as members. Everyone in favor say amen."

There arose a chorus of "Amen," the loudest from the man with the mustache. Everyone surged forward to shake our hands and introduce themselves to us. My earlier indiscretion seemed to have been forgotten. I hoped that it would simply disappear amid all of the goodwill that was washing over us.

When everyone was gone from the sanctuary Brother Gray turned to Dad with a sheepish grin. "Sister Gray and I wanted to have you all come over for lunch, but Sister Gray is not feeling so well."

Dad's hands dug into my shoulders, and I winced. My sins were still remembered.

"Perhaps if Sister Gray is feeling better tonight we can have a time together after the evening service," Brother Gray added.

Dad and Mom were gracious and watched as Brother Gray hurried through the door to his living quarters.

We all walked quietly out to the car. The drive home was equally as quiet. We filed into the house, and Mom put Paul into his crib so she could prepare some sandwiches for lunch. Linda,

Roger, and I looked at Dad. He turned and studied us. His eyes moved from one child to the other until they rested on me. There was fire in that look. I figured that it was a prelude to hell, and my knees began to shake. Dad pointed to our old beat up sofa.

"Linda, you and Roger sit there. I want you to see the consequences of being a sinner," he said in a low voice. They quickly took their seats and waited with expectant looks for the show to begin.

Dad bent down and put his face close to mine.

He started out quietly by reminding me of what I had done. His face got red, and his voice got louder as he moved on to how my actions had embarrassed him and all of the family. He told me that our ancestors had never included a person as sinful as me. His voice rose another couple of decibels as he described what I was going to feel like when he finished with me. Sweat broke out on my brow. I just wanted to die right then and there and be spared the gruesome intermediate steps.

Suddenly Mom appeared in the room with an open Bible in her hand. She stood between Dad and me.

"Jim, he is just a boy—just a boy! Let me remind you what the Bible says in Ephesians. 'And, ye fathers, provoke not your children to wrath: but bring them up in the nurture and admonition of the Lord.'" Mom's voice had a pleading edge to it. "Please go easy on him. The move has been hard on all of us."

Dad looked at me, and I saw that most of the fire was gone. He still had that strong glower, but his shoulders slumped a little bit. When he was angry he seemed to grow in height, and a burning fire flew from his eyes scorching everything within view. Now he seemed to shrink, and he pursed his lips as if in deep thought. I prayed that God would bless Mom for trying to save my life.

"Dale, what you did was wrong. You know that, don't you?" he asked in a quiet voice. I was so scared that all I could do was nod. "You are going to go without lunch today. You are going to lay in bed all afternoon. When we go to church tonight you will apologize to Sister Gray in front of her family. Do I make myself clear?"

My mouth was hanging open. I forced myself to answer, "Yes, sir."

Dad sighed and went into the kitchen.

The death angel had passed me by, and I was back in the land of the living. I dutifully walked over to the bed and lay there as the rest of the family ate lunch. I thought about my conversation with Andy and his question about being held in the hand of God. Maybe this was proof, I thought. As I considered it I decided that it was only proof that Mom loved me more than Dad. I was still thinking about this as the rest of the family finished lunch.

"Everyone has to take an afternoon nap," Dad declared. "I don't want to hear a peep out of any of you."

Roger joined me in the bed and was soon asleep. Paul was sleeping quietly in his crib, and Linda was motionless in her room. A quiet stillness descended on us, and soon I heard Dad snoring softly.

I firmly believe that the devil knows who among us is weaker than the others and marks the weak ones for torment and destruction. He had already wreaked havoc on me once that day. Now he was at it again as I lay in the bed. My thoughts wandered to the idea of being protected by God and how you could know. I turned over in my mind how to figure out if I was held in the hand of God. A plan formed in my mind, and I decided to follow through on it. Looking back on it I am amazed that my stupidity knew no bounds in those days. There were times when my teachers declared that I might be a genius, but the devil knew better than that.

I left the bed and walked into the kitchen. Quietly I picked up a chair and maneuvered it by the cabinet where Dad kept his gun and bullets. I climbed up and opened the cabinet to have a look.

The gun and holster were sitting there ready for use. I ran my hand over the leather and touched the cold steel of the gun. My eyes fell on the box of bullets. The top was off of the box, and I could see the blunt end of the bullets sticking up. I reached out and plucked one out of the box. It was smooth, and I knew it had been engineered to be lethal.

I took it in my hand and stepped down from the chair. I paused to listen, but the family was all sleeping quietly. I opened the kitchen door and snuck out into the warmth of the afternoon.

Mr. Garza was working on one of his wrought-iron doors and didn't pay any attention as I slipped around the corner of the house. I walked over to the brick that I used to kill the mice. Picking it up, I weighed it in my hand and considered my next actions. Everything seemed to be in order in my head so I decided to proceed on.

Mr. Garza looked at me with curiosity as I walked past him and headed for the porch. I walked up onto the porch and set the bullet down so that it was pointing away from our part of the house. I picked up the brick and brought it down with a sharp swing to crush the end of the bullet. Nothing happened.

Mr. Garza was watching me closely now. He started to walk over in my direction, craning his neck in order to have a better look at what I was doing. He saw the bullet on the porch, and his eyes widened. I figured I had one more chance to fire off that bullet.

Mr. Garza started running toward me, and I gave one more mighty swing. I heard Mr. Garza say, "Mother of God!" just as the brick hit the bullet. There was a loud explosion, and the bullet hit something, ricocheted off with a whine, hit Mr. Garza's metal trash box, and whined off into the distance. I was stunned.

Mr. Garza grabbed my arm and turned me around so that he could look at me. Quickly he ran his hand over my body, turning me this way and that, to see if I had been hit by the bullet.

"You stupid boy," he cried. "What were you thinking?"

I smiled. "I was trying to figure out if God held me in His hands." I told him about my conversation with Andrew on the reservation. "I figured that if I could make the bullet go off and not get hurt then I would know if I was held in God's hands."

Mr. Garza muttered to himself and ran his hands through his

hair. "That is tempting God. You must never tempt God like that! He will answer, but you will pay for it."

The front door opened, and Dad walked out. "What is going on here? I thought I heard a gun go off."

Mr. Garza told Dad about the whole thing in graphic detail. "He could have killed himself, or me, or some passerby. He said that he was testing to see if he was held in God's hands."

Dad grabbed my arm so hard that it hurt. "Thank you, Mr. Garza," he said through clenched teeth. I saw Mom, Linda, and Roger crowd into the doorway. "I will take it from here." Dad swung me off my feet and propelled me past Mom and into the front room. He kicked the door closed behind him without letting go of my arm. He turned me to face him, and the fire was back in his eyes. "You stay right here, and I will be back in a minute."

I was shaking from the shock of the explosion, and the great anger I had seen rekindled in my dad. Linda and Roger sat back on the old sofa with eyes as big as saucers. Mom wrung her hands as she stood there looking at me.

"What were you thinking, son?" she asked. "What has gotten into you?"

Dad reappeared in the room carrying one of his Mexican made leather sandals. He called them *huaraches*. It was long with a thick leather sole. He held it by the heel and swung it against a chair. It made a swishing sound, and when it hit the chair it cracked like a whip. I winced, and I knew this was going to be the end.

I looked up at Mom and said, "Mom?" She swung into action.

"Jim, remember that he is just a boy. Please don't go hard on him. Remember the Scripture?"

Dad grinned at her, but his eyes lost none of the fire. He reached over and picked up a Bible and began to thumb through it. He found what he was looking for and thrust the Bible at me.

"Dale, read to your mom Proverbs 23:13 and 14," he commanded me.

In a quavering voice I read "Withhold not correction from the child; for if thou beatest him with the rod he shall not die. Thou shalt beat him with the rod, and shalt deliver his soul from hell."

Linda gasped. "He said 'hell'," she whispered loudly.

Mom turned white and sat down heavily next to Linda and Roger as if her legs could no longer hold her up.

Dad stood over me. "Bend over," he said in an angry tone. I knew I deserved this beating and more, so I obediently bent over. Dad laid it on thick and heavy with his huarache. Each time he hit my bottom it lifted my feet off the floor. I began to cry after the third hit, and I was just a sobbing puddle of repentant boy by the time he finished.

"Go to the bed and stay there until it is time for church," Dad commanded. I forced my sore legs to move me over to the bed, and I gingerly crawled up on it. My tears streamed from shame and pain. I lay quietly on my side with my eyes closed. The rest of the family went into the kitchen, and I heard Mom and Dad talking quietly. I lay there for the rest of the afternoon, separated from my family and separated from my God. I prayed for forgiveness, but I didn't feel forgiven.

I must have fallen asleep because the next thing I knew someone was roughly shaking my shoulder. I opened my eyes a slit to see my sister standing there.

"Hey, sinner," she said with a smile. "It's time to wake up and go to church."

I tried to roll over, but my backside was so sore that I couldn't do it. I groaned as I eased myself off the bed and stood up.

"Sinners get what they deserve," my sister taunted. She turned and walked away.

I found that the pain receded a bit as I began to move. I was sore and stiff, but I was able to hobble out to the car. The drive to church was quiet. Mom didn't look at me. Roger made faces at me. Dad watched me in the rearview mirror. I didn't want to go to church, but I didn't have a choice. I was sure that everyone had abandoned me because of my great sins.

When we arrived at church I noticed a few adults standing outside as if they were waiting for us. Dad shook hands with a few of the men, and they all waited outside to talk while Mom herded us kids into the sanctuary.

I sat in the uncomfortable hard pew while people filed in for the evening service. My sore behind kept me from sitting quietly. I squirmed, trying to find a comfortable way to sit. The Gray family walked into the sanctuary and sat in the pew opposite ours. Sister Gray seemed to have regained her composure. John and Wesley leaned forward to look at us and then leaned back to sit very upright in the pew.

Brother Gray walked to the front and smiled at everyone.

"Tonight we will have a short time of worship," he said with a wide smile. "I think we should have a time of singing, a time of prayer, and then all go to our houses to get ready for the week ahead of us." He looked over at Dad. "Jim, why don't we have a song and then a prayer? Just continue that until we have sung ten songs and prayed ten prayers? You can lead us."

I was glad that my sins didn't keep Dad from being a leader at the church. He confidently walked to the front and began leading the congregation in singing their hymns. People would shout out their favorite song and we would sing it with gusto. Then Dad would ask for a volunteer to pray, and somebody would stand to deliver a short but heartfelt prayer to God. When the service ended everyone shook hands and exchanged hugs.

"Why don't you come back here to the house, and we can have some sandwiches and chips," Brother Gray said to Dad. "I think we all need to get to know each other better." He smiled at Dad and Mom and pointed to the door, which I guessed led back to their house. Dad nodded and followed Brother Gray. Mom picked up Paul, and the rest of us followed Dad.

I was very surprised by the size of the house at the back of the church. There was a spacious kitchen and dining area, two bathrooms, and three bedrooms. It seemed a lot bigger than our apartment. Brother and Sister Gray had one of the bedrooms. The four boys all slept in one bedroom, and the girl had her own bedroom.

Brother Gray escorted us into the kitchen/dining area where his family was already seated around the table. We stood there looking at them, and they just sat there looking at us. Dad cleared his throat.

"My son, Dale, has something to tell you." Dad looked down at me and squinted his eyes a little. "You do have something to tell these people, don't you, Dale?"

Everybody looked at me expectantly, John and Wesley with their mouths hanging open. I nodded and began the short speech I had practiced in my head.

"I am sorry for taking a Tootsie Roll and shaping it like a dog turd and throwing it on the floor and pretending to eat a dog turd," I said quietly and quickly. Dad reached over and thumped me hard on the head.

Linda said in a loud whisper "He said 'turd'."

"We don't say 'turd.' That is low talk, and we just don't need to use it. Now apologize again," Dad said in a low growly voice.

"I apologize for saying 'turd' because it is wrong to say 'turd' in public," I said with my head hanging down. Dad sighed heavily, and John and Wesley giggled.

Brother Gray gave a hearty laugh. "That is quite all right, boy," he said to me. "Let's have some supper."

We ate sandwiches and chips, and there was even soda pop! When Brother Gray finished he turned on their TV. He changed the channel until he found the *Red Skelton Show*. All of the adults made their way to the living area. The older Gray kids made for the back door. Dad looked at us in a speculative way.

"Linda, you and Roger stay here with us," he said. "Dale, you can go play with the Gray boys."

I looked over at John, and he shrugged. He turned away, and I followed him back to his bedroom. Wesley was already there sitting on the floor.

"Where are your older brothers?" I asked. John jerked his thumb to the wall behind him.

"I think they went out to be with some friends," he said. "They try to stay away from the house as much as possible."

I nodded. If I could I would stay away from my house as long as possible during the day. John and I sat on the floor by Wesley. He was putting a puzzle together, and we just watched him for a few minutes. I was getting bored when John looked up and smiled.

"I know what we can do," he said brightly. "We can play this game that we call 'alligator catch a monkey.' The way it works is that one of us is the alligator and sits in the middle of the room. The rest of us jump from bed to bed like monkeys over the head of the alligator and try not to get caught. If you're caught then you become the alligator until you catch someone else."

"Sounds like fun," I agreed. "Who gets to be the alligator first?"

John pointed at Wesley. "He always gets to start. He likes being the alligator. He may be small, but he sure is quick."

Wesley smiled and nodded. "I'm quicker than snot," he said with a big grin.

I looked around the room to plot my path of escape. My bottom was still sore, but I figured I could still make a jump or two. There was a bed on each wall, one for each boy. Two beds had windows over them. It looked like an easy game to me because there were plenty of beds to jump to.

John and I got onto beds across the room from each other. John said, "Go!" and we started jumping from bed to bed to escape Wesley. He was quick, just like he said. He almost nabbed me a couple of time, and I stopped to catch my breath. I noticed that he had turned his back to concentrate on John, and I launched myself to another bed.

While I was in mid-air I saw Wesley turn quickly and make a grab for my legs. I twisted my body and just avoided capture. When I twisted, it changed my trajectory, and I landed on the bed in a way that caused the mattress to throw me against a window ledge.

I heard, rather than felt, a loud crunching sound. I went limp and rolled off the bed. I opened my eyes, but found that I could only see out of one of them. Wesley was looking at me in horror, and John jumped down to quickly help me to my feet.

"We need to get you some help," John said in a worried tone of voice. He supported my arm and steered me down the hall to the living area. The adults were watching TV and laughing so they didn't see us at first.

"I think Dale might need some help," John said loudly.

Brother Gray turned to look first, and the smile disappeared quickly from his face. Sister Gray took one look and headed for the kitchen sink where she threw up for the second time that day. Dad came over and peered down into my face.

"Can you see?" he asked.

"I can see out of my left eye, but I can't see anything out of my right eye," I said.

Mom began to cry. She covered her mouth with her hands, and her shoulders shook from the heavy sobs escaping her throat.

"The boy needs a doctor," Brother Gray said. "He needs a doctor fast, but the closest one is in Albuquerque." He bit his lip, and a small frown creased his forehead.

"We do have a veterinarian," he said quietly. "She can't give medicine, but she might be able to sew things up." He hurried over to the phone and made a call. I could hear him speaking to someone in urgent tones. He hung up and came back over to us.

"OK. The vet said that she will do what she can. You can go right to her clinic." Brother Gray drew something on a piece of paper and handed it to Dad. "Just follow these directions, and you will get there quickly. You can leave the other kids with us."

Mom picked up Paul and hugged him close. "The little one is coming with us," she said between sobs. "Linda, you look after Roger, and we will be back soon to get you."

Dad hustled us out to the car. There was a swift urgency in his every movement. He didn't look at me, but Mom rubbed my shoulder, and it was some comfort. By the time we arrived at the vet's clinic the pain had begun to set in. It rolled over me in waves, and I didn't know if I could stand it. Dad helped me out of the car and we walked to the clinic together. I was shivering, probably from shock.

The door of the clinic opened, and a tall, thin woman in blue jeans beckoned us inside. She bent down and looked at me as Dad explained what had happened. She nodded and took me by the arm.

"I am going to take him back here to look things over and work on him," she told Mom and Dad. "I can't give him any medicine, but I think I can help him."

She walked me a few steps toward the back and then turned around when she heard Mom and Dad following.

"I don't want you back there with us while I am working on the boy," she said quietly. "You will just distract him and maybe make things worse."

Dad looked like he was going to object. He stared at the vet for a minute and then nodded. He took Mom by the arm and steered her toward some chairs in the outer office.

The vet put her hand on my back and kind of pushed me along until we came to a room with a big metal table. She turned on the light and began to take things out of some cabinets by the wall.

"Climb up on that table so I can have a good look at the wound," she commanded.

It took some effort because I was still shivering, but I finally got up on the table and sat there watching the vet. She had a tray that was on a stand that had wheels on the bottom. She was quickly setting bottles and instruments on the tray in a very precise manner. I noticed that she had some large squares of cloth that she was soaking with something from a bottle.

"I need to clean your wound a little bit," she said in a kind tone of voice. "This might hurt some. Can you stay real still while I work on you?" she asked.

"I will try," I replied in a quavering voice. "But I'm shivering, and it may be hard to do."

She nodded and proceeded to gently wipe my right brow and eye. Soon I could see again. "There's that eye," she said with a smile. She held the cloth to my brow as she looked closely into my eye. "I think your eye is going to be just fine," she said in a warm tone of voice. "You just had a flap of skin and a bunch of blood keeping you from seeing with that eye."

She turned to the tray and picked up a needle. Expertly she poked some thread through the needle eye and evened it up.

"I am going to have to close up that wound," she said earnestly. "I can't give you anything to deaden the pain. I need you to bite on this and not move or make any sounds."

She shoved a tongue depressor between my teeth and quickly set to work. It hurt badly, but I tried to be brave. Honestly it didn't hurt as much as Dad's spanking.

"God must hold you in His hands," she said as she drew the thread through my skin. "Another quarter of an inch lower and you would be blind in that eye. That cut went clear to the bone."

I was stunned by what I heard. I took the tongue depressor out of my mouth.

"What did you say?" I asked in a quavering voice.

She stopped working and looked at me for a few seconds. "I said that the cut went clear to the bone."

"No. I meant the thing you said about God's hands," I told her.

"Oh, that." She shoved the tongue depressor back into my mouth. "That's just an expression we use in these parts. It means that God is looking out for you."

My pain went away as I thought about what she said. She finished sewing me up and slapped a huge bandage over the wound. She gave me some aspirin for the pain. I crawled down off the table, and we walked back to where Dad and Mom were sitting waiting for us. Mom came over and hugged me.

"He is going to be just fine," the veterinarian said. He sat real still and didn't moan or cry or anything. He was very brave."

Dad was holding Paul, and he looked at me in a way that made me think he was almost proud of me. He paid the vet and ushered us back to the car. When we arrived at the Grays' house at the church Dad made Mom and me stay in the car while he went in to get Linda and Roger. The drive home was very quiet.

Mom put us all to bed and sang her song. I lay on my side and tried to go to sleep. Roger rolled over so that he could look at my face.

"You are ugly," he said. "Linda said you are a sinner."

"You're ugly, too," I told him. "I may be a sinner, but Jesus forgives me, and I am held in the hands of God."

I rolled over onto my sore backside. I was convinced now that God did hold me in His hands. I drifted off to sleep thinking about the goodness of God. I just hoped I could measure up to His expectations for me. The next day I was going to be starting at a new school, and I was worried about it. I knew that God would hold my hand as I went through the next few days, and that made all the difference.

SIX

A DIFFERENT LANGUAGE

I had always enjoyed going to school. It had always seemed to me to be a place filled with interesting books and children.

And school had always smelled better than my house, too. Where we lived before, my dad used to smoke all the time, and the smell had permeated everything we owned. Since we only bathed twice in a week I could never manage to wash out the stink. At my old school, none of the other kids wanted to sit beside me because of the smell of the smoke, and I'd never blamed them.

I had attended a school in first grade for about two months before I was transferred to another school. My teacher at the second school was a product of a finishing school, which used to be required of all young people in the south from a certain socio-economic class. She was proper and quiet and kind.

I generally liked her, but there was one particular thing about her that I didn't like. It was her habit of requiring every child who requested to go to the bathroom to kiss her on the cheek before they left the room to go. She wore quite a bit of powder on her face, and her cheek was a bit furry with fine hair. I liked her, but for some reason it just didn't seem right to have to kiss your teacher in order to go to the bathroom.

One day during lunchtime I found that I had to go to the bathroom. I approached the table where all the teachers sat eating lunch together and asked for permission.

"You may go to the bathroom as soon as you kiss my cheek," she said in her prim and proper way.

"I don't want to do that," I replied. "I just really need to go to the bathroom."

"No kiss, no bathroom," she said with finality.

I stood there for a minute looking her in the eye, and then I just let loose.

A steady stream of pee went down my leg and formed a pungent puddle on the floor. All of the teachers looked at me with horror and disgust. There were gasps and groans. The lunch ladies came over and mopped everything up. I had to go home and change clothes. I was never asked to kiss her cheek again.

On the other hand, this same teacher had allowed me to take a book home and read it for myself. It was the first time that I had a fun book from school that I could read any time I wished. I still remember details about it to this day. She turned out to be a fine teacher, once we had established our boundaries.

I hoped that I wouldn't have to go through something like that at my new school.

I was really looking forward to the first day of school in New Mexico, but I woke up with a headache. My forehead hurt where the stitches had been placed. My eyes seemed to hurt when I opened them. My head pounded as I dressed for school, found the mousetraps, and emptied them outside.

I walked into the kitchen where Dad and Mom were talking quietly and finishing their cups of coffee. Mom set a plate in front of me and patted me on the head. Dad looked at me over his coffee cup rim as he took a sip.

"I'll be taking you and Linda to school for this first day," he told me. He set his coffee mug down with a thump on the table. "I am just going to warn you right now that I don't want any trouble from you at this new school. Yesterday was a disaster, and we started off on the wrong foot with the church. We are *not* going to do that with school. Do you understand me, boy?" Dad looked me right in the eye and held my gaze.

"Yes, sir," I replied. I took a quick swig of milk hoping that Dad would look away, but he just kept his eyes locked on mine. I nodded to affirm that I understood. He gave a little sigh and picked up his mug. He had a skeptical look on his face, but I was determined to do well at this new school. Dad reached into his shirt pocket and took out a piece of paper that had been folded up. He scooted it across the table to me.

"Unfold that, and read it out loud," he commanded.

I unfolded the paper and oriented it so that I could read it. "To Dale's teacher," I read. "If Dale gets into any trouble at school please let me know. You have my permission to discipline him in any way that you see fit. If Dale gets into trouble at school then he will be disciplined at home as well. Sincerely, James E. Sims."

I looked at Dad, and he smiled back at me. "That's right," he said. "I just want you to know where I stand. If I hear of any nonsense going on at school and it involves you I will personally make sure that you get the spanking of your life."

I shivered a little bit when I heard that. I thought I had already received the spanking of my life. I wasn't sure my life could handle many more of those.

He reached across the table and grabbed the note out of my hands. After refolding it and putting it back in his pocket he took a long self-satisfied sip of his coffee. "Now, eat your food, and let's go to school."

The note scared me. I thought about it as I finished my eggs and toast. I thought about it as I rinsed off my plate and fork and placed them beside the sink. I thought about it when Linda came back from Mrs. Woodley's apartment. I was really bothered about it because I suspected that if the note fell into the wrong hands I could be blamed for something that wasn't my fault by someone who didn't like me. Then I would suffer unjust consequences at school and at home.

Dad doused my head with Vitalis and tortured my hair into a shape that met his approval. Linda and I followed him out to the car and sat quietly while he drove the short distance to school. We each had our school supplies and a little extra money in our pockets to pay for lunch. Linda seemed to be really excited. I was a bit concerned. My forehead hurt where the stitches had gone in. My lips were red and chapped because I kept licking them. My eyes were still watering from the Vitalis fumes. I was worried that I wouldn't make a good first impression.

Dad parked the car, and we piled out. He made us stop and stand in front of him for a final inspection. He smiled at Linda and stroked her hair, and she smiled back at him. He looked at me, and the smile disappeared. He lifted my chin with his hand so that he could get a better look at my forehead. The stitches were covered by a large white bandage that had puckered overnight. Dad shook his head and turned his back.

"Let's get you set up in this new school," he said over his shoulder. "Just stay close to me. Follow behind me wherever I go."

The school was a one-story concrete block building with a lot of windows. All around the building there were kids screaming and running and playing on the grounds. I noticed that they all had black hair and dark skin. Dad led us through a door and down a hallway to a room with a sign over the door that read "Office."

We marched in behind Dad who walked over to a desk and began to talk to a lady who looked like a Navajo. She smiled at us as Dad explained that we had moved here without school records, and Linda was starting first grade even though she hadn't been in school in the town we had moved from.

The lady behind the desk maintained her calm as Dad tried to explain things to her. Finally she held up a sheet of paper and pointed to it.

"Mrs. Woodley wrote us a note about your family. She has requested that Linda be in her class. We will put Dale into Mrs. Garza's class." She smiled at Dad. "I will take them to their classes. Do they have lunch money?"

Linda and I dug out our money and gave it over to the lady. She counted it and said that it was enough for lunch for all week.

"Do you want them to walk home or take the bus home?" she asked Dad.

He rubbed his hand across his jaw and looked at us as he considered his answer.

"I think they can take the bus home," he said.

"I will make sure that they get on the right bus," the lady told him. Dad nodded to show that he was appreciative. "Is there anything else that I should know?" the lady asked. Dad pulled the note to my teacher out of his shirt pocket.

"This note is for Dale's teacher. It gives her permission to discipline him if he needs it." Dad handed over the note and looked down at me with a glower. The lady read the note and looked at me with that inscrutable stare that I came to expect from the Navajo.

Dad turned to us and kneeled down. He held Linda by the shoulders and smiled at her.

"You learn as quickly as you can from Mrs. Woodley. I am sure that you will be a good student." He gave her a quick hug and then turned to me.

"Dale, at this school you will be one of only a handful of white kids. If you are going to do well at this school you have to think like an Indian boy and act like an Indian boy. Can you do that?"

"Yes, Dad," I told him with conviction. "I will do that to the best of my ability," I promised.

He gave me a dubious look and ran his hand through his hair. "Don't forget about that note to your teacher. Stay out of trouble."

If Dad had only known how I interpreted those words about

being an Indian he would have never spoken them. His little speech set my feet on a path that made things a lot more interesting for all of us.

Dad left us with the lady and hurried out the door without looking back. The lady smiled at us and came around to our side of her desk to hold our hands. We followed her down the hall to the classrooms.

"My name is Mrs. Zonni," she said. "I work in the office every day. If you need anything you should just come and ask for me."

We nodded, and she smiled again. She had a nice smile and carried an immense amount of calm with her. As we walked down the hall she would stop at each classroom and tell us who the teacher was in that room and what grade she taught and how long she had taught and where she had come from. She told us about some of the other children, about a problem with sheep on the reservation, about the approaching cold weather, and about the rising cost of milk.

We finally stopped at Mrs. Woodley's room, and it was good to see her friendly face behind the desk. She motioned for Linda to come into the room. When Mrs. Zonni was sure that Linda was in good hands she gave a short wave goodbye and guided me on down the hall.

"Do you know Yas and his uncles, Andy and Amos, from the reservation?" I asked.

Mrs. Zonni stopped and looked down at me. "The Code Talkers? Yeah, I know them. I know the mother of Yas. She is a good woman. She makes good fry bread."

That was interesting. Mrs. Zonni had just confirmed that Andy and Amos had told me the truth about their names. Dad was wrong, and somehow it made me feel better about things.

"I met them on the reservation on Saturday. They named me Young White," I said with some pride.

Mrs. Zonni looked sideways at me out of the corner of her eye.

"Here at this school you will be called Dale. Don't tell anyone that they call you Young White on the reservation."

I started to ask why, but then I remembered what the Navajo men had told me about someone's name being private. I figured it only applied to Indian names, not white names.

We didn't go far before she stopped at a large classroom with many windows that looked out onto the school yard. On every wall there were bookshelves covered with books. There was a young lady with dark skin and shiny black hair sitting behind the teacher's desk. She looked out at us and smiled, motioning with her hand for us to come into the room.

"This is your teacher, Mrs. Garza," Mrs. Zonni told me. "She is one of the best, and I think you will like her class." She handed some papers over to Mrs. Garza and discussed them for a few minutes. I heard them talking about the note from Dad, and Mrs. Garza shot a glance at my bandaged forehead before turning back to speak with Mrs. Zonni.

In a few minutes Mrs. Zonni got up to leave. "Dale, I am going back to the office now," she said with a smile. "Remember that you can come and ask me anything, and I will help you." She left the room, taking her immense calm with her.

Mrs. Garza studied me quietly. I could tell that she was trying to figure out what kind of challenge I was going to present in her classroom. I tried to smile, but my head hurt and my lips were chapped.

"Why do you have that bandage?" she asked me.

I fingered the patch on my brow. "I was playing alligator catch a monkey, and I hit it on a windowsill. I got stitches from the animal doctor."

"Does it hurt?" she asked with concern in her voice. She didn't say anything about the animal doctor, and I figured that it must have been a common occurrence for her to sew people up.

"It hurts a little, and I have a headache," I told her.

She looked out the window and then back at me. "I don't know what alligator catch a monkey is, but I wouldn't play that game again if I were you. I also think you should stay inside and not go to recess until the stitches come out."

I nodded and mumbled a "Yes, ma'am," through my chapped lips.

She pointed to a desk in one of the middle rows. "That desk will be yours. You can put your things in there."

I walked over to the desk and began to settle in. It was one of those desks with a wooden top that was also a lid for kind of a tub that held all of your school stuff. I lifted the desk top and put my pencils, erasers, Big Chief tablet, crayons, and ruler inside.

Mrs. Garza came over and looked at the way that I had stacked everything in there. She gave a short nod of her head as if she were satisfied. She turned her gaze on my lips and studied them for a moment. It made me nervous, and I licked them.

"Don't do that," she commanded. "When you lick your lips it makes them worse." She went over to her desk, opened the top drawer, and took something out. She walked back over to my desk and held it up for me to see. It was a small plastic jar. The label read "Petroleum Jelly."

She unscrewed the lid and dipped a finger in the goo. Leaning over she smeared some on my lips.

"Don't lick that off. We will put some more on during the day, and it will heal those lips," she said with a smile. She carried the jar back to her desk and wiped her finger with a paper tissue. "Now I am going to run up to the office for a few minutes, and I will be right back." She pointed at the bookshelves lining the walls. "You can read a book if you want or just sit quietly."

I watched her leave the room and then swiveled my head to get a good look at the room. Along one wall were windows with book-shelves under them. I walked over to the windows and leaned on the top of the bookshelves to see out. I saw dozens of kids running and laughing and playing on a large dirt playground that had a few straggly patches of grass sticking up in random places. I saw some movement out of the corner of my right eye, and I turned my head to get a better look.

I was surprised to see a sheep wandering around on the playground. It was nibbling on what little grass was available, chewing in a determined manner as it wandered from clump to clump. I saw some Indian boys talking excitedly and pointing at the sheep. They made a few hand motions and nodded their heads as if they had decided something. Slowly they walked away from each other. They seemed to be going in different directions, but then I noticed that they were making slow and deliberate movements toward the sheep. It looked to me as if they were trying to sneak up on the animal. Finally they had surrounded the sheep, just standing there quietly as it continued to tug on the grass clumps.

I held my breath in suspense as I tried to figure out what they were going to do. A boy on one side of the sheep made a quick movement and grabbed it by an ear. A boy on the other side grabbed its other ear. Two boys in the back ran up, each grabbing a hind leg. The sheep stood trembling as if it was paralyzed by fear.

There was a boy standing off to one side who seemed to be stepping backward from the whole affair. Suddenly he leaned forward and with a running leap he quickly jumped on the back of the sheep. The other boys let go, and the sheep began to make high arcing leaps.

The boy on its back hung on tight, and the other boys whooped and laughed as the sheep tried to dislodge its unwelcome rider. Finally it jumped high and came down with a stiff-legged jolt, making the boy on its back lost his grip. He rolled off onto the ground as the frightened animal continued to leap around the playground. It looked like fun to me, and I was disappointed that I had to stay inside. Turning from the window with a sigh I went back to my desk.

I sat for a few minutes reflecting on what I had just seen. It looked more exciting than alligator catch a monkey. Although it looked dangerous, those boys had not been hurt. In the meantime I was sitting at my desk enduring a throbbing forehead. I considered that maybe Indians were better at physical things than white people. I wondered if I could ever be as good as an Indian kid at running or jumping. I wasn't sure if I could be as good as the Indians, but I figured I should try because my dad told me to try.

I began to look at the chalkboard and think about how to get better at certain things. I was really looking beyond the chalkboard and into space as I made my plans, but I knew something wasn't quite right. I concentrated on what I saw written up there on the board, and fear settled on my soul. I rubbed my eyes, and I squinted at the words. After a few minutes I had to admit to myself that I couldn't read anything that was written on the chalkboard. I could see things just fine. I simply hadn't seen anything like it before. There were loops and squiggles and dashes, some linked together and some separated by a space.

I knew then that I was in trouble. It appeared to me that all of the work in class was done in Navajo writing. I couldn't read or write Navajo. I figured that kids learned that in first grade. Linda would learn it, and she would be just fine. They would probably put me back in a class with Linda, and I would have to repeat a grade.

Dad had made it clear that I was supposed to "think like an Indian boy and act like an Indian boy." He had made me promise him that I would try to fit in. I was panicking. How was I ever going to catch up and fit in? I certainly didn't want to repeat first grade, and I didn't want to fail my dad.

"O God, please help me!" I prayed in desperation. And then God opened my eyes.

I noticed that along the top of the chalkboard were a series of placards. On each placard was a letter of the English alphabet followed by another thing with loops and squiggles. There was a separate placard for each capital and lowercase letter of the alphabet. By using those placards I was able to decipher what I saw written on the chalkboard.

God had given me an answer! I would teach myself to read and write Navajo as quickly as I could, and nobody needed to know. I would just have to fake it until I figured everything out. I couldn't go out to play on the playground because of my stitches so I would use recess time to teach myself. If I could get to school early I could use the time before class to work on it.

Quickly I reached into my desk and pulled out my writing tablet and a pencil. Slowly and carefully I copied everything written down on the chalkboard onto a page of my tablet. It took up the top half of the page. Slowly and carefully I translated it into English using the placards that had been fastened above the chalkboard. That took up the bottom of the page. Now I could compare the two on one page. Once the translation was complete it was easy to read. It was an assignment that everyone was supposed to turn in to the teacher.

What a relief it was to know that now I had a way to understand the language. I used another page of my tablet to copy what was written on each placard. That way I could work at home in the evening and make even quicker progress.

A bell rang announcing the beginning of the school day. The playground emptied as the children ran into the building. I hid my work while Mrs. Garza came into the room and gave me a small pile of books for my lessons. She walked over and stood by the door greeting each child by name as they entered the room. She smiled and gave out hugs. I was sure that I would enjoy being in her room. I certainly intended to stay there even if I had to work extra hard at learning to read and write Navajo.

When everyone was seated at their desk Mrs. Garza went to stand at the front of the room.

"Good morning, class," she said with a smile.

A chorus of voices answered, "Good morning, Mrs. Garza."

She gestured toward where I was sitting. "We have a new student in our class. His name is Dale, and we need to make him feel welcome."

I looked around the room and saw some kids laughing while others recoiled in shock.

"He is ugly," one girl whispered.

I wasn't surprised to hear it. My lips were red, cracked, and swollen and they were covered in petroleum jelly. I had a huge bandage on my forehead over my eye. My hair had been soaked in the vile Vitalis and had been forced into some kind of swept back look.

Mrs. Garza walked over to a tall, thin Indian boy that was sitting behind me. "Jerry, I want you to help Dale get used to things. Will you do that for me?"

Jerry kind of gave a low groan and hung his head, but I saw him give a slight nod. Some of the other Indian kids snickered. I felt sorry for Jerry. I wouldn't want to have the responsibility of taking care of a new kid in class, especially one that was considered ugly. Mrs. Garza seemed oblivious to all of that. She had us stand and give the pledge of allegiance to the U.S. flag. Then she began her lesson for the day.

As the morning went by I noticed that the class seemed to be divided into two groups. Each group got different assignments. She would spend time with one group while the second group did an assignment. I couldn't really see any differences in the two groups. I did see that the room was packed with students so I figured that was her way of handling a very large group of people.

At recess time a bell rang, and all the kids rushed out to play. I stayed in the room and looked wistfully out a window as Mrs. Garza spread another liberal amount of petroleum jelly on my cracked lips. My eyes roamed across the bookshelves. On one of the lower shelves I saw a book about Davy Crockett.

"Mrs. Garza, can I check out that book and read it?" I asked.

She took the book from the shelf and handed it to me. "There is a little pocket on the inside cover. In the pocket is a paper. You write your name and today's date on the paper and give it to me," she said with a smile.

I did as she asked and took the book back to my desk. Mrs. Garza watched me for a few minutes and then left the room. Even though the book was interesting I was determined to stick to my plan of learning to write in Navajo.

I pulled out my Big Chief tablet and flipped to a new page. At the top I wrote "I will learn to write in Navajo. I will become like them." I used the placards to write it out as exactly as I could using the swirls and dashes. I copied it out three times just to be sure. The bell rang, and I quickly closed up the tablet. I opened up my new book and acted as though I had been reading it during the whole recess. Mrs. Garza and all the kids came back into the room, and soon it was business as usual until lunchtime.

When the bell rang for lunch I put everything into my desk and closed the lid. I sensed someone beside me and turned to see Jerry standing there.

"Hurry up!" he said. "We will be late for the bus."

Quickly I followed him out of the room and down to the front of the school. "Where are we going?" I asked.

"Lunch," he said quickly. Jerry pushed me ahead of him out of the front door of the school and up the steps into a large yellow school bus parked out front. The bus was full of kids from the school. I looked for my sister, but I didn't see her. Jerry pushed me into a seat and slid in next to me. The door closed, and the bus lurched out of the drive and down the road.

Jerry turned and looked at me with contempt in his eyes. "You sure are ugly, even for a white kid," he said with snort. He sniffed the air around me. "You smell terrible," he said holding his nose. "What did you do to your head?"

I told him about alligator catch a monkey and how I had hit my head on the window sill. I also told him about the Vitalis in my hair and petroleum jelly on my lips. He puckered up his lips, and I could tell he was chewing on the inside of his mouth as if he was in deep thought.

"Do you live in town?" he asked.

"We moved in right next to Mrs. Woodley, the teacher," I told him. He recoiled as if I had hit him. He leaned away from me.

"You mean the haunted place? The place that is haunted by the ghost of old man Woodley?" he exclaimed.

"Yeah, that's the place," I replied. "But my mom prayed the ghost out of there, and it isn't haunted anymore."

He looked a little dubious, but he shrugged and turned to talk to the boy across the aisle from him. They both turned to look at me. I tried to smile, but my cracked lips hurt so much that I only managed a grimace. Both boys shook their heads and turned their attention away from me until the bus ground to a stop. I saw that we were in a parking lot full of busses unloading children. Jerry stood up and motioned for me to follow him.

"Where are we?" I asked as we jumped out of the bus and ran into a building.

"This is the high school," he said over his shoulder. "Everyone comes here to eat lunch."

We hurried down a hallway following the smell of food to a large cafeteria. We stopped at a table where a lady sat looking at a list. She asked for a name, found it on the list, made a check beside it, and moved on to the next kid. I told her my name, and she looked up and down the list.

"You are not on the list," she told me. "You must pay for your meal."

I explained about giving my money to Mrs. Zonni at the school. The lady nodded and wrote something on her list. She motioned for me to go get some food and turned her attention to the next kid in line. I hurried forward to join Jerry. He handed me a metal food tray and a fork and spoon. We inched forward to where some ladies were putting food on students' trays. I watched as every child ahead of me received a ladle of brown beans, two tortillas, and two small cartons of milk. Steam rose off of the beans as they formed a small pile on my plate. Carefully balancing my tray, I followed Jerry over to a table and sat next to him. I looked up and down the table at the faces of all of the Indian kids. They were concentrating on putting beans on tortillas and rolling up the tortillas. Some of them were simply shoveling beans into their mouths. I wiped the petroleum jelly off my lips with a paper napkin. Confidently I lifted a spoonful of beans to my lips and let them slide into my mouth. All of the skin on the roof of my mouth instantly blistered. I tried to spit out the beans, but that burned my tongue and lips as well. Tears welled up in my eyes. I opened up one of the half pints of milk and chugged it down. The cool milk helped some, but the pain was still intense. I started blowing on the beans hoping that it would cool them off. I kept testing them only to have the hot beans burn more and more of my lips. Jerry watched me and finally said, "We are leaving in a few minutes. You have to put up your tray, and get in line for the bus."

I was miserable. I was hungry, and my mouth, throat, and tongue were blistered and sore. An Indian boy came by and saw the food left on my plate. "Are you going to eat that?" he asked me.

I shook my head, and he took my tray out of my hands. Quickly he gulped down the beans and the remaining carton of milk. He rolled up the tortillas and stuffed them in a front pocket of his jeans. I was shocked at how quickly he could eat the hot beans. Once again I was convinced that the Indians were just physically different from us stupid and weak white people. I pondered that fact as I stepped up in the bus and sat by Jerry. I curled up in the seat and let the tears fall silently. Jerry watched for a minute before leaning close to me.

"Don't cry," he commanded in a hard tone. "The other kids will make fun of you."

"I don't care," I croaked through cracked and burning lips. "I hurt, and I'm hungry."

Jerry looked around to see if anybody was paying attention. He touched my knee and whispered, "Straighten up, quit crying, and I will tell you the secret of eating the food."

I wiped my eyes on my shirt sleeve and sniffed. Slowly I sat up straight and tried to compose myself. Jerry looked around again as if he would get in trouble for telling me this wonderful secret. The bus lurched and swayed as Jerry explained things.

"You can't just start pouring the food into your mouth. You have to take a little swig of milk and hold it in your mouth for a few seconds. Then you take a bite. The milk coats your mouth and helps you eat." He smirked at me. "Didn't they teach you anything at the white school you came from?"

I shook my head in the negative, and Jerry snorted. "That's what I thought. So you are ugly *and* stupid," he said in a mocking tone of voice. He turned his back on me and started talking to the kid across the aisle.

The bus stopped in front of the school, and we piled out onto the driveway. I stopped to watch some other busses pull up. I stood there until I saw my sister step out of the last bus. She was so busy talking to an Indian girl that she didn't notice me. Evidently she was having fun at school. All I wanted to know was that she was safe. I walked into the school and down the hall to my new classroom. Mrs. Garza was waiting at the door.

"You are late, Dale. Is everything OK?" she asked. I nodded and took my seat. Mrs. Garza went to her desk and returned with her jar of petroleum jelly. She used her finger to put some more goop on my lips. I heard some kids snicker, but I didn't care. It made my lips feel better.

The afternoon went just like the morning until 3:00. Right at that time an Indian girl showed up in the classroom with a box. She stood expectantly by the door. Mrs. Garza was working with a reading circle when the girl walked in, but she didn't miss a beat when she made her announcement.

"The peanut girl is here. If anyone wants a bag of peanuts they can get one from her now," she told us.

I was starving because I had not eaten lunch and a bag of peanuts looked good to me. I got up and joined the group of kids going to get their peanuts. When I got to the girl she moved the box with the bags of peanuts away from me.

"This is only for Indians," she told me. "You don't look like any kind of Indian to me."

"What do you mean when you say that these are only for Indians? Why can't I have some?" I asked in a perplexed tone of voice. Suddenly Mrs. Garza was beside me with her hand on my shoulder guiding me out into the hallway. She stopped and turned me around to face her.

"Dale, many of these children are very poor. The Bureau of Indian Affairs provides these peanuts so that those kids can get extra protein during the day. It is only for Indians, not for whites. Do you understand?" she asked me in a quiet voice. Even though I didn't quite understand I nodded as if I did. She patted my shoulder and steered me back to my desk.

I sat there for a few minutes thinking about this new world to which my parents had brought me. There was so much I didn't understand. I wasn't sure that I would do well in this place. I felt something nudge my elbow, so I turned around. Jerry had poked me with a ruler. I started to protest, but he hissed at me.

"Turn back around and face front," he said in an angry whisper. "Put your hand back here, and I will give you something."

I faced to the front and slowly put my hand behind me. I felt something slick in my hand and pulled it around front to have a look. Jerry had put a plastic bag of peanuts in my hand. I turned and smiled at him as best I could through my chapped and blistered lips. He hissed at me again and motioned for me to turn back around. As I was turning away I noticed a small smile on his face. I ate the peanuts and reflected on the fact that I might be ugly and stupid, but I might have made a friend, and God held me in his hands.

When the bell rang to dismiss class I gathered up my Big Chief tablet and walked down the hall to Linda's classroom. She was talking with Mrs. Woodley and waved goodbye as she left the room.

We walked to the office where Mrs. Zonni was waiting to take us to our bus. She talked to the bus driver and gave him instructions to drop us off by the house.

Linda and I sat together as the bus lurched out of the driveway. I was sure that the ride would be short because I remembered the route Dad drove to get us to school that morning. It turned out the ride wasn't short enough. We hadn't gone 100 yards when Linda began to sing. She sang "This Little Light of Mine" in a sweet but loud voice.

"What are you doing?" I whispered to her. "Don't do that. It's embarrassing."

She just smiled at me and kept on singing. Some of the kids around us snickered and began to whisper to each other behind their hands. When the bus pulled up in front of the house I jumped off without even touching the steps. I left Linda to fend for herself as I ran to the house. Mom was on the front porch with Roger and Paul.

"How was your first day of school?" she asked as I ran past her. I threw my tablet on the roll-away bed and immediately headed back outside. "Stop right there," Mom demanded. I came to a shuddering stop right beside her. "Sit right here and tell me all about your first day," she said, patting a spot beside her on the step. I made room for Linda as she walked by to go into the house. She stuck her tongue out at me and walked past as if I were an insect to be ignored. I sat next to Mom and wished for the interview to finish swiftly.

"Who is your teacher?" Mom asked with a smile. "What is your room like? Tell me about your school."

I told her briefly about Mrs. Garza, the room full of the books, the boys with the sheep, and taking a bus to lunch. I didn't tell her about the lessons in Navajo language because I wanted time to catch up. Mom listened carefully as she kept an eye on Roger and Paul. She nodded in all the right places. I suspected that she had more questions, but she saw me squirming.

"Dale, I know that you want to run around for a little bit. Just help me out by taking your brother with you," she said wearily. "If you can help me that way then I can get supper started."

I nodded and looked at Roger. His eyes were crusty, his nose was running with a greenish kind of snot, and his pants weren't zipped up. He saw me looking at him and used his shirt sleeve to wipe his nose. I helped him zip up his pants and motioned for him to follow me. I really didn't want him with me, but Mom needed help, and I was glad to provide it. I waited for him to catch up so that I could hold his hand.

Together we walked across the street and followed it on the other side of the road from the house. Soon we were standing in front of the Catholic church building. It had been built around a large open courtyard that was separated from the street by tall wrought-iron gates. I wanted to see if Miguel and Maria were there. I also wanted to see if there were any nuns. I didn't know what a nun looked like, but I figured that I would recognize one if I saw her. A side door of the church opened, and a woman dressed in some kind of black dress with a black and white head covering scurried across the courtyard. She was almost on the other side when she stopped and slowly pivoted to look at us. She lifted one hand and shaded her eyes as if she were looking at a mirage. Slowly she walked over to the gate. She smiled at us and bent down to get on our level.

"Where did you two little raggedy boys come from?" she asked in a kind voice. Roger pointed back across the street to our house. She looked toward our house, and I saw her mouth form an "O" shape. Her gaze came back down to us. "You are from that family, are you?" she asked. I nodded and she kept her eyes locked on us. "What are you here for then?"

"I have some friends named Miguel and Maria who go to school here. I was just hoping to talk to them a little bit," I said.

She put her hands on her hips and looked over our heads toward the Colonia. "They moved away yesterday," she said quietly. "Sometimes the kids come and stay, but mostly they move around a lot."

She turned her attention back to us. "Do you go to church?" she asked.

I nodded. "We just joined the Baptist church down the street," I told her.

"Ah!" she said in a sorrowful voice. "So, you are going to hell then."

"No, ma'am," I replied quickly. "I accepted Jesus as my Savior last year, and God holds me in His hands." I pointed to my brother. "But I think he is going straight to hell because he has some kind of plague from God."

The lady looked down at Roger and gasped loudly as he sucked up some snot. She crossed herself and mumbled a prayer. "I think that maybe both of you are going to hell because you are Baptists," she said with conviction.

I didn't want to argue with an adult so I decided to change the subject. "Are you a nun?" I asked.

She smiled and nodded. "Yes, I am Sister Mary Catherine of the Order of St. Joseph." She studied us for a moment. "Do you know any of the catechism?" she asked.

I had never heard of the catechism. "What's that?" I replied with curiosity.

"Ah, poor soul," the nun said with a catch in her throat. "You don't know about the catechism?"

I shook my head in the negative, and the nun folded her hands in front of her as if she were praying.

"It is all kinds of things that a good Christian should know," she said with sincerity. "I will give you one example. Do you know what a transgression is?"

"Sure," I replied. "It is kind of like a 'trespass,' only against God Himself." I thought for a minute and then began to recite the Lord's Prayer.

"Our Father who art in heaven, hallowed be thy name. Thy

kingdom come, thy will be done on earth as it is in heaven. Give us this day our daily bread, and forgive us our trespasses as we forgive those who trespass against us. And lead us not into temptation, but deliver us from evil. For thine is the kingdom, and the power, and the glory forever. Amen."

The nun smiled and nodded. Just then I heard Mom call us to supper.

"I have to go. That's my mom calling for us," I told the nun. "Maybe we can talk later," I said with a smile.

The nun didn't say anything. She just stood looking down at us. I waved, and we ran back across the street to the house.

I held the kitchen door open for Roger and walked in after him. Dad was already at the table listening to Linda as she told him about her day at school. He looked tired from his first full day at the sawmill. Mom was busy putting food on plates and the plates on the table. Paul was in his high chair spreading food all over his face and into his hair. Mom finally sat down. Dad gave a short prayer, and things were silent as we all ate our supper. When Dad finished eating he pushed his plate away from him and turned his attention on me.

"I heard all about Linda's day. How was your day?" he asked, searching my eyes to see if I would tell him the truth.

"My day was like Linda's," I said. "The teacher wouldn't let me go out for recess. We went to another school for lunch. My teacher's name is Mrs. Garza. She put some stuff called petroleum jelly on my lips because they were chapped. She assigned a kid named Jerry to help me."

Dad nodded and turned to wipe some food off of Paul's face. "So you stayed out of trouble?" he asked.

"Yes, sir," I replied. "No trouble today."

Roger piped up just then. "Dale said I was going to hell," he told Dad with a smile.

"What!?" Dad roared as he rounded on me.

Roger nodded. "The nun at the church said that we were going to hell, and Dale said that only I was going to hell because I had a plague from God."

Dad's eyes became slits as he glowered down at me. "I don't want you over there talking to those idol worshipping Catholics. Do you understand me?"

I nodded and hoped that I wouldn't get a spanking for saying "hell." Dad turned away from me and looked at Mom.

"I am going out to the church to talk to Brother Gray for a few minutes," he told her. "I will be back soon."

I helped Mom clean up the kitchen while Linda went next door for her lesson with Mrs. Woodley. I played with Roger and Paul so that Mom could have a break. After an hour Linda was back, and it gave me some time to work on my Navajo while she played with Roger and Paul. I retrieved my tablet from the bed and grabbed a pencil. I decided to work at the kitchen table. Slowly and methodically I worked on the language. I was so engrossed in my work that I didn't see Mom and Dad standing there. I hadn't even heard Dad come back to the house.

Dad spoke first. "What are you working on?"

I jumped in my seat. "Just some writing homework," I squeaked out. I held my breath and prayed that they wouldn't ask too many questions.

Mom looked over my shoulder and nodded. "You are a good student," she said with a smile.

Neither one of them remarked on the strange loops and swirls of the letters, which was just fine with me. They left me alone to continue my work. I noticed as I worked that some of the Navajo letters looked vaguely like the English letters. I worked for a solid hour copying the letters over and over again. I was making progress, and I was sure that I would soon have the Navajo writing mastered.

That night I fell thankfully into bed. I was already planning my work for the next day. I was thankful that God held me in His hands. I was thankful for a friend like Jerry, even if he thought I was stupid and ugly.

Mom put Paul in his crib and then stood where Linda and we could see her. She said a short bedtime prayer and then sang for us.

"Good night, my God is watching o'er you.

Good night, His mercies go before you.

Good night, and I'll be waiting for you.

So, good night, may God bless you."

I went to sleep with a clear conscience. In my dreams I wrote the large swirls and loops of the Navajo. My skin began to change color, and I started looking like an Indian boy. In my dreams the Navajo letters surrounded me and covered me. I heard the Medicine Man chanting, and he threw dust on me. I was in Navajo land in my dreams all night long.

The next morning my head felt better. There was no headache, and I was more confident about my ability to do my work at school. My morning routine went by quickly, and soon Linda and I were running out the door to the bus stop. There were several children already there waiting for the bus. Linda started talking to a girl who was in her class. I was fidgeting, hopping from foot to foot, ready to get to school. I interrupted Linda's conversation.

"Linda, get on the bus with that girl. I am going to run on up to the school without waiting for the bus."

Linda's mouth opened in astonishment. "Why aren't you waiting for the bus?" she protested.

In my haste I didn't answer her. I took off running down the road toward the school. The morning was cool, but I sweated anyway. When I got to the school I went directly to my room and sat down to work on the letters. I didn't see Mrs. Garza so I assumed that she wasn't there yet. Then I heard her voice just over my right shoulder.

"What are you working on, Dale?" she asked. She had been working in the back of the room, hidden by a bookshelf.

I quickly closed my writing tablet. "Nothing," I lied as I tried to sneak the tablet into my desk.

"Don't lie to me, Dale," Mrs. Garza said. "Give me that tablet."

With dread in my heart I handed the tablet over to Mrs. Garza. With sorrow in my voice I confessed to the whole thing. I saw Mrs. Garza's eyes shift from the tablet to the placards to my face.

"Please don't put me back into first grade," I begged. "I hated the way I had to wait for the other kids to read. I hated the simple assignments. Please, please, please don't put me back in first grade!"

Mrs. Garza sat down heavily in a chair that was close by. She held my tablet in her hand and studied it closely. I noticed that she covered her face with her hand, and soon I saw her shoulders shaking. It looked like she was crying. I just knew that she was upset with me and that I would have to go back to the detestable first grade.

Finally she removed her hand from her face. I saw that there were tears in her eyes, but I also saw her smiling. Then I heard her laughing. She was laughing out loud, and the tears just seemed to stream from her face as her shoulders shook. After a few minutes she seemed to gain control of herself.

"Phew," she said letting out a long breath. "I needed that!" She looked at me and almost started to laugh again but exerted a great effort of will to keep from doing so.

"Dale, let me explain this to you," she said as she wiped the tears from her eyes. "This is a combined second and third grade class. The language on the chalkboard is English, only it is cursive handwriting, not block letters. The cursive is for the third grade class. You are not supposed to learn that until next year."

I was so relieved that I didn't know what to say. No wonder that some of the letters on the placards looked vaguely like English letters. It was as if a large boulder had been removed from my shoulders.

"Can I keep your work?" Mrs. Garza asked. I nodded, and she neatly tore the pages out of my tablet. "You stay inside and don't go out to play until your stitches come out. Do you understand? I am going down to the office for a few minutes."

I nodded and took out my book on Davy Crockett. Now I could concentrate on reading it.

That day went way better than the day before. I knew what to expect, and I could handle all of the new things in a different way, even with more of the petroleum jelly on my lips.

At the end of the school day as I walked to the bus I noticed Mrs. Zonni standing in the hall. She folded her arms over her breasts and looked down at me.

"Writing Navajo, huh?" she asked. "I have never heard anything so funny in my life." She laughed heartily as she turned to walk back into the office area.

Something came of all of that. To this day my cursive handwriting is atrocious, mainly because I learned it on the fly. My wife says it looks like Navajo writing to her.

SEVEN

CALLING A TRUCE

A n uneasy truce existed at church all because of a day when Brother Gray had to go out of town, and he asked Dad to preach the sermon on a Sunday.

We had been attending church for a couple of months, and this was Dad's first chance to show the congregation that he could preach. He wasn't given much time to prepare, but he dug into studying the Bible and writing notes on paper. I heard him reading his notes out loud and mumbling to himself as he made slight corrections.

On Saturday afternoon he made Linda and me sit on our old sofa while he practiced his sermon on us. I tried to listen closely and pay attention, but Dad's voice just seemed to drone on forever. The longer I listened the more confused I got. I just wasn't sure what the sermon was all about or what Dad was trying to say to us.

He finally wrapped it up and then looked expectantly at us. Linda just smiled and jumped off the sofa to go play in her room without saying anything. I sat there thinking through what I had heard. It didn't make much sense to me. I knew he was going to ask me about it, and I anxiously considered my answer.

"Well?" Dad asked. "What did you think?"

I shrugged. "I thought it was good," I said with a grin "I'm just a kid, so I didn't understand most of it, but I thought it was good."

Dad's eyes narrowed to slits, and he looked hard at me for a minute. "Bah!" he said in exasperation. "Get out of here," he commanded.

I scuttled off the couch and ran into the front yard. Even out there I could hear him mumbling to himself. He was tense that evening, and I doubt that he slept much that night. The next morning was just as bad. He doused my hair with Vitalis three times and kept twitching my clothes into shape. I was miserable and uncomfortable by the time we got to church.

It turned out that all of Dad's worries were for naught. I think he did a good job in the pulpit because most of the men came forward to shake his hand afterward. Mom praised him on the drive home, and he seemed to be quite satisfied with himself.

All of that changed, though, when Brother Gray got back into town. He and Dad had a conversation that made Dad angry. He came home and stomped around for a bit. Mom set him down at the table with a cup of coffee and shooed us kids out of the room. I stopped just outside the door and heard some of what they said to each other, just enough to kind of piece things together.

Evidently Brother Gray had heard that Dad had preached a good sermon. He got jealous and reminded Dad that the church was his church, the pulpit was his pulpit, and the people were his people. He told Dad to stick to leading the singing and working with the kids at church.

Dad was very agitated. Mom reached up and smoothed back some of Dad's hair. She spoke quietly to him and rubbed his back for a few minutes. I could feel the tension leaving the room. After a few minutes of silence Mom came out of the kitchen and beckoned us over to her.

"Come with me, children," she said with a wide smile. "Your dad wants to talk to you for a minute."

Mom carried Paul in, and the rest of us followed. When we were all assembled in the kitchen Dad looked at us with a serious expression on his face. He cleared his throat and sat up a bit straighter in his chair.

"Because I am a leader in the church, people watch our family closely. If you children don't behave in church then people will think that I am a bad leader. Do you understand what I am saying?" he asked while looking straight at me.

I nodded my head, and he shifted his gaze to Linda. She smiled at him and flipped her hair.

Dad's expression softened a bit, and he looked over at Roger who was shuffling his feet nervously. Roger stopped his shuffling and stood very still. His nose was running, and he snuffed real hard and loud so that all of the snot retreated back up his nose. Dad passed a weary hand over his eyes. Mom handed Paul over for me to hold while she used an old dish cloth to clean Roger's face. She clamped the cloth over his nose which made him screw up his eyes.

"Blow real hard," she commanded. Roger gave it everything he had, and a veritable stream of snot gushed into the cloth. Paul pointed and laughed. He was squirming in my arms so I put him down while Mom wiped all of the stuff off Roger's face. Paul toddled over to where Dad was sitting and hung onto his pants.

Dad waited until Mom was finished with Roger before he began to talk again. He pointed a finger at me. "Dale, you are the oldest, and I expect you to set the example. When you are in Sunday school I want you to show proper respect to Sister Gray. Sing the songs, and answer the questions. No more back talk! Understand?"

I gritted my teeth and looked down at the floor. "I'm sorry, Dad, but that lady is an idiot. I don't like her, and I don't trust her."

Dad came up out of his chair, grabbed my arm, and spun me around. He quickly spanked me hard a few times. He turned me back around to face him. "She is an adult, and you will treat all adults with respect!" he shouted into my face. I nodded bleakly, and he sat heavily back into this chair. He continued to stare at me while I tried to control my emotions.

"You will set an example," he told me again slowly, stressing each word in a grim way. "You will protect your sister and brothers. You will help your mother whenever she needs help. You will make sure that Roger blows his nose and remembers to zip up his pants after going to the bathroom. Is that clear? Do you understand?"

"Yes, sir," I said quietly. He continued to stare hard at me for a few moments.

"If the other children misbehave then I will hold you responsible for what they do," he told me with a serious set of his jaw. "You will be punished if you can't get Linda and Roger to behave. Do you understand?"

I was shocked. "I don't think that is fair, Dad. I can't control them." Dad turned red in the face, and for a minute I thought that he was going to spank me again.

"I don't care if you think it is fair or not. I need your help," Dad told me in a low voice.

That put things in a different light for me. Dad was asking for my help. I determined then and there to be as helpful to Mom and Dad as I could.

That is when the truce at church was established. I helped get Roger and Linda ready for church every Sunday morning. Since Paul was getting bigger and more vocal I began to help with him as well.

I dutifully marched into the Sunday school room where Sister Gray dispensed nonsense and made us sing songs with a dubious message. I didn't ask questions, but I did answer every question that was put to me. I answered quickly and respectfully.

I kept Roger and Linda in line during that time as well. I always loaded up my pockets with little Tootsie Rolls and squares of toilet paper. I gave the Tootsie Rolls to Linda and Roger when they became fidgety. I used the toilet paper to blow Roger's nose when the snot ran out. That kid had an inexhaustible supply of snot and boogers. At the end of each Sunday school time I had a small pile of used toilet paper sitting beside my chair. Time seemed to drag out into eternity while I was in the room with Sister Gray. Sometimes she would say something that I knew was false. It took every ounce of my willpower to keep from saying anything. Yet, I kept my peace because Dad needed my help.

Dad established some kind of truce as well. He continued to lead the singing and help with the youth of the church, but he was never asked to preach again. I figured that Brother Gray just couldn't stand to be compared to someone else. The sermons were boring and seemed to always be about one of three topics: hell, bad behavior by women, and the flawed teachings of the Catholics, Mormons, and Lutherans or others.

One day I decided to bring to church a book about Davy Crockett. It was way more interesting than the sermon, and it kept me quiet and occupied. After church Dad asked me what I was reading. He got angry with me when he saw the book about Davy Crockett and told me that the only book he wanted me to read during church was the Bible. I found a Bible and decided to read it all the way through starting in the Old Testament. That became quite an education for me!

The Bible has sixty-six books, thirty-nine books in the Old Testament, and twenty-seven books in the New Testament. The Bible that I took with me to church was an old one that Mom had almost worn out. It was called the King James Version, and Dad assured me that it was the only translation that was approved of by God. Out in the margin of each page were numbers and letters and a list of verses. Mom called it a chain reference and showed me how to use it to find other verses in other books of the Bible that referred to the same topic. She also showed me how to use something called a concordance. It was located in the back of the Bible and had common phrases and words listed alphabetically. A person could look up a word in the concordance and find all the places in the Bible where that word was used.

The King James Version was hard to read at first, but I soon got used to the cadence of the old English. I also discovered that I could automatically translate in my head, exchanging an old word like "shew" for "show" or "thou" for "you." I found that I could use the chain reference and the concordance to get a better understanding. If that failed then I waited until I got home and used an old dictionary to look up the meaning of words.

Dad was happy to see me reading the Bible. Sometimes after church, as we were sitting around the table eating lunch, he would ask me about what I had been reading in the Bible. I think he wanted to make sure I was really reading and not just faking it.

One day he asked me where I was at in my reading of the Bible.

"Dale, what were you reading in the Bible this morning?" he asked while shoveling food into his mouth.

I put down my fork and looked at him. "I have been reading about King Solomon. Sister Gray said that Mr. Corbin who owned all of that land over by the big mesa was as wealthy as Solomon. I got to thinking about it and decided to look up everything I could about Solomon."

Dad nodded and chewed slowly on a bite of fried chicken. "What exactly did you find out about Solomon?" he asked.

I smiled, pleased that Dad was interested. "I started reading about him over in first Kings," I said. "He was wise, wealthy, and powerful."

I told the story of the two women who each claimed the one baby and how Solomon had solved the problem. "He was the son of David who had killed the giant," I continued. Dad still looked interested so I was encouraged to continue the story. "Solomon built the temple in Jerusalem, and he talked with God." Dad nodded again, and I took it as a sign that I could go on with my story. "Solomon also had 700 wives and 300 concubines." Mom had been sipping out of her coffee mug. She lowered it just a bit and looked at me over the rim. Linda put down her fork and turned to me.

"What's a concubine?" she asked.

"I had to look that up in the dictionary when we got home. It means a woman who you are not married to, but you live with her and have coitus with her." Mom turned a bright pink and dropped her coffee mug, which promptly smashed into pieces. Dad had just taken a bite of a potato, and I heard him inhale sharply. The potato got stuck in his throat, and he began to cough trying to dislodge it. Mom stood up and began to whack him hard on the back.

"What does that mean?" Linda asked loudly over Dad's coughing. Mom stuck out her hand with her palm open toward me before I could answer. She looked like she was trying to stop a car that was going to hit her.

"Stop right there, young man," she commanded as she continued to pound hard on Dad's back.

"But I know what it means, Mom. I looked it up in the dictionary," I assured her.

The potato became dislodged from Dad's throat. He gave a last powerful cough that caused it to fly through the air and hit Roger in the eye and making him cry, which caused Paul to cry.

Dad took a deep breath and reached across the table to grab my ear. He pulled me away from the table and into the living room. He sat down, bent me over his knee, and began to spank me until I cried for mercy, and his arm got tired. He let go of me, and I stood in front of him crying.

"I don't know what is wrong with you!" he shouted at me. "Why are you talking about those things?"

I hiccupped a few times and said, "I—I—I was only answering your questions. I—I—I thought you wanted me to read the Bible. I —I—I don't understand why you are so angry."

Mom came in and stood behind me. She gently turned me around and hugged me. "You started it, Jim," she said to Dad. "You told him to read the Bible. You asked him what he was reading. You can't blame him for trying to understand things."

I heard Dad say, "I didn't know that our son was a pervert.

Imagine what it would have been like if we hadn't stopped him from telling everything to his sister."

I hadn't heard the word "pervert" before and determined to look it up in the dictionary. That afternoon was the last time that Dad asked me what I was reading in the Bible. I continued to read it anyway, and God blessed the reading of it.

Dad was upset that he wasn't allowed to preach anymore. He groused around the house for a few weeks complaining to Mom. One evening she had just had enough.

"I don't want to hear another complaint," Mom told him. "You just have to find a way to preach or teach somewhere other than the church." Dad took her words to heart, and that is how the Bible study began out at Johnson's sawmill.

Dad worked at the sawmill five days a week as a logger. The men he worked with were rough and tough. They did a little bit of everything all the way from logging to standing guard at the mill overnight.

One day he started taking his Bible to work and inviting men to join him for a Bible study over lunch. A couple of guys began to sit with him and listen and ask questions. The group of men participating grew until there were ten or twelve men who began to read the Bible for themselves. Dad had his own small congregation out there at the sawmill.

One Friday evening there was a knock at our kitchen door. Dad opened the door, and Mom stood behind him to get a look at our visitors. I peeked around Dad's arm, and in the doorway stood the largest man I had ever seen. He looked like a giant to me. He filled the doorway, but I noticed that he wasn't alone. There were two Indian men standing in the shadows just behind the giant.

"Hello, Tom," Dad said in surprise. "What can I do for you?"

The giant shuffled his feet a bit and then said in a low, rumbling voice "I come to talk to you about being saved. When you read the Bible to us at the sawmill it made me start to thinking about things. I've been at war with God all my life, and I want to call a truce."

Dad turned to Mom and asked her to take us children into the other room. As we followed her into the living room he opened the kitchen door wider so that the giant could come inside. The two Indians started to come in as well, but Dad barred their way.

"Where do you boys think you're going?" Dad asked. "I don't know you, and I don't just let strangers into my house."

Tom turned around and pointed at the men. "Those men are my friends." He pointed at one and said, "That feller is Andy, and the other man is Yas. They help run Tinian Mission, and they have been helping me when the need for a strong drink comes down on me."

Dad fixed them with a wild glare and said, "Wait right there." He walked over to the cabinet and pulled out his pistol. He loaded it in a way that let the men see that he was using real bullets. When he finished he rolled the cylinder back into place with a heavy click that showed he meant business. He held the gun out in front of him and walked back to the door.

"Now, you two Injuns just back off from the house about ten steps, then turn and walk away." Andy and Yas spoke together quietly for a few minutes. I could tell that they were angry and confused. They did not seem to be afraid as they looked at Dad with inscrutable expressions.

"What is this, Jim?" Tom asked in a shaky voice. "I've known these men for years. Andy and his brother Amos are good Christians. They started Tinian Mission. Yas over there is starting a club for Indian boys to teach them how to be good people and to be leaders in the tribe."

I could tell that Dad was dubious because he kept the gun pointed at Andy and Yas. He turned to look at Mom and us kids watching from the living room. He seemed to wrestle with his doubts for a few minutes, and then I saw him give a small nod of his head as if he had made a decision.

"You Injuns come on into the house real slow-like, and we will sit around this table and talk," Dad said quietly. He moved to the far side of the table and sat down. He was still holding the gun, and he had it pointed toward the two men as they entered the room. Tom sat next to Dad while Andy and Yas sat facing them across the table. Andy motioned toward the gun.

"What is this about, Reverend Jim?" he asked. "I have seen you many times on the reservation, and you have never felt threatened there, have you?"

Dad moved the gun just a bit. I noticed that he had taken his finger off the trigger. He cleared his throat. "The man who used to live in this apartment was killed by an Injun who stabbed him right through the heart. The man's name was Woodley, and he was murdered by stinking Injuns just like you." Dad sounded angry, and he slapped his hand down hard on the table. "I am not going to let my family go unprotected."

Andy shook his head. "It was a sad thing about Mr. Woodley, but he wasn't killed by an Indian. The man who stabbed him was a Mexican."

Dad half rose from the chair and pointed his finger at Andy. "I saw the pictures of the man in the paper. He looked Injun to me. Scratch a Mexican, and you find an Injun I always say."

Andy shrugged a little and folded his arms across his chest. "You have nothing to worry about from Yas and me. We are Christian brothers, and we came to support Tom. Perhaps you can just talk to Tom about his soul, and forget about us."

Dad clamped his jaws together, and I could tell he was thinking it over. He kept the gun pointed in the general direction of the Indian men, but he turned to Tom. "OK, Tom. You said that you wanted to talk about getting saved. Do you know what that means?"

For the next thirty minutes Dad and Tom talked about God, the souls of men, and how Jesus made a way for man to have peace with God. The longer Dad talked the calmer he got. Yas and Andy were very quiet, and Dad seemed to forget they were even in the room. Tom hung his head, and large tears dropped from his eyes.

When Dad asked him if he wanted Jesus in his heart Tom couldn't even speak. He just nodded his giant head. Dad told him that he had to pray out loud, confess his sins, and ask Jesus to come into his heart and change his life.

When Tom prayed he spoke in a low rumbling voice that could barely be heard. When he finished Dad put his arm around his shoulders.

Andy and Yas both said, "Amen."

Tom lifted his head and smiled through his tears. "Thank you, preacher Jim," he said. "Now I want to be baptized by you. When can we do that?"

Dad told Tom to show up at the church on Sunday morning, and he could be baptized. Tom looked down at the tear-stained table top. "Jim, I don't know how I'm going to do this because I am afraid of water when it gets over my head."

Dad rubbed his chin and then smiled at Tom. "Don't worry. What we will do is practice a little bit right now. Stand and I will show you how it works." Tom stood up, and Dad held out his right arm. "Now all you have to do is hang onto this arm, and I will put you down into the water with it and then use both of my arms to raise you back up out of the water. It will only take a couple of seconds."

Tom looked relieved, and he shook hands with Dad. Then he reached over and shook hands with Andy and Yas. "Praise the Lord," he shouted at the top of his lungs. Then he left with his two friends, and we could hear him praising Jesus as they walked down the street.

Mom led us into the kitchen as Dad shut the door. We watched as he unloaded the gun and put it back into the cabinet.

Mom walked over and hugged him. "I am so proud of you," she gushed. "Your ministry among those loggers is bearing fruit. Now you are becoming the minister that God called you to be." She kissed him and gave a quiet chuckle. Dad looked thoughtful.

"I need to go over right now and talk to Brother Gray about baptizing Tom on Sunday," he told her.

She nodded and patted him on the back as he left the house.

Our church was very small. We had a baptistery that sat where most churches would have a choir loft, right behind the pastor's lectern down by the front row of pews. When we heard that Brother Gray agreed to let Dad do the baptism we kids got very excited. There had been one baptism since we came to town. We noticed that water slopped out over the edge of the baptistery during that one. We decided that we would sit on the front row because water would slop out of the baptistery, and we had a good chance of getting wet. The only thing that irked me during baptism time was the actions of one of our deacons. He would trim his nails and yell "Amen!" at random intervals. *Click, click.* "Amen." It was annoying.

The time for the giant logger to be baptized came at the end of another boring sermon. Dad stepped into the water and motioned for the logger to step down into the water. Dad said the words and then laid Tom down into the water. The deacon watched and trimmed his fingernails from the back of the church –"amen!"

Tom began to thrash around in the water. He had lost his footing and couldn't get back up out of the water. Dad was trying to help him and was getting all wet. Water was sloshing around every-where, and my sister, brothers, and I were getting wet.

A large hairy hand emerged from the depths of the baptistery water and grabbed hold of Dad's tie. Dad wasn't a tall man, but he was a strong man. He had been a Shore Patrolman and a wrestler for the U.S. Navy. I saw him brace himself as Tom grabbed hold of the tie. He seemed to be gaining control of the situation when Tom's feet just slid completely out from under him.

Dad's face took on a look of desperation, and then he simply collapsed under the weight of the giant. Dad looked like one of those fishing bobbers as he went under and came up a couple of times.

I heard a *click* and then a roar of pain from the back of the church. I turned to see the deacon holding his little finger as blood poured out. He had been so engrossed in what was happening in the baptistery that he had clipped off part of the tip of his little finger.

Finally Dad and the giant logger regained their footing and sloshed out of the baptistery. It is still the most memorable baptism I have ever witnessed.

A few months later I saw the logger at a grocery store in town. He was telling the owner of the store about how he had given his life to Christ, and he was a new man. He explained to the store owner about salvation and redemption and urged that man to give his life over to Christ.

The logger paid for his groceries, and I walked out of the store behind him. I stopped him and reminded him of all of the events that had happened at his baptism. He leaned down and listened politely.

"Boy," he said in a deep growl. "None of that stuff matters. What really matters is that I did what God asked me to do, and I am a new man now. Through Jesus I made a truce with God. Jesus gave me a new life, and I don't intend to waste it."

I thought a lot about Tom and his salvation experience. I think that Dad did a good job considering all of the circumstances. I still felt ashamed of the way he treated Andy and Yas so I was a little worried when later that week Dad told me to get ready to go with him out to the reservation. I prayed that God would help me understand things in a way that was different from my dad. I was quiet as we drove up to Tinian Mission.

Dad stopped the car and looked over at me. "I am going to get to the bottom of this thing about the mission. We can't have some Injuns going around lying about who started it." His eyes blazed with righteous indignation.

I nodded, hoping that he would calm down before we left the

car. He set his jaw in a determined manner, and I knew that he would not calm down.

I followed behind him as he walked into the mission, and I saw that Andy, Amos, Yas, and some other men were sitting on chairs just inside the door. Dad walked right past them as if they were invisible. I think that all Indians looked the same to him.

I waved to the men, and they kind of gave me a slow nod in acknowledgment.

Dad walked into the back room where Mr. and Mrs. Roberts were sitting at a table talking to each other. Dad didn't even say "hello" or "excuse me." He just walked right up and put his hands palm-down on the table, leaning across the table to speak to the couple.

"I heard that some Injuns started this mission, and I came to get the truth, to get to the bottom of all of this," he said quickly and angrily. "I don't like it when people lie about God's work."

Mr. Roberts smiled and motioned to a chair. "Have a seat, Jim, and we can talk about this."

Dad hauled the chair around and plunked himself down as if he could hardly wait. I walked over to the window and stood leaning against the wall. Mr. Roberts folded his arms across his chest, leaning back in his chair.

"Jim, the truth is that two Navajo men started Tinian Mission. I can't pronounce their Navajo names, but they are called Amos and Andrew. We call Andrew by the shortened form of the name, Andy. I know that you have seen them around." He motioned toward the window as if he was including the whole reservation area. "Those men were stationed in the military as Code Talkers in the South Pacific, and they came to know the Lord."

While he was speaking, Mrs. Roberts left the room and came back leading Andy and Amos. They all walked around the table so that they were facing Dad. Mrs. Robertson smiled and motioned with her hand to the two men.

"Jim, let me introduce Andy and Amos to you. They are the

men who started this mission." Mrs. Robertson put her hand on Andy's arm. "These men wanted the mission, and they wrote to the Southern Baptist Convention asking for help in making it successful."

Dad glared at the two men. I saw his eyes narrow as he looked at Andy. He pointed at him and said, "I know you. You were at the house with Tom."

Andy gave a hint of a smile. "Hello, Preacher Jim," he said quietly.

Dad looked steadily at both men. "I see that you couldn't make a go of the mission so you had to call in white men to make it work."

Amos chuckled softly and said something to Andy in Navajo. The men shook their heads and gave soft sighs. "That is what I like about you, Preacher Jim," Andy said. "We never have to wonder how you feel about things."

Dad kind of bristled and then seemed to settle back in his chair. I could tell that he wasn't quite sure whether it was a compliment or an insult. He swiveled his head to look at Mr. Roberts and back again at the Navajo men.

Amos gave a slight cough as if he were clearing his throat. He shuffled his feet just a bit and then pointed his chin at Dad.

"Preacher Jim, I was wondering if you would do the funeral for a woman who died out here this morning. She is the daughter of one of the tribal leaders. They are not Catholic, so the priest won't be involved. We don't want Bother Gray to say the words because we don't trust him. I heard how you helped Tom, and I want a real Christian to preach the funeral service." Amos looked over at Andy who gave a slight nod of assent.

I could tell that Dad was both surprised and pleased. He rubbed his chin as if he were deep in thought. "When is this funeral?" he asked.

Amos spoke up, using his hands to paint a picture in the air. "Some men are making a good coffin for her right now. We have some ceremonies to perform this morning, and there will be a big lunch for everyone. There will be some dancing and singing in the afternoon." Amos stopped and consulted for a minute with Andy. "My brother thinks that if you come about 5:30 it would be good. Yas will do the translating."

Dad looked at the men to see if they were joking or serious. He studied Andy for a long time. "I saw you, a supposed Christian, stake another Indian to the ground and torture him until he cried. Don't deny it! I saw you do it with my own eyes."

Andy turned and called out softly.

Yas walked into the room and talked briefly and quietly with Andy. He turned to Dad and asked "What is your question?"

Dad pointed an accusing finger at Andy as he spoke to Yas. "I saw that man stake you to the ground and torture you. I heard you scream and cry out." Dad's face was red, and he shook with anger. "Why would you have anything to do with him after the way he treated you?"

Yas nodded slowly. "Andy is my uncle. I know it looked bad, but he was helping me. I was addicted to drugs and alcohol, and I asked him to help me beat the delirium tremens as I shook off the effects of the alcohol." Yas put his hand on Andy's shoulder and smiled. "This man was saving my life. He helped me to kick the bad stuff. He staked me to the ground so that I wouldn't hurt myself or anyone else."

Yas looked down, and I could tell that he was embarrassed at the admission of his addiction. "I wasn't in my right mind," he said quietly.

Dad's face showed equal amounts of surprise and cynicism. His mouth opened and closed a few times before he could get any words out.

Yas pointed at me. "I don't remember much about that time, but I do remember seeing your son. He looked at me, and I saw the peace that passes understanding in his eyes."

Dad half rose from his chair. "You leave my son out of it, you hear?" he shouted at the men. "He is just a kid and not too bright at that. He is impressionable, and I don't want you mixing up his thoughts."

The Indians looked at me, and I just shrugged.

Andy turned back to Dad and spoke solemnly. "I think you are wrong about the boy. I think he understands more than you give him credit for. We have given him the name of Young White, but we will call him Dale." Andy looked at me, and I saw the hint of a smile. "He is safe on this reservation. You have my word on it."

Dad kind of huffed a bit and then seemed to settle down. He looked at Mr. Roberts, who smiled back at him and nodded his head. Dad clasped his hands and then slowly released them. He took a deep breath and looked up at the Indians.

"All right! I will do the funeral this evening, but only if I get to preach. Is that clear?" Dad said with a stern look at the men.

Amos nodded. "That is what we want. Thank you. We will see you then." The men turned away and filed out of the room,

As we left the reservation, I could tell that Dad was already thinking about the sermon. He had his car window rolled down and rested his left arm on the windowsill. When he got home he told Mom all about the visit and then got out his Bible in order to prepare the sermon.

Brother Gray made a surprise visit to the house right before we were to leave for the funeral. The preacher kind of paced back and forth and looked as if he was thinking hard about it. He finally stopped pacing and turned to face Dad.

"Jim, I think it is just fine for you to do this funeral, but I don't think you should expect much from them savages. Watch your family close, and don't let 'em snatch one of your young'uns," he said seriously. He glared around at us and then abruptly left. We looked at each other in surprise. I had never felt threatened while I was on the reservation.

Mom looked down thoughtfully at us kids, and I could see fear welling up inside of her.

That afternoon the whole family piled into our car and drove down the dusty road to the reservation.

Linda and Roger were excited because it was their first time around the Indians. On the drive out to the reservation they pestered me with questions. I could answer some of the questions but not all of them.

Dad turned in his seat and told us to shut up and be quiet or he was going to turn the car around and leave us back at the house.

Linda and Roger were wide-eyed as they saw all of the things that I now took for granted. Everything that seemed ordinary to me was new and exotic to them. When we finally pulled up at the mission all of us were fidgeting and ready to get out of the car.

"Dale!" Dad said in a voice that startled me. He turned around and glared at me. "You are to keep Roger and Linda close to you. If I find that they have been harmed or have wandered off I will whip you so hard that your hide will come off."

I gulped and nodded to show that I understood.

We piled out of the car, and I took Roger by one hand and Linda by the other. Both of them tried to squirm away, but I was stronger than them, and I held on tight until they gave up.

An Indian man that I had never seen before came up and held his hand out to Dad.

"My name is Bill," he said quietly. "I will show you to the place where we are having the funeral."

Dad cautiously shook his hand and then wiped it on his pants. Bill noticed and kind of gave a soft chuckle. He turned and motioned with his hand for us to follow him.

Dad and Mom walked hand in hand right behind him, with Mom holding Paul. I kept a tight hold on Linda and Roger's hands and dragged them along with me.

Bill walked us out to the dusty, wind-blown edge of the village. There I saw a bunch of tall poles that created a boundary for a large square. The poles were covered with many large sheets of dirty white canvas. In the center of the square, raised up on a wooden platform, was a wooden coffin with the top open. Around the coffin were hundreds of Indians milling around, occasionally throwing things into the coffin. They made very little noise, and I thought it was strange that the people seemed so quiet. There were logs set out along the boundaries of the square. Around the coffin were about a hundred folding chairs. Some older men were sitting on the logs playing drums.

To the pounding of the drums, the people moved backward and forward to the coffin. The Medicine Man was there dancing and shaking gourds and throwing some kind of white powder on the people. I watched in fascination as I was swept up into the whole drama of the event. I looked up at my dad's face and was surprised at the grim look in his eye and his tightened jaw. He turned to Bill.

"Does that evil old witchdoctor have to be here?" he asked, pointing directly at the Medicine Man. Bill sucked in his breath and ducked his head. I wanted to tell Dad that it was impolite to point directly at something, but I held my peace.

"It is just a custom, Preacher Jim," Bill said quietly. "We Christians know that it doesn't mean anything, but it does bring peace to the People when they see him do his work."

Mom took my hand and pulled me over to some of the folding chairs close to the coffin. She was holding Paul, I was holding Linda's hand, and she was holding Roger's hand. We followed her like small boats in the wake of a large ship.

As we sat looking at the coffin I began to pay closer attention to what the people were throwing into the coffin. I saw people throw cigarettes, whiskey bottles, dresses, shoes, jewelry, knives, feathers, cloth, blankets, hats, frying pans, photographs, and dolls. The people looked very poor, but everything that went into the coffin was of really good quality. Some things were still in the store's plastic wrappers.

As I watched I sensed that someone had sat beside me. I was surprised and delighted to see that it was Jerry, my friend from school.

"Hey!" I said.

"Hey," he replied with a smile. "What are you doing here?"

I smiled and sat up a bit straighter with pride. "My dad is going to preach the funeral service," I said solemnly. "Andy and Amos asked him to do it."

Jerry looked at the coffin and then back at me. "She was a Chief's daughter. She went to some college back in the east, and she wasn't the same when she came back." He scratched his head and nudged a rock with the toe of his sneaker. "She died because she drank too much," he said sadly.

"Why are the people throwing all of those things in the coffin?" I asked him. He watched the people dancing back and forth in front of the coffin before answering.

"We believe that a person makes a long journey after they leave this life," he told me with utmost sincerity. "All of those things we put in the coffin will help the person as they make that journey." His eyes never wavered as he explained things to me.

We watched the dancing and quiet wailing until the people began to tire and to sit down on the chairs. Soon a group of women began to move through the crowd bringing bowls and water cups.

Dad came and sat between Mom and me. He was sweating in his suit, and he had a slight coating of dust on his hair. When the women came to where we were sitting they did something differ- ent. All of the women had thick black hair that they wore long. The woman with the bowls took hold of her hair and carefully wiped out a bowl and handed it to Mom. She did the same for Dad. Jerry sucked in his breath.

"That is a sign of the greatest respect," he said just loud enough for Dad to hear. The woman came to me and did the same with my bowl. I noticed that there were bugs in her hair, and it bothered me so much that I lost my appetite. I waited until she had gone on further down the row before saying anything.

"Dad," I said in quiet desperation. "I can't eat out of that bowl. That woman had bugs in her hair."

Dad lowered his face down to mine and growled, "You will eat everything that is put into your bowl. You will eat it all and not complain. Do you understand me?"

The woman with the cups did the same thing when she handed the cups to our family. Soon other women came down the line bearing kettles of beans and stacks of fry bread. I accepted everything and forced myself to eat and drink. I was so hungry that I soon stopped worrying about the bugs in the hair.

Finally a man stood up and walked to the platform on which the coffin sat. He called for other men to help him. About six or eight large Navajo men climbed onto the platform. Together they closed the lid on the coffin. It was so full of things that it would not close tight enough to latch it. The men sat on the lid to force it down, and a man on the ground reached up to latch it tight.

After the men had all sat down, Bill, our guide, motioned for the whole crowd of people to sit. There were not enough chairs or places to sit on logs, so many of the people sat on blankets on the ground. Everyone was busy eating, and the quiet hum of conversation filled the square. The sun was going down, and it was getting cooler.

Bill came over to talk to Dad, and I saw Yas detach himself from a group and walk over. The men spoke softly to Dad and I saw him take up his Bible. He stood and was escorted by Bill and Yas to the platform. Dad climbed up onto it and began to address the crowd in English. Yas translated as he spoke. Dad had to keep turning around in order to address the people who were sitting on all sides. He spoke for about an hour, and Yas was animated as he translated. He used his hands in an expressive way to explain what Dad was saying. Everyone listened politely. I don't remember much of what Dad said, but I do remember the last thing he talked about.

Dad raised his voice and shouted out to the crowd "God does not want to be at war with the Navajo. He has made a truce, a way for you to live at peace with Him. Accept Jesus, and be at peace!"

When Dad was finished speaking and praying he came down

off the platform and was escorted back to us by the men who had closed the coffin lid. It was getting dark, and Jerry told me that we needed to leave before the rattlesnakes started coming out.

Dad led the way toward the car, and Mom gathered us kids to follow after him. He was stopped by Andy, who seemed to just appear out of the shadows.

"Thank you, Preacher Jim," Andy said while holding out his hand for Dad to shake. "I liked what you had to say about a truce. I tell you that the People are at truce with you because of today. We will watch after your family. We will make sure that the children are safe. You do not need to fear us."

When we drove away from the reservation I saw Dad look back in his rearview mirror. Perhaps he believed in the truce, but he sure looked skeptical to me.

Perhaps it would have been different if he knew then the price that the Navajo were willing to pay—and the price that some would soon pay—to keep us safe.

EIGHT
BRAVE FAMILY

OCTOBER 1962

According to my Indian friends, snow came to our area early that year. The first snowfall was light, but the following days brought more and more until there was a sizable amount piled up.

We all bundled up in our warmest clothes for the bus ride to school. Mrs. Garza made sure that we hung up our coats, hats, and gloves in the right place before the lessons for the day started. When it was time for recess, there was a mad dash for the coats. Even though it was very cold outside we preferred to brave the cold and have time away from our books.

I stood huddled in a doorway to keep out of the wind and to watch the other kids on the playground to see how they were handling the cold. I saw my sister over by the swings. She was exchanging caps with an Indian girl. They were giggling at the way that they looked in each other's caps.

Out of the corner of my eye, I saw kids starting to form a long line. Usually the kids ran around every which way during recess. To see kids forming a line was so unusual that I gave it my full attention.

Jerry came and stood by me as I quietly watched the line forming up.

"What are they doing?" I asked him. He grinned and slapped me on the arm.

"We need to be part of this!" he said excitedly. He pushed me ahead of him to stand in the line. We stood right behind a boy named Reuben whose nickname was Butterfingers because he wasn't any good at catching things.

"What's going on?" I asked again. Reuben kind of snickered, and Jerry gave out a groan.

"Man, you don't know anything, do you?" he said in disgust. I shrugged my shoulders, and Jerry said something to Reuben in their language. They both laughed, which made me a little angry.

"Watch that guy at the front of the line," Jerry told me. "We will do whatever he does."

There were three boys a few feet in front of the line. They were trampling down the snow while other kids were urging them to move faster. I noticed that they were breaking a trail in the snow that went down a slight hill and ended at a flat place about thirty yards away. When they finished the trail they ran back up the hill to stand at the back of the line.

The kid at the front of the line ran up to where the trail started, jumped sideways, and kind of skidded on the snow for a few feet. When he stopped skidding he quickly ran to the back of the line, and the next kid in line ran to the trail and did the same way. He went just a bit farther than the first kid before he also ran to the back of the line.

It didn't take me long to figure out that we were helping to create a long smooth path for kids to slide on. We all took turns making it just a little longer until the whole length of the trail was smooth and packed. After that it was just a matter of seeing which kids could slide on their feet for the whole length of the trail. Most kids wiped out, and we all had a good-natured laugh at their expense. I noticed that the kids with the bigger feet seemed to be the ones who went farther down the trail.

I was standing behind Jerry and Reuben, trying to stay warm while waiting for my turn to slide down the hill, when I heard Jerry say something about Yas.

"What did you say?" I asked him. "Did you say something about Yas?"

Jerry turned and looked at me for a minute as if he were trying to figure out whether I was worthy of receiving an answer. He finally said, "Yas has a new girlfriend. Her name is Mary Frahwah."

I shrugged at the news. I was still too young for a girlfriend myself and wasn't sure what that meant anyway.

"She is only half Navajo," Reuben said with a sneer. "She is half Pueblo. Her mom is Navajo and was married to one of the big time drunks from the Pueblo tribe. Mary lives with her mom in a hogan on the reservation."

"Shut up, Reuben," Jerry said quietly. He turned to me and whispered, "Don't listen to him."

Reuben pushed Jerry and said, "Why are you taking up for someone when everyone knows that it was her dad that led the men to the treasure."

"What treasure?" I asked. Suddenly I was very interested in Mary Frahwah.

It was Reuben's turn to slide down the trail. I watched him wipe out. Jerry and I followed right behind with the same results. When we got back in line I immediately repeated my question.

"What treasure?" I asked again.

Reuben made a face and said, "Everyone knows that story. A long time ago there were some Spanish soldiers who were killed fighting the People up in the mountains. They were buried up there in a cave with all of their armor and money and gold and everything. The People covered up the cave entrance and we were the only ones who knew where it was. One day Mary's dad got drunk and led some white guys there. They took everything they could carry out of the cave. Now the spirits have been disturbed. Some of the elders went up there and hid the entrance to the cave so that nobody can find it anymore."

"Why is that such a big deal?" I asked.

Reuben laughed out loud.

"You really don't know much, do you?" he said. "Mary's dad got killed for disturbing the spirits. There is always a price to pay for disturbing the spirits of the dead."

"Who killed him?" I asked. "How do you know it was the spirits?"

"Mary's dad was found dead by the side of the road in town. There wasn't a mark on his body, and even the vultures and little animals wouldn't go near his body. That's how I know!" Reuben said it emphatically and looked me right in the face as he was saying it. I could tell that he really believed that what he was saying was true.

Jerry snorted. "A lot of the People have drank themselves to death and died by the road or under a tree or in their car. That doesn't mean the spirits are mad at them. It just means they were controlled by the drink."

Reuben shrugged and faced forward, ending our conversation.

Jerry winked at me, and then he sidled up to Reuben.

"A man was killed right at Dale's front door, and his ghost haunted their place until his mom prayed and made the ghost leave," Jerry told him in a quiet voice. Reuben looked around quickly, and I nodded to show it was true.

Reuben stepped out of line and looked at me hard for a few seconds before leaving to go to the back of the line.

Jerry chuckled and shook his head. "Reuben is very superstitious," he said with a smile. "That story will keep him and his gossip away from you."

The school bell rang, signaling the end of recess, and we all groaned. As we walked in I decided to ask Jerry a question that had been bothering me.

"Jerry, do you remember when my dad preached that funeral on the reservation?"

He looked at me a little funny and nodded.

"Well," I continued, "nobody was making a lot of noise or crying out loud. If she was the daughter of a chief then why weren't they making more noise?"

Jerry nodded again and looked past me into the distance. "The People think that if you make too much noise it will attract the attention of the spirits to you. Nobody wants that." Jerry looked at me in a thoughtful way. "Somebody needs to explain this stuff to you."

"I thought that's what you were doing," I said and clapped him on the shoulder.

"No, I mean someone older who can help you understand the People," he said as he rubbed the top of his head. Suddenly his eyes widened, and he smiled. "Yas has decided to take a group of us boys on the reservation and teach us how to be men. He said that he is going to teach us about our past and teach us how to prepare for the future. I am in that group, and maybe you can be too."

It sounded good, but I was doubtful. "I don't live on the reservation, and I'm not a Navajo," I said. "Maybe this is only an Indian thing."

Jerry smiled and held the door open for me as we walked into the school building. "I'll ask him if you can be part of the group on the days you come out to the reservation."

I thought about being part of a group like that all the rest of the day. I remembered that Andy had told me that I could never be an Indian no matter how hard I tried to be one. He also told me that he wanted me to understand them. I figured that maybe being part of the group would help me to have an understanding.

I also thought about Mary, the treasure, and her dad the rest of the day. It was a sad story. I thought about the effect of alcohol on

141

people. In my mind's eye I played back the images of those poor Indians who had gotten drunk in town and had been laid on the ground under the trees in back of the bar. I didn't feel sorry for them because it was their decision. I didn't despise them because their situation seemed kind of desperate and sad. I knew it wasn't right, but I just didn't know how I felt about those folks.

I was still thinking about those things that Friday evening as our family sat around the table eating supper. Dad was telling Mom that he was going out to the reservation on Saturday to check on the well pump. Mom started to reply, but she stopped in mid-sentence. Her mouth was open, but no words were coming out. I saw a look of horror slowly work its way up to her eyes. She put her left hand over her mouth and pointed a shaky right hand at my sister.

"What is that in your hair?" she wailed. We turned to look at Linda who was busy scratching her head. Mom got up and quickly began to part Linda's hair. "Jim, our little girl has lice!"

Dad got up and looked for himself as if he just couldn't believe what Mom said. He and Mom looked at each other in dismay. Somehow, without having a conversation or uttering a word, they came to some mutual agreement and launched into action. Dad picked up Linda and held her out away from himself. Quickly he carried her over to the kitchen counter and sat her down next to the sink. Mom went into the other room and came back with a towel, a hairbrush, a bottle of Vitalis and the electric clippers that Dad used to cut the hair on us boys.

"Dale, you take Roger and Paul into the other room," Dad commanded before turning back to help Mom with Linda.

I picked up Paul and led Roger by the hand into the living room. I got a ball, and we sat on the floor rolling it back and forth to each other. I could hear Linda weeping softly and Mom apologizing for having to brush her hair so hard. Then I heard the buzz of the electric clippers. I knew from the sound that they were cutting through hair, and I heard Linda go from weeping to actual crying loudly.

I crept to the door of the kitchen and snuck a look. All of Linda's long hair was lying in a little pile on the floor in front of the sink. Mom was lathering Linda's head with some kind of shampoo. When Mom finished with the shampoo she toweled dry her head and what little hair she had left. I was shocked at the way Linda looked. Her head seemed smaller without all the hair.

Dad reached over and grabbed a bottle of Vitalis that was on the sink. He opened it and poured a generous amount on Linda's head. She began to wail and writhe as he held her arm to keep her from running away. My parents were quick to hug her and comfort her.

I wondered why there was no sympathy for Roger or me when we had that vile stuff poured on our heads. It was obvious to me in that moment that Linda was always going to be treated differently from us boys. I wasn't jealous, but I sure would have liked an explanation.

Mom and Dad repeated their treatments, and then Mom led Linda to her bedroom. Dad came into the living room and stood there grinding his teeth as he looked toward the bedroom. I could hear Mom talking quietly to Linda in soothing tones.

"Dale, get a broom and come in here," I heard Mom call. Her voice had a kind of edge to it, and I looked at Dad to see if he also heard it.

He glowered at me and jerked his thumb in the direction of Linda's room. "You heard your mom. What are you waiting for? Get after it," he said with a growl.

I ran into the kitchen, found the broom, and just as quick as I could took it to the bedroom. Mom was sitting on the bed with Linda, and they were both looking at something on the floor. Mom pointed at it with a shaking hand.

"Pick that up with the broom," she commanded. "Don't touch it with your hand. Carry it into the bathroom and put it in the bathtub."

I looked closely at the thing on the floor and discovered that it was the knit hat that Linda had gotten from the Indian girl in the schoolyard. I pushed the broom handle under it and carefully lifted it up. "Why am I using this broom, Mom?" I asked.

"Because it has lice in it, that's why!" Mom said in a loud voice. "Don't mess around with it. Just carry it carefully to the bathtub and drop it in. Don't jostle it around either. I don't want any of those bugs falling off."

I concentrated on carrying it with great care. Once in the bathroom I tilted the broom handle and let the cap slide into the bathtub. I bent down and looked at it closely. I saw a little bit of movement, and soon I was able to see a few bugs crawling around on it. I shivered a little bit and hurriedly left to go back to Linda's bedroom.

Mom was still trying to comfort a sobbing Linda. She shot me a look and said, "Go get the dustpan, and bring it back here to sweep up."

As I ran into the kitchen to get the dustpan I saw Dad pacing back and forth in the living room. His fists were clenched, and I could tell he was very angry.

I grabbed the dustpan and sped back to Linda's bedroom. Quickly I maneuvered the dustpan with my left hand while balancing the broom against my upper body. I swept the floor as best as I could. Mom watched me closely, and when I finished she told me to dump everything outside and leave the broom and dustpan on the front porch for now.

I went out through the kitchen door, and as soon as I stepped away from the side of the house the wind the tore the dustpan from my hand, sending it skittering along the driveway. I quickly ran after it and caught it right before it went into the street. I turned around and fought the cold wind back to the house. Tears were torn from my eyes as I placed the broom and dustpan on the front porch.

I quickly scuttled back inside where it was warm. Dad was putting on his coat. He grabbed a paper sack and went into the bathroom. I could hear him muttering under his breath as the sack made crinkling sounds. Soon he was striding back into the living room. He had the paper sack in his hand, and it was obvious that something was in it. I figured it was the knit cap, but I didn't know what he was going to do with it.

"Dale," he barked at me. "Put on a coat and gloves. You are coming with me to the reservation."

I quickly squirmed into my coat and pulled on my frayed gloves as I walked out to the car. Dad fired up the car, and soon we were following the tracks through the snow of cars that had gone before us along the reservation road. Dad was silent as he drove, but I noticed that he gripped the steering wheel with an extra amount of tightness. I couldn't tell if it was to keep control of the car because of the snow or if he was just very angry.

We pulled up at the mission building, and Dad grabbed the paper sack as he left the car. He was taking giant strides, and I hurried through the snow to keep up with him. It was evening, and the sun had already gone down. It was so cold that Dad's breath came out like steam blowing out of a mad bull's nostrils.

There were lights on in the mission building, and Dad threw the door open wide with a little extra force. I followed him inside and saw Andy, Amos, Yas, and Mr. Roberts sitting at a table talking to each other in low voices. They looked up, startled at the sight of Dad standing there. Dad slammed the door shut behind him and hurled the paper bag onto the table. It slid a little bit along the surface before it stopped in front of Mr. Roberts. The men stared at the bag for a minute and then looked up at Dad.

"Today my daughter came home from school with head lice," he said in a low angry voice. "She got it from an Indian girl who gave her a cap. I put the cap in that bag so that you can see it. I think somebody did this on purpose in order to get back at white people."

Mr. Roberts opened the sack and pulled out the cap. He spread it out on the table, and the men looked it over. I could hear Amos,

Andy, and Yas talking about it quietly among themselves. Mr. Roberts shook his head and said something to Andy who shrugged.

"Jim, I don't think this was done on purpose," Mr. Roberts said with a slight smile. I could tell that he was trying to calm Dad down as he talked. "You know that many of the people out here have problems with head lice. They don't always have enough water to wash themselves the way they want to. The school nurses help a lot, but it is a hard thing to stop because of the living conditions."

Dad turned red in the face. "Dirty, filthy savages," he shouted. "I don't want my children infected by the Indians."

Amos, Andy, and Yas sat up real straight in their chairs. I could tell that they were offended and angry. They sat silent and unmoving, and somehow their silence was louder than Dad's shouting.

Mr. Roberts stood up and walked over to Dad. I noticed him put a hand on each of the men's shoulders, giving a squeeze as he walked past them. Each of the Indian men seemed to calm down a bit after that.

Mr. Roberts stood right in front of Dad and looked him in the eyes.

"Jim, these men are your brothers in Christ. They are also fellow veterans who served their country well. You owe them some respect and kindness because of those things." Mr. Roberts just stood there waiting for Dad to respond.

Dad looked away from Mr. Roberts and then shifted his gaze to the floor. He cleared his throat a couple of times and then nodded as if he had made some decision. He looked up, his eyes roving over the faces of the Indian men.

"How can I keep my daughter healthy out here when all I see and hear about is head lice, tuberculosis, parasites, alcoholism, and a thousand other diseases?" Dad asked the men.

They looked back at him with stony gazes. Mr. Roberts shook his head. "That's the way it is with mission work, Jim," he said in a soft voice. "You have to take the good with the bad. My wife and I came out here to help, and we realized that it was not going to be easy. When God calls people, He gives you a choice. You can either stay where you are or you can go where He leads."

I went over to the window and looked out at the sky. Snow was falling heavily, and I couldn't see the stars, but I knew they were up there. I felt the same about God. He was out there, but I just couldn't see Him. The adults in the room seemed to feed on anger. I knew that there should be peace, but Dad was determined to keep it away from us. I shut my ears to the angry voices and thought about the cold outside of the room and the welcome heat inside the room. I smelled the wood burning in the stove along with the metallic smell of unwashed bodies. I heard the crackle of fire and the edge to the voices of angry and disturbed men.

"What do you say, Jim?" Mr. Roberts said in a kind voice. "Can you forgive these people and get past this?"

Amos spoke up before Dad could say anything. "You told us about a truce with God, and I promised you a truce between us. The people will not do anything to hurt your children, and we will not do anything to hurt you. The problem with the lice was just bad luck. Now that your children know, they will not borrow our hats again. We ask you to do the Christian thing, Preacher Jim."

I turned around to look at Dad. He was standing with his head bowed and his fists clenched at his sides. I heard him let out a long sigh, and he slowly straightened out his fingers. He put his hands together and rubbed them in a slow and deliberate way. He raised his head and looked at each man in turn.

"You are right," he said. "I was just upset because my daughter had to have most of her hair cut off, and I hate seeing her hurt. I apologize for what I said."

The men got up from the table and came over to shake Dad's hand. Mr. Roberts motioned for Dad to follow him over to the table. I continued to stand by the window, just watching to see how things developed. Nobody paid attention to me. It was as if I were invisible to those men.

On the table were the well-worn plans for the water well, each part correctly labeled with the dates of when it was last replaced. The men began to discuss the problem of frozen pipes and how difficult it can be to pump water in sub-freezing temperatures. Mr. Roberts was writing on a piece of paper as the men came to some decisions concerning the pump.

Dad looked over the list and nodded. "I can go into Albuquerque tomorrow morning and get those parts. If I leave early in the morning I should be back in the afternoon to help make the repairs," he told them.

The men at the table spoke together in their language for a few minutes, and then Andy turned to Dad and spoke.

"If you really want to show that you are sorry I think you should leave your son with us tonight. Let him stay with us here overnight, and we will take him home tomorrow afternoon."

Dad looked at me and then shrugged. "Sure. He's not too bright, and I think it would be okay," he replied. "But what would that prove?"

Andy grinned. "It would prove that you trust us with one of your children. It would also give us an opportunity to explain our ways to your son so that he might understand us."

Dad cast a doubtful look my way. I could tell that he wasn't too concerned about leaving me with them. I didn't know what was going through his mind. He kind of grunted and waved a dismissive hand toward me. "He might be able to understand some things, but I doubt it."

Dad spoke for a few more minutes and then turned to leave. I hurried to catch up to him before he went out the door.

"Dad," I said quietly as I tugged on his sleeve. "Why do you always bring me with you out here to the reservation? I thought you were doing it so that I could learn."

Dad chuckled and shook his head. "Son, you are the oldest child. Your sister always obeys, and she helps your mom with your brothers. Paul is too young to get into much trouble. Roger is a good kid who obeys his mom and his sister. But you. . ." He sighed and bent down so that he was looking me right in the eye. "You are always in trouble. I give you a simple job to do, like catch mice, and you get in trouble with the neighbor. You try to shoot off guns or hang around with kids from the Colonia in back of the house. I can't leave you with your mom because you will give her too much trouble, and you know her health is poor. I can't trust you so I keep you close."

I didn't know what to say to that. Dad was right. I seemed to always be in trouble, but I tried to be helpful. I felt tears dropping on my cheek, and I was afraid that the Indians would make fun of me if they saw me cry.

Dad just looked at me and shrugged. "I will see you tomorrow," he said with finality. "Don't give these people any trouble or they might scalp you."

I looked back at the men sitting around the table. They quickly ducked their heads and looked down at the tabletop. Dad opened the door, and a blast of cold air blew inside before he could close it. I walked to the window and watched as he hurriedly got into the car and drove away until the taillights were swallowed up by the falling snow. I felt abandoned and very much alone.

I sensed someone coming up behind me. Soon I felt a hand on my shoulder, and I looked up to see Yas standing there.

"Come over to the table and sit with us, Young White," he said quietly. He put a little pressure on my shoulder and spun me around to face the table. Then he kind of pushed me a step at time to a chair at the table. He motioned for me to sit. The men began to talk in quiet voices about the well and how to repair it.

After about ten or fifteen minutes Mr. Roberts got up from the table and announced that he was going home. He shook hands with all of the men, opened the door, and stepped out into the darkness. The men at the table sat silent. I didn't have much to say so I sat silent as well. Then there was a knock at the door. Yas got up and hurried to answer it.

Imagine my surprise when a young Indian woman came in

followed by seven boys. When the boys took off their caps I immediately recognized them. They were in my class at school. One of them was Jerry. Yas walked over and shook each boy's hand. He turned to the woman and smiled. She said something quietly and reached out to hold his hand. He turned around and looked at me.

"Young White, this is my friend Mary. She is going to help me with some things here on the reservation," he said proudly. He jerked his chin in my direction. "Mary, this is Young White. We also call him Dale."

Mary lifted her free hand and gave me a little wave. Her smile made her whole face light up, and I immediately liked her. "Do you want me to call you Dale or Young White?" she asked me.

I thought about it for a few seconds. "When we are on the reservation you can call me Young White. Anywhere else maybe you should just call me Dale," I said with a smile. I sensed that I could trust her.

The other boys came and sat at the table with me while the men stood and talked among themselves. Andy and Amos left us with Mary and Yas. It was obvious to me that something was going on, but I wasn't sure just what.

I turned to Jerry who was sitting next to me. "What is going on?" I asked. "Where did Andy and Amos go?"

Jerry shrugged. He looked around the table and pointed his chin toward Yas. "He and Mary called a meeting for tonight. Remember how I told you that Yas is taking a group of us to teach us how to be men and to teach us about our past? Well, this is that group," Jerry said proudly. I looked at my friends around the table, and they all nodded their heads in agreement.

Yas and Mary were standing at the window looking outside and talking quietly to each other. I saw them lean forward to look at something, and then Yas turned around. "Put your coats and gloves on, and follow me," he commanded as he opened the door and walked outside.

We quickly squirmed into our coats and ran out after him. The wind was howling, and snow was swirling through the air. It seemed to me that there wasn't as much snow falling, but it was certainly getting colder. Yas and Mary walked ahead of us, and we followed without talking.

Soon we were at a hogan that had a horse tied up outside. The horse had a blanket and saddle on it as if someone had already ridden it. Mary went in first followed by Yas.

We crowded in after them, jostling each other in our haste to get in out of the cold. I smelled something cooking, and I looked around to see what was going on in the hogan. An older woman was standing over a cast-iron stove that glowed a pleasant orange. She was stirring a pot that had steam coming off it. Two beds, a small table and four chairs, a cabinet, and a couple of benches filled the interior of the hogan. Strings of red chili peppers hung from the support timbers. I noticed Amos sitting on one of the benches, and I wondered if he was the one who rode the horse over.

We all took off our coats and kind of spread out to find places to sit. The hogan was warm and smelled of stew, fry bread, musty blankets, burning wood, and the coppery smell that I always associated with the Indians. I was comfortable among my friends and those good people who treated me so well.

Yas walked over quietly and spoke with Amos. They seemed to be making some plans, but I couldn't hear what they were saying. Amos got up from his bench and walked out of the door.

"Stand up and follow me," Yas commanded. He looked over at Mary, and I saw her nod as if they had communicated without talking. Yas turned and walked out the door. We boys followed after him.

Right outside the door was Amos mounted on the horse. He had a large burlap bag in his hand. I saw him use his knees to urge the horse forward. Yas walked just behind the horse and motioned for us to follow him. We obediently walked single file behind Yas who carefully followed in the path that the horse was breaking through the snow.

I noticed that the snow had stopped falling, and the clouds were parting to show a sliver of the moon. Light seemed to emanate from the snow, and even though Amos on his horse was some ways ahead of us I could see him clearly. We continued to walk on until I was sure that my feet were going to freeze off. Jerry looked back, and I followed his gaze. We had come so far that we couldn't see the village anymore.

"Where are we going?" I asked Jerry in a whisper.

He just shrugged and kept trudging along.

We were about in the middle of the group. The horse made a trail in the snow. Yas made it a bit better, and the kids right behind him kind of packed the snow down. By the time Jerry and I were walking on it there was more packed snow and less powdery snow on the trail.

It seemed to me that time kind of slowed down. I didn't know how long we walked or how far, but I knew I was very cold. I was walking with my head down and just putting one frozen foot in front of the next one. I was tired as well, and maybe that is why I didn't notice that the kid in front of me had stopped. I ran right into him, and he pushed back with a grunt. I straightened up and looked around just like everybody else was doing.

Amos had jumped down off the horse, and he was having a quiet conversation with Yas. Both of them turned around and walked to us. Even though Yas began to speak loudly to us, his words seemed to be smothered by the snow.

"Tonight you will test your manhood," he said. There was a quiet intensity about him that made us pay special attention. "I want you all to take off your clothes and put them in that sack." He pointed at the sack that Amos was holding out in front of him. We looked at him with our mouths open.

"Won't we freeze to death?" Jerry asked in a quavering voice.

Yas nodded slightly. "You don't have to do this if you don't want to. You can turn around right now and run home. If you do that, though, you will not be one of us ever again."

We looked at each other trying to make sense of this. Finally, one of the bigger boys started taking off his clothes until he was naked. He put everything in the sack and wrapped his arms around his body, shivering and hopping from foot to foot in the snow. The rest of followed suit until all of us boys were naked.

Amos tied up the mouth of the sack and jumped on the horse's back. Yas jumped up on the horse behind him.

"I want you all to count to two hundred. When you have counted that high you can begin to run back the way we have come," Yas told us.

He pointed at the trail that we had made in the snow. "You must all come back together and at the same time. You cannot leave anyone behind. Do you understand?"

We all nodded weakly with shivering heads. Yas looked at each of us in turn, bending down from the horse and looking right into our eyes. "I will see you back at the hogan."

Amos clucked to the horse which gave a short jump and then headed back down the trail at a trot. We watched them go in silence until we could no longer see them.

The bigger boy who had been the first to take off his clothes snorted in disgust. "While we were watching them go we could have been counting rather than just standing here freezing." He began to count quickly, and we all joined him, our voices quavering from the cold.

It seemed to take forever to get to two hundred. My fingers were cold, and I wasn't sure I could even move them. When we got to two hundred we all began to run, slipping and sliding along the snowy path. The bigger boy took the lead, and the rest of us kind of strung out behind him.

"Buddy up," he commanded. "Help each other along. If someone starts to get in trouble we will all help out."

Jerry and I ran side by side. I heard one of the smaller boys behind me crying softly, but he still seemed to be running. Our breathing sounded ragged and forced. One kid had kind of a wheeze that came out at the end of each breath.

I was so cold that I began to wonder what it would be like to simply fall into the snow and go to sleep. I was seriously considering it when something began to change. My body heated up, and I could feel my hands again. The cold didn't seem so cold, and my legs still seemed to be strong. My feet were like blocks of ice, but soon I found that I didn't care as much.

The boy in the lead began a chant in Navajo, and the others joined in. I didn't know the words, but there was a recognizable tune. I droned along with the tune, not saying words but simply chanting "ungh, ungh" in time with the others. It helped pass the time.

Suddenly one of the boys let out a yelp. "I see the tops of the hogans," he yelled to us. "We are close. We will make it."

We picked up the pace a bit, and soon we could smell the pinion wood burning in the fireplaces. The boy in the lead slowed down a little and let us catch up to him. "Is everyone here? Check with your buddy, and make sure that nobody is missing."

We looked around and did a quick head count. Everybody was there, and we soon arrived at the hogan with the horse tied up outside. We lifted the blanket at the door and hurried inside without hesitation to find our clothes laid out in neat bundles scattered over the room.

We each spied our own clothing and hurriedly dressed. The clothes had been heated by the fire, and they were still warm.

Yas told us not to put on our socks or shoes yet but to sit down and let our feet thaw out. Mary gave us each a small cloth that had been heated by the fire. She showed us how to rub our feet slowly until feeling crept back into them and to use the heated cloth to rub them.

When Yas and Mary were convinced that we were fine and that there was no sign of frostbite they began to give each of us bowls full of goat stew. They also gave us each small cups filled with some kind of hot tea.

Yas asked us about our run back to the village.

"I heard John crying," one boy said. "But he finished the run just like the rest of us."

Another boy piped up. "I looked around to see if Dale was still with us, but he was so white that he blended in with the snow, and I thought we had lost him."

Everybody howled with laughter. I felt a sense of belonging, of comradeship with those boys. We had survived a hardship together. We had helped each other, and we had successfully met a challenge.

Yas smiled and nodded. "I want each of you to remember this night. You are now part of the Brave Family. You are all brothers now. You will now know that sometimes you cannot control what goes on outside of you, but you can control what goes on inside of you. Now you know that you are strong."

We all nodded as we gratefully slurped our stew and ate the chunks of meat.

"You know that my name means 'snow,'" Yas continued. "I got my name over in Korea. I got stuck in a foxhole during a snowstorm. I was wounded badly. I was there for a night and a day. A medic happened to hear me call out for help. He pulled me out of the foxhole and took me to the hospital. I had to have some skin removed and some toes cut off. I was in pain, and the hospital put me on painkillers, and I got hooked on them. Later, when they took me off them painkillers, I started drinking booze to kill the pain. The booze made me useless. It sucked the life right out of me."

Yas sat down on the floor, and Mary came to sit by him, holding his hand. "I started going to a mission place where they gave out free food, sang hymns, and the preacher told everyone about the Bible. I came to believe in God and Jesus Christ. You should too. One day God told me to come back here. I knew that I had to break the hold that booze had on me. I tried to quit sometimes, but I would get the

DTs and go crazy. When I came here my uncles, Amos and Andy, helped me to get out from under the booze. Now I am telling you this so that you don't make the same mistakes I made. I want you to be better than me, stronger than me. I know you can do it."

We all nodded to show that we understood. In that moment I went to war against alcohol. It was slowly destroying my grandfather, and it had almost destroyed my friend, Yas. I decided that I would hate it for the rest of my life. Even if everyone around me drank beer, wine, or liquor I would never bend, and I would never use it myself. I remembered seeing Yas staked to the ground and how the medicine man danced around him. I remembered Yas shouting and saying crazy things. Now I knew why all of that was happening. I also knew that I never wanted to go through anything like that myself.

Mary stood up and left the hogan. We continued to sit silently. I was hoping that Yas would talk some more, but he was silent. We were all trying to recover from our ordeal, and the silence was making a few of us nod off. In few minutes Mary came back leading a very old Navajo man by the arm. She shooed some boys off a bed and helped the old man sit there.

"This is Grandfather," she told us. "He is the oldest man among us. Tonight he will tell you about the people so that you will know the legends and the stories."

The old man cleared his throat, and Mary brought him some tea. He swayed slightly on the bed and said something to Jerry.

"I am supposed to translate for you," Jerry told me. "I am supposed to tell you what old Grandfather will be telling us."

The old grandfather began to speak, and he told us some of the tribal history stories, especially regarding the long walk and their Trail of Tears. He also told us some of the Navajo myths and legends.

We were quiet for a while when he finished with his stories, and then he broke the silence by asking me, as a white person, to tell some stories. The only stories I could think of were out of the Bible.

I told the story about the children mocking Elisha because he had a bald head and how two bears came out of the woods and attacked the children. Then I told the story of how a man gathered some gourds to put into a stew for a lot of people to eat. When the people began to eat they said that the stew was poisoned and warned everyone not to eat it. Elisha was there and saw what was happening. He told one of the men to bring him some flour, and he threw it into the pot. Then he told everyone to go ahead and eat the stew. When they tasted it they found that it was good, and everyone was able to eat and get fed.

Jerry translated for me to the old grandfather.

The old grandfather listened attentively as I told the stories. "How do you know these stories?" he asked me. I was embarrassed to admit it, but I told him truthfully that I had been bad in church, and to punish me my dad made me read the Bible silently during the church services. Dad didn't tell me what to read so I scanned through the Bible until I found the interesting stories and only read those.

The old man nodded and then turned and said something to Mary. She got up and scrounged around in a wooden chest that was stored under the bed. She came up with a Bible and handed it to him. He handed it to me and said, "Find those stories, and read them to us."

I obediently turned to the stories of Elisha and read them out loud. Everyone was quiet as I read.

Finally, the old man held up his hand for me to stop reading. He said something in Navajo to Jerry who listened and then told me that the grandfather was pleased with my selection of stories. The Navajo have bear stories, and they also have gourd stories. He thanked me for sharing with them.

Then the old grandfather heaved himself up off the bed, his

bones creaking and joints snapping with age. Mary hurried to help him and then led him away back to his own hogan.

Yas stood up to address us. "Tomorrow we will all go into town. There we will face a challenge together. We will help some people. Tonight, though, you must sleep here in this place. You have done well. Tomorrow you will do well."

We each found a place on the floor. There were plenty of good thick blankets, and we stayed warm all night long.

We were quietly awakened by Yas and Mary early the next morning. We shook out our blankets and, folding them neatly, we created a pile in one corner of the room. Then we took turns trotting out to the toilet to do our morning business. It was very cold outside, but I was no longer afraid of the cold.

Back at the hogan we were all given some fry bread and a small glass of milk. While we were eating I heard a large truck rumble up to the hogan. Soon, Andy came in, scooped up the blankets, and carried them outside. I followed him and stood there as he piled them in the back of the truck. Yas came out followed by the other boys.

"We are going into town this morning," he told us. "Today is head pay day when all of the people receive their head money. You know that many of the people will go into town and get drunk. After they get too drunk to walk they are laid out in back of the saloon. Sometimes they suffer from the cold. Sometimes they are robbed or abused by people in town as they lay outside. Today we will help them. We will cover them with blankets. We will stand guard over them and protect them."

Yas jerked his chin toward the truck. "Get in the back, and we will make the trip to town."

All of us piled into the back of the truck and covered up with the blankets. There was a very strong wind blowing from the north. It had a fresh smell to it that made me feel alive. As the truck moved toward town it slid in the deep ruts of the road. The back of the truck fishtailed this way and that, jostling us as the wind whipped our hair around. We were quiet as we made the trip. I remember looking around at each of the boys and thinking that I was glad to be part of the Brave Family.

We finally reached town, cold and stiff but ready to help. Andy drove the truck to one of the larger bars. Even though the bar wasn't going to be open for another couple of hours there was already a line of people waiting outside in the cold. Andy motioned for us to jump down out of the truck. We each handed him a blanket before jumping down into the ice and snow of the road.

Yas waved his arms as if he were gathering some chickens, and we walked over to stand close to him.

"I brought some fry bread with us. It is up in the front of the truck," he told us. "One of you get that bread, and we will hand it out to the people in line. Many of them have not eaten today so that they can be first in line."

"Why should we worry about these people?" one of the boys asked. "They are drinking up their money and hurting themselves and their families. Why should we even feel sorry for them? I just feel sorry for their family. I am ashamed to see how some of the people ruin themselves in front of the whites."

One of the boys came around the side of the truck with the fry bread, and he handed it over to Yas. We all waited to see what Yas would say. I really understood all of that because my grandfather was a drunk. I knew the problems that he created for all of us in the family.

Yas weighed the bag of bread in his hand as he craned his neck to look back at the line of people queueing up to drink themselves into oblivion. When Yas turned back around to look at us there was sorrow showing on his face.

"We don't know what devils are causing our people to do this." He looked at each of us in turn. He had a way of looking at you as if he could see right down into your very soul. "All I know is that I was like them once, and now I am not like them. That gives me hope that those people in the line maybe have a better future. It gives me hope that the People might be stronger and better in the future. Perhaps what we do here today will be the beginning of a new time for the People."

We all looked at the ground and then kind of sideways at each other. We were ashamed for even questioning the motives for helping.

Yas reached out and put his hand on my arm.

"Dale, you are white. You are not one of the people," Yas said softly. "You do not have to help with this. I can see your house from here. Why don't you go on home?"

I was shocked! Wasn't I part of the Brave Family? I thought for a minute before replying.

"My family has always tried to help. You know that I helped my mother hand out bread and milk at this very place when we first came to town." I looked around at the other boys, and I saw many of them looking back at me with curiosity. "I am part of the Brave Family. I want to help today."

Jerry grinned real big and held out his hand. I shook it, and the other boys extended theirs as well.

Yas smiled and said, "Let's go on over and start handing out pieces of bread."

I will never forget that morning. We handed out the bread to the people. Some of them thanked us, but most just took it and turned away so that we would not see them eat it. Andy had brought some hot coffee in a thermos, and he let people take small drinks until the coffee was all gone.

When the bar opened up there was a general rush by the people in line to get in and start their drinking. Yas led us to the back of the bar, and we waited in the cold for about an hour until the first drunks were carried out back and laid down on the snowy ground. Yas directed us to cover up three people with one blanket. While the people slept we stood guard.

I saw a white boy across the street watching us. He was wearing a good coat and wool cap. He sat on a tree stump and watched as we cared for the drunks. Finally he came across the street to talk to us. As he got closer I recognized him as a boy that was in the grade ahead of me at school. His name was Hutch Bernandez, and his dad owned a run-down hotel, the bus depot, and a lot of land that backed up onto the Pueblo reservation. Hutch walked back and forth in front of us, inspecting us as if we were strange creatures. He stopped right in front of me.

"Why are you helping all these drunk Indians?" he asked. "You look stupid doing this, you know."

"My family always helps people who need help," I told him. I meant my mom and dad, but I also meant the Brave Family.

Hutch looked up and down the line. "Can I join you?" he asked in a wistful tone of voice. "I want to help, too."

We all looked at Yas. He walked over and began to ask Hutch some questions.

Just then Hutch's dad came over and demanded to know what was going on. Yas explained it clearly, and the man kind of nodded. He rubbed his jaw and kind of pushed some snow around with the toe of his boot. Without looking at Hutch he said, "You go home now, boy. We will talk about this later."

He squared up to Yas and looked him right in the eye. "I appreciate what you are doing here, but it is not something my family will be doing."

Yas nodded and started to say something, but Hutch's dad cut him off. "If you are looking for a job I got one for you. I need help on the reservations cutting trees, tending to a sawmill, and occasionally doing some dynamite blasting for the government. If you are interested you should be waiting outside my house early every morning."

Yas nodded, and they shook hands.

That afternoon I walked back to my own house. Over supper I told my dad and mom about my experiences. Dad shrugged when I told him about running naked in the snow. He laughed out loud when I told him about being a member of the Brave Family. Then he reached over and plunked me hard on my head.

"You are an idiot," he told me. "Now go clean out the mouse traps and reset them for tonight."

His criticism hurt, but I was still proud to be part of the Brave Family. Little did I know that this was the beginning of a time which would change my whole life and set my feet on a life path that made me so different from my family and my friends.

NINE

FIGHTING BACK

DECEMBER 1962

T hings seemed to be different for me once I joined the Brave Family. My time at school had a new feel to it. I was more focused, and I was able to pay more attention to the details of my work.

I also began to be included in the conversations among the other boys. Jerry had just about been my only friend, but now I had other friends. We even had nicknames for each other. The name they chose for me was Ghost because I was white and could move quietly. Jerry was called Peanut because he ate peanuts all the time. We used our nicknames during recess, but we reverted to our regular names during class, unless we forgot.

One day Reuben asked to borrow a ruler, and I tossed it over to him. It bounced off his hand and landed on the floor. "Reuben, you have butterfingers," I said happily. I leaned over and said, "Butterfinger, butterfinger" in a half-mocking tone. Reuben smiled and picked up the ruler.

I felt a hand on my shoulder and turned to see the very disapproving face of my teacher. She bent down so she could look me right in the eye.

"Dale, how would you feel if someone called you a name?" she asked in a quiet voice. I blushed even though I knew that I was only using Reuben's nickname. "You must apologize to Reuben right now."

I spun around in my chair and looked at Reuben. His eyes were wide, and his mouth was open. I hoped that he would defend me and tell our teacher about the nickname thing. He stayed mute so I didn't see that I had much of a choice.

"I . . . I . . . I . . . apologize, Reuben, for calling you a butterfinger." I said it loud enough for everyone to hear. He kind of nodded and shrugged. I looked up at Mrs. Garza to see if she accepted my apology to Reuben. She still had this rather grim look on her face.

"Dale, I expect better from you. I want you to write the words 'I will not call Reuben names' one hundred times on a piece of paper. You will also stay inside during recess time, both morning and afternoon, for the next two days," she told me. "Do you understand me?" she asked quietly.

I nodded and took a deep breath. Writing the words was not going to be hard. Missing recess was going to be real punishment. The confinement of the classroom was only made bearable by having a recess.

That afternoon I watched my friends rush outside to play in the cold and snow. I sat forlornly at my desk and laboriously wrote out "I will not call Reuben names" on line after line of paper. Mrs. Garza sat at her desk and graded papers. When I had finished twenty-five lines on my paper I raised my hand. Mrs. Garza caught the movement and looked up from her work.

"Would it be all right if I just took a little break and looked outside for one minute?" I asked in a plaintive voice. Mrs. Garza arched an eyebrow, and I could tell she was considering my request. "I have already completed writing the sentence twenty-five times." I saw the beginning of a smile. "I am only asking to look for one minute."

She shook her head, but the smile widened a little bit. "Okay," she said. "One minute and one minute only."

I immediately ran over to the windows and stared out at the other kids having fun. I saw a small knot of my friends laughing and throwing snowballs. I looked over toward the swings and saw my sister talking to an Indian girl, maybe the girl who had given her the cap. My sister's hair had been cut very short. It made her head look small. Dad wasn't the greatest barber, and even from a distance I could tell that it had been cut unevenly. Linda seemed to be having a good talk with her friend.

As I was watching I saw John and Wesley Gray push the Indian girl aside and stand in front of Linda. It appeared to me that they were taunting her because of her short hair. John reached out and pushed her. She fell into the snow and began to cry.

I gasped and began to bang on the window. How dare they do such a thing! While Linda was on the ground, I saw John straddle her and then sit on her. He pushed her so that she was lying on her back, and then he lay flat on top of her. Wesley threw his head back, and I saw him laughing. Enough was enough! Nobody, and I mean nobody, was going to pick on my sister.

I turned away from the window and ran as fast as I could for the door. Mrs. Garza yelled at me, but I didn't pay attention. I was trying to get to my sister before something really bad happened to her.

I could hear Mrs. Garza running down the hall after me, but I was faster than her. I hit the outside door hard without breaking stride and slogged quickly through the snow and mud over to the swings where John was trying to kiss my sister.

She was yelling, "No, No!" and trying to squirm away from him. I reached down and grabbed John by the collar. Hauling as hard as I could, I rolled him off Linda and tossed him into a puddle of snow and mud.

His brother Wesley shouted something like, "You can't do that to my brother!"

I made a fist, rounded on him, and hit him hard right in the mouth. He lost his balance and landed next to his brother in the puddle.

I helped my sister to her feet and gave her a hug. I told her to run back into the building, find a teacher, and tell her what was happening.

I heard angry voices and somebody crying behind me. Wesley was bleeding from his mouth. He held his mouth open, crying with great gasping sobs while John looked at him with concern. John stood up and helped Wesley to his feet.

"You knocked my front teeth out," Wesley lisped. He opened his mouth, and sure enough there was a big gaping hole where his teeth had been.

"Good!" I replied angrily. "You mess around with my family, and I'll knock out the rest of your rotten teeth," I said with a raised fist.

John let out a bellow and ran at me. I waited until he was close before trying to hit him. The mud and snow made things so slippery that I lost my footing and missed.

He tackled me, and we both fell to the ground. We rolled around in the mud scratching, clawing, screaming, and spitting. We couldn't really get a grip on each other so neither one of us was hurt.

I was finally able to stand up, and as soon as I could manage it I began kicking at John. I didn't aim for a particular spot; I just wanted to hurt him. Suddenly I felt many hands on me dragging me away from John.

I found myself in the clutches of several teachers. A couple of others were pulling John up out of the mud. The teachers hauled John, Wesley, and me into the building and down the hall to the room right outside of the principal's office.

Linda was already there sitting on a bench along one side of the small room. I sat down heavily beside her.

John and Wesley tromped noisily into the room. They saw an

empty bench that was right across the room from us and sat down over there.

I looked at them, and they glared at me.

"Let me see your teeth," I said to Wesley. He removed a bloody rag that he had been holding to his lips and opened his mouth wide. The nurse had given the rag to him so that he wouldn't bleed all over the floors. The gap seemed even bigger that it had before. "What happened to the teeth? I asked. Wesley shook his head and cried.

"He swallowed them," John said angrily. "You knocked them out, and he swallowed them. You are an evil person, and I hate your guts."

I shrugged. It wasn't like other people hadn't already called me names. My own dad said I was just a trouble maker.

I looked over at Linda. She was looking down at the floor with her small head bowed.

"Are you all right?" I asked.

She nodded and then looked sideways at me.

"You are covered in mud, and you look ugly," she said.

I thought about that for a few seconds, and somehow it seemed funny to me. I started to snicker, and then I laughed out loud.

Linda smiled and then reached for my hand. She leaned in close and whispered, "Thank you. I think you are the best big brother ever." We sat there holding hands and enjoying the comfort that we gave to each other. John and Wesley continued to glare at us with narrowed eyes and tight lips.

The principal hurried in and looked first at Linda and then over at the Gray boys. He made a little exasperated sound at the back of his throat and turned so that he was standing right in front of me. "Tell me what happened out there by the swings," he said in a voice that sounded like an iron bar falling on concrete. He folded his arms across his chest and waited. The man seemed to be nine feet tall, and his face was dark and glowering. Mrs. Zonni came from the office and stood beside him. She also folded her arms across her chest.

"I saw John Gray over there push my sister on the ground and then jump on top of her. He was trying to kiss her, and she kept saying 'No,' but he wouldn't leave her alone. Nobody was doing anything to help so I ran over there and pulled him off her. Then Wesley threatened me so I hit him just as hard as I could. Then John got up and attacked me, and we fought and rolled around on the ground. Then I got up and tried to kick the snot out of him until some teachers got their hands on me." I said all of that very quickly without drawing a breath. My chest was heaving with the effort of trying to control my emotions. I still had ahold of Linda's hand. She nodded as I spoke, and when I finished I looked over at her.

"Dale told the truth," she told the principal. "John and Wesley were mean to my friend and pushed her around. Then John began to make fun of me because my hair had to be cut off because of the lice that I got. Then John pushed me on the ground, and then he laid on top of me and began to try to kiss me. I yelled for help, but nobody seemed to care. Then Dale came running over and beat up John and Wesley."

She craned her head around so that she could look past Mrs. Zonni to see the Gray brothers. "I hate you!" she shouted at them. "I hate you, and my big brother saved me."

The principal looked at us for a few minutes in silence. He tapped his foot and kind of looked thoughtfully over to the side. Suddenly he whipped around and marched over to stand in front of the Gray boys. "Tell me what happened, and don't you lie to me, John Ray."

John's eyes got big, and he gulped real loud. I could tell that he was trying to come up with a good story. The minute he opened his mouth I knew he had decided to lie.

"Well. . .Wesley and me was just walking around when we seen this Indian girl making fun of Linda, cause of her hair and all. We pushed her away. Then I reached over to pat Linda on the shoulder, to kind of comfort her, you know. When I did that, she fell down in the snow. I reached down to pick her up, and I lost my balance and fell on top of her. Since the snow and ice was so slickery I couldn't get up. The next thing I knew ole crazy Dale was pulling on me and shouting at me. Then I seen him turn around and pop poor Wesley right in the mouth. He knocked out his teeth, and poor Wesley swallowed 'em. Then crazy Dale tried to kill me and knock out my teeth. If it wasn't for them good teachers he would have done it, too!"

Linda jumped up and pointed right at John Gray. "You are a liar, John! I hope you burn in hell!"

Mrs. Zonni walked over and hugged Linda who was crying tears of anger and frustration.

The principal looked back at me as if he were deciding what to say. He cleared his throat a couple of times and finally put his hands on his hips.

"We have called your dads. They will be here in a few minutes," he said menacingly. "Dale, your teacher brought me a note from your dad that said if you get in trouble at school you will also be in trouble when you get home. He said that I can discipline you any way that seems fit. I think I will wait until your dad gets here, and we will decide what that means."

My anger was starting to melt away, slowly being replaced by a mounting dread. I knew first-hand how Dad punished when he was angry. I looked across the room at the Gray boys and saw the bloody rag held to Wesley's mouth and the hatred that had set in around John's eyes. I hoped that the truth would win out, but I wasn't very optimistic that would happen.

After another ten minutes Dad and Brother Gray stormed into the room.

Dad came over to us and immediately grabbed Linda and hugged her tight. "Are you okay?" he asked with concern in his voice. Linda nodded, and he held her close to him for a few minutes.

I could hear John and Wesley telling their lies to Brother Gray and adding extra detail to make it sound more gruesome. Brother Gray was getting red in the face, and occasionally he would turn kind of sideways to look over at me.

"Dale!" Dad said loudly. "What is wrong with you? Trouble seems to be part of your life all the time these days." I saw a red flush on his neck which was the signal that he was getting very angry.

Brother Gray came over to stand by Dad. "What are you going to do with this devil child, Jim? He knocked out Wesley's teeth. He is uncontrollable. I think he is spending too much time among them savages on the reservation. If you want to be a minister, Jim, you have to be able to control your own household! That's what the Good Book says in first Timothy chapter three verses four and five. How can I let you be a leader in the church if you can't control even your own son?"

I could tell that Dad was bothered by what Brother Gray said. He looked at me for a few seconds and then turned to the principal. "Do you have a paddle handy?" he asked. The principal nodded and went to fetch it out of his office.

"But Dad. . ." I began to say. He cut me off with a low growl. He rounded on me and got down on my level.

"Shut up, Dale. The evidence of your wrongdoing is sitting right there in front of us." He pointed at Wesley who had begun to cry again. "Do you deny that you knocked out his teeth?"

"No, Dad," I said quietly. "But he had it coming to him, and I would do it again if I was in the situation again. You should have seen what they did to Linda," I said forcefully.

Dad spoke to me through gritted teeth. "Linda looks just fine to me. What I see is Wesley Gray holding a bloody rag to his mouth because the place where his two front teeth used to be is still bleeding. What I heard on the phone was that you were already in trouble in the classroom, and Mrs. Garza had made you stay inside for recess. Somehow you thought you were above the rules and ran out of the classroom. Then you immediately began to beat up John and Wesley."

The principal returned with a paddle that was about three feet long with holes drilled in it. Back in those days punishment at school was allowed and condoned. Almost every principal had a big paddle that he or she used to impress on miscreants that poor behavior would not be tolerated. The principal handed the paddle over to Dad. He took a couple of practice swings and then grabbed my ear, using it to lift me off the bench. He spun me around, bent me over and began to spank me hard. Every blow knocked a grunt out of me and left my backside feeling as if a fire had been lit on it. He gave me five strong shots and then stopped. I didn't cry, but I hurt so much that I couldn't straighten up.

I had been spanked before, and I knew that if I just hunkered down I could take anything Dad dished out. What he did next, though, just about tore out my heart. He looked over at Wesley Gray and said, "Come over here, Wesley."

Wesley turned white, but he managed to get to his feet and walk slowly to us. Dad looked from him to me and then handed the paddle over to Wesley. "Here, Wesley. Take this paddle and give Dale five big wallops with it. Don't hold back now. Put everything you got into it."

Wesley handled the paddle uncertainly. He looked over at his dad, who nodded his head in grim satisfaction. He looked at his brother who said angrily, "Give it to him, Wes. He deserves it."

Wesley threw down the rag and opened up his stance a little bit as if he were getting ready to bat a ball. He swung and connected hard with my backside.

I had decided not to give him the satisfaction of crying out in pain. Yet, Dad had already softened me up, and that first hit really hurt. I bit my tongue to keep from crying out. I bit down harder with every blow until I felt blood in my mouth.

John Gray cheered when Wesley finished and handed the paddle back to Dad. The paddle got handed over to the principal who took it back to his office. Dad spun me around and pushed me hard so I was forced to sit back down on the bench. I was hurt, angry, frustrated, and humiliated. The injustice of it all was almost more than I could stand. My own dad didn't believe me.

The principal decided that we could all go home for the rest of the day. He lectured us about making good choices. He told me that I would still have to write the sentences, and now I would miss recess for the rest of the week. As far as I could tell, the Gray boys got off free.

Dad picked up Linda and commanded me to follow along. When we got to the car he put Linda in the front seat and me in the back. It seemed to be a long quiet ride to the house.

Mom met us at the kitchen door. She had received a visit from Jewel Gray who had heard something from a teacher at the school. Mom had gotten a sketchy outline of how things went down and was very worried. She fussed over Linda and put a hand on my head. I busted out crying, and Mom hugged me. She took me into the other room and quickly made out the folding bed. I took off my shoes and socks and crawled under the covers. Dad was watching all of this, and he didn't seem too happy that Mom was being compassionate.

"No supper for you tonight, Dale," he said in a hard tone of voice. I nodded because I had kind of expected it. I didn't say anything because my tongue still hurt.

Roger and Paul came over and stood beside the bed. They began to make faces at me, but I didn't respond.

Mom and Dad went into the other room, and I heard chairs scrape as they positioned themselves at the table. Although they spoke quietly, I heard their whole conversation. Dad gave his take on what happened, and it sounded a lot like John Gray's lies.

Mom was quiet as Dad told her how exasperated he was with me. When he finished they were quiet for few minutes. I heard them slurping coffee from their mugs.

"Linda," Mom called out. "Come over here and talk to us." I

heard Linda's shoes tap on the kitchen floor as she walked to the table. Mom's voice was soft and sweet as she spoke.

"Linda, I want you to tell your dad and me what happened out on the playground. Don't lie to us. Tell us the truth, exactly as it happened," Mom commanded.

Linda told the truth, exactly as it happened. There was a stunned silence as my parents tried to come to grips with this new version of events.

"Dale saved my life," Linda said. "He helped me."

I heard Mom kiss her and tell her to go to her room and wait there. When Linda had shut the door to her room Mom and Dad took up their conversation again.

"I don't care what she says," Dad growled. "I know what I saw. Linda is just very young and doesn't understand. I do think Dale is spending too much time with those savages. I will still take him out to the Reservation, but he is going to stay right beside me all the time."

That night I lay in bed suffering while the family ate supper. Afterwards Linda played with Roger and Paul over by my bed. When eight o'clock rolled around Mom put everybody to bed. She stood where we could all hear and sang a song to us.

"Good night, my God is watching o'er you. Good night, his mercies go before you. Good night, and I'll be waiting for you. So, good night, may God bless you."

Although my brothers fell asleep quickly, I found that sleep would not come for me. My bottom hurt and my tongue hurt. A little while later Mom and Dad went to bed, and the house became quiet. I heard Linda's door open, and I saw just her shape as she made her way over to the bed in the dark.

"Dale," she whispered. "I brought you some supper." I felt her hand touch mine, and she slipped me something.

"What is it?" I asked.

"A biscuit and a piece of chicken," she told me.

I brought it to my mouth and took small bites. My tongue still hurt, and I had to be careful as I chewed. The food tasted delicious. Linda stayed by the bed until I finished. She took the chicken bones from and me and walked into the kitchen to throw them away. When she came back she stood by the bed again for a few silent moments.

"Thank you, Dale, for saving me. You are a good big brother, and I love you." She leaned down and kissed my forehead before silently slipping back to her room.

I spent quite a bit of time that night thinking about what had happened. I knew what I saw, and I knew that I had done the right thing. It seemed to me that liars had won out, and once again I was disappointed in the adults. I couldn't decide if they were stupid or blind. I just knew that they were wrong. I had paid a penalty for doing the right thing. The more I thought about it, the angrier I got. Right before I went to sleep I made up my mind that from then on I would always do the right thing, regardless of the outcome. The bad guys might win every now and then, but the good guys were bound to win sometimes as well.

A few quiet weeks went by after that. Word went around at school, and my friends treated me with respect and kindness. John and Wesley were shunned and seemed genuinely surprised that nobody liked them. I finished my penance of writing and missing recess.

Things seemed to get back to normal.

That is, until Dad brought a TV set to the house.

One evening Dad came home lugging an old used black-and-white TV console. He had bought it cheaply at a second hand store in Albuquerque. He set it up in the living room, and we sat mesmerized by the technology that brought the world into our small apartment. Since it was a Friday night Dad told us we could stay up late. A movie came on, and after some discussion Mom and Dad decided to let us watch it.

I don't remember who was in the movie, but I sure remember the plot. Some American archaeologists went to Egypt and uncovered an ancient tomb. There was a curse on anyone disturbing the tomb, but the Americans went ahead and plundered it anyway. They went back to the U.S. with their treasure and took with them an old Egyptian who could read the ancient language and help catalog the treasures.

What the men didn't know was that the old Egyptian guy was a member of a sacred priesthood charged with killing anyone who disturbed the tomb. The old Egyptian gave dolls to the children of each of the archaeologists. At night the dolls would come alive. They would sneak into the bedrooms of the archaeologists and climb up on the bed. Using a long needle-sharp skewer they would pierce the men in the heart so that they died.

One man woke up right before being skewered and fought off the doll. He chased it to a warehouse where he saw the old Egyptian casting spells. The man was able to kill the dolls along with the old Egyptian by burning down the warehouse. One doll escaped, though, and at the end of the movie was plotting revenge.

That movie scared the living daylights out of us kids. One reason was that Linda had about a hundred dolls. Dad had built a shelf that ran around the walls of her bedroom. When she kept her bedroom door open we could see all of Linda's dolls.

More importantly they could see us. It seemed that their eyes followed you wherever you went. That night Linda kept her bedroom door open as she slept. I slept on the part of the folding bed closest to her room. Paul slept next to me and was hemmed in on the other side by Roger. Mom had recently taken him out of the crib and put him in bed with us. I had to get up with Paul twice every night and take him to the bathroom or else he would wet the bed.

"Dale, do you think Linda's dolls come alive at night?" Roger asked in a whisper.

"No! Don't be stupid," I whispered back. In the back of my mind, though, I had the same question.

I began to adopt strategies to thwart the dolls. I slept with my hands over my heart so that if they tried to skewer me it would hurt my hands first and wake me up so that I could fight them off. I slept on my side because the dolls always went in through the chest. Mostly, though, I just barely slept, and I jumped at every sound.

This went on for five or six days. I was a walking zombie during the day, and I dreaded the night.

Finally, I decided that enough was enough. One afternoon while Linda and Mom were outside I got a sharp knife from the kitchen, went into Linda's room, and cut the heads off of every doll. I immediately felt better even though I knew that there would be a price to pay.

Sure enough, Dad spanked me with an old leather sandal until his arm just got tired of swinging. That night I slept great, although I couldn't sleep on my backside for a few nights afterwards.

The day after the beheadings Linda came to me and said, "I know why you did that, and I feel a little better as well. But those were my dolls, and you are stupid. Somehow you have to replace my dolls."

After I became an adult I sent Linda a doll for her birthday almost every year until her death in March of 2000.

Something about being part of the Brave Family resonated deep inside of me. I knew that there were people who needed help sometimes. I also knew that adults didn't always get it right. I felt that it was my responsibility to help the poor and oppressed. I decided that I would spend my life helping those who could not help themselves. I would stand up for what was right even if it cost me.

I determined to be brave, and that determination may have saved my life.

TEN

BAD MEDICINE

FEBRUARY AND MARCH 1963

D ad took me to the reservation every time that he visited with the Roberts. He kept me close and told me to keep my mouth shut and sit by him. He said that he took me with him so Mom wouldn't have to deal with me. I saw Amos, Andy, Yas, and Mary, but I wasn't allowed to speak to them. I always smiled and waved. Dad would watch me closely to make sure that I remained silent. I obeyed even though it was hard to do so.

This went on for a month until Mary brought a friend with her to see Dad.

One Saturday Dad took me with him to the reservation. There was a problem with the well again. I had tried to tell Dad about how some men broke the well, but he refused to listen to me. Evidently my credibility was very low with him, and he simply regarded me as a problem child.

That Saturday I sat with him as he made a list of well parts to purchase in Albuquerque. Mr. Roberts was discussing the repairs with Dad as Mrs. Roberts tutored a Navajo girl over in the corner of the room. The door to the outer office was closed, and the quiet of the room was making me nod off a bit.

Suddenly the door opened, and in walked Yas's friend, Mary. There was another woman with her who looked a little familiar to me, but I couldn't place her. Mary and the other woman walked around so that they were facing Dad across the table.

He and Mr. Roberts looked up to see what they wanted. The woman with Mary turned and looked at me.

"Hello, Dale," she said. As soon as I heard her voice I recognized that she was Mrs. Zonni from school. She was dressed differently than when I saw her at school, and I guess that's why I didn't recognize her at first. She had on a blue shirt and blue jeans. She wore a lot of turquoise jewelry.

"I came here to tell your father the truth about what happened at school. I think he deserves to know."

"What do you mean?" growled Dad. "Has he been in trouble AGAIN?"

"No, no," said Mrs. Zonni softly. "Dale has been a model student. I am Mrs. Zonni from the school office. I was there when you spanked Dale and when you let Wesley Gray spank him."

Dad got kind of a grin on his face, and I could tell that he was ready to ignore Mrs. Zonni. "So?" he asked with a sarcastic tone of voice. "Dale got exactly what he deserved."

Mrs. Zonni's face lost all expression. It could have been carved from stone. She drew herself up and straightened her shoulders.

"Mr. Sims, I want to tell you what I saw and heard. Please let me tell you about that day," she said in a quiet voice.

Dad leaned back in his chair and stretched out his arms so that his hands were resting on the table top. He drummed a kind of rhythm with his fingers, and I could tell from the expression on his face that he was trying to decide what to do. Finally he shrugged and crossed his arms. "Sure. Go ahead and tell me what you came here to say."

Mrs. Zonni started to speak, but he stopped her with a raised hand. "I already know everything about that day. I am not sure why you would even want to talk about it. But if it makes you feel any better, then go right ahead."

I saw Mrs. Zonni tighten her hands into fists. I don't think she liked to be interrupted or talked down to. She took a deep breath and let it out slowly. She turned to Mary and said something in their language. Mary just nodded and replied without taking her eyes off Dad.

"I was working in the office that afternoon when your daughter, Linda, came running in," Mrs. Zonni said quickly and quietly. "She was crying, and so I hugged her. I asked her what was the matter, but she was crying and sobbing. She pointed back down the hall, and I figured that whatever was going on had to be happening outside because Linda had snow on her back when she came into the office. I ran outside just in time to see Dale and John Gray fighting and rolling around on the ground. I called for some other teachers to help, and we pulled the boys apart. Then we took Dale, John, and Wesley to the principal's office."

She looked at me for a few seconds. "Do you remember that, Dale?" she asked.

I nodded, but I didn't say anything. It seemed to me that she was just telling me about things that I already knew. She pursed her lips and glanced sideways at Mary who seemed to be encouraging her to continue.

"While we were marching the boys inside I heard John talking to Wesley and he said, 'I shouldn't ought to have pushed Linda down to get a kiss from her. If I had stayed on my feet I could have had my kiss and still be ready to slug Dale.' I stopped him and asked him if he really started all of that, and he said, 'Yes.' He was the one who should have had the spanking." Mrs. Zonni looked down at me and her eyes softened. "Dale ran to the aid of his sister. He stopped a bully from hurting his sister."

Dad slapped his hand down on the table angrily. "Dale disobeyed his teacher and left the room. He hit two boys and

knocked Wesley's front teeth out. He started a fight, made a distur-
bance, disobeyed a teacher, and hurt people."

Mrs. Zonni put her hands on the table and leaned in toward
Dad. "The people respect Dale," she said through clenched teeth.

Dad came up out of his chair and leaned forward toward Mrs.
Zonni. "The people? The people?" he shouted. "And just who are
these people you are talking about? People who like savage lawless-
ness? People who think it is funny when one boy loses his front
teeth because another boy is violent and out of control?"

Mrs. Zonni didn't budge. "The people is what we call
ourselves. We, the Navajo, are the people. We are the *Dineh*. We
respect Dale because he ran to help his sister. We respect him
because he fought off two bullies. We respect him because he got
her out of harm's way. We respect him because he obeyed you and
took a spanking from you even though he did nothing wrong. We
respect him because he bit his tongue rather than cry out when you
and that other boy spanked him. We respect him because he is
brave and good."

Mrs. Zonni heaved herself up to her full height and looked at
Dad with flashing eyes. "The people think he is brave and a hero.
We think that your son will be a great man someday."

Dad looked as if he were going to reach across the table and
strangle Mrs. Zonni. Then he kind of turned his head and looked at
her sideways. He grinned and sat down. He started to chuckle and
then he began to laugh. He laughed so hard that tears formed at the
corners of his eyes.

Mrs. Zonni and Mary looked at him as if he had gone crazy.
Mr. Roberts put his hand on Dad's shoulder and asked him if he
was okay.

Dad just nodded, and his laughter gradually subsided as he
wiped the tears from his eyes. When he got his wind back he
straightened up in his chair.

"You say that the people," he said with a sneer, "believe that
Dale will be great some day?" He waved a hand in my direction.

"That boy is willful, stubborn, disobedient, bad, violent, and an idiot to boot. He won't become great. He will be in prison if he doesn't get himself killed first." Dad pointed at Mrs. Zonni, and his eyes squinted. "Now, leave my son alone. You are only encouraging him to make more trouble."

I wasn't really surprised by anything Dad had said because he had already made himself very clear on how he felt about me. It was Mrs. Zonni and her words that surprised me. I had never heard anybody say that I was respected and could be great.

Mrs. Zonni turned to Mary, and they spoke softly for a few minutes while Dad tapped his fingernails on the tabletop impatiently.

Suddenly Mrs. Zonni turned and looked down at me. She began to sing in a chanting kind of way. Her voice rose and fell, and even though I didn't understand the words I listened intently. The song didn't last long. Mrs. Zonni finished it with a single note that she held out for a long time. She stopped and put her hands out toward me, fingers up and extended, palms open. She held that pose for a moment and then dropped her hands.

She looked at Dad and said, "I sang an old Navajo blessing over your son. He will do great things, and you will never understand those things. I have blessed him, the people bless him, and God will bless him."

She turned and walked out of the room followed by Mary.

Dad watched them go and then yelled loudly "Bah! You dirty Indian witches. Leave my family alone. I don't want to see or hear of you interfering with my family ever again." He reached over and plunked me hard on the head. "Don't fall for that evil witchcraft stuff, boy. We are Christians, and don't you forget it."

Dad turned to Mr. Roberts with an incredulous look on his face. "Have you ever seen anything like that?" he asked.

Before he could answer Mrs. Roberts spoke up. "I have seen things like this before. There is nobody quite as superstitious as a Navajo. But I will tell you this: if they believe that they gave your son a blessing then they will honor that and stick by it to the end. They put great stock in those blessings, and all of the Navajo who know about it will honor it. The same with a curse. If they curse somebody then they certainly expect that person to suffer greatly."

Dad shook his head sadly. "Those savage barbarians," he said in a sorrowful voice. "Only God can make a difference in their lives."

I wasn't sure why Dad was so upset. I couldn't see any harm in getting a blessing from someone, even if they were an Indian and spoke in a language I didn't understand. I wondered what it meant to get a blessing, and I wondered how I would even know if I was being blessed.

Over the next few days I thought about it many times. The boys at school seemed to know about the blessing. They treated me differently than before. They gave me extra food from their plates at lunch. They sat close beside me and helped me with little things.

Then one day things began to change.

Mom had heard about the blessing, but she hadn't said anything to me about it. One day, while Dad was gone, she asked me to sit with her at the table. She looked at me and smiled. "Dale, I want you to tell me about the blessing," she said in a quiet voice.

I thought for a moment before replying. "Mrs. Zonni from the school office gave it to me. She sang a song that she said was a blessing. Then she held her hands out to me like this," and I held out my hands just like Mrs. Zonni had done.

Mom nodded and rested her chin in her right hand as she looked at me.

"Did Mrs. Zonni say anything else?" Mom asked.

"She said that she blessed me, the Navajo blessed me, and God blessed me. She said that I would be a great man one day. She said that I would do great things," I replied.

Mom didn't move. She just kept staring at my eyes.

"What did your dad say after that?" Mom asked in a quiet voice.

"Well. . ." I hesitated because I didn't want to get into trouble again. Mom seemed to understand because she reached across the table and took hold of one of my hands, holding it in her warm, soft hand.

"Dale, you can tell me anything," she said. "What we talk about here will just be between the two of us, understand?" she said with a small smile. I nodded and took a deep breath.

"Dad called Mrs. Zonni a witch and said that all of that stuff was evil witchcraft stuff, and because we are Christians I shouldn't pay any attention to it," I said quickly, running it all together as I tried to blurt it out.

Mom nodded as if she understood. She kept ahold of my hand but looked away from me for a minute, staring out of the kitchen window. Her eyes narrowed, and I could tell that she was trying to think through something. Finally, she turned back to look at me.

"Do you want to be a great man someday?" she asked. I didn't know what to say so I just nodded. Mom gave a little sigh, and a sad look crept into her eyes.

"Son, I want you to be a great man, I really do," she said kind of wistfully. "But life can get in the way. We don't always become the people that we want to be. I have heard people say that you can be anything you want to be if you will just try really hard. I don't believe that. I have seen too many people try and fail. We fail because we are weak. Sometimes we do stupid things that keep us from achieving what we should in this life. Sometimes we get physically hurt, and sometimes we get spiritually hurt. . .it just sort of happens."

Mom looked down at the tabletop and then back up at me. "One thing I do know, though, is that God has a plan for the life of everyone. I believe that God can bless you with or without an Indian blessing. I think that if you will put your trust in the Lord then He will guide you to be a good person. You may not be a great man, but you can certainly be a good person. Do you understand?"

I nodded and rubbed the side of my nose. The skin on both

sides of my nose had been itching lately, and I just idly scratched it without giving it much thought. Mom watched me for a moment.

"Does your nose itch?" she asked.

I nodded and scratched again.

She looked closer, studying my face. "What is happening there at the corner of your mouth?" she asked with great concern. She reached over and grabbed my chin so she could hold my head up and get a better look. She ran a finger over a crusty patch that had appeared on the right corner of my mouth. She quickly left the table and walked to the sink to wet a washcloth. She brought it over and carefully wiped the corner of my mouth. She studied the spot for a few more minutes.

"We'll show your dad when he comes home for supper," she said. "We don't have to say anything to him about our conversation, but I think he needs to see this."

That night over supper Mom casually asked Dad to look at my mouth. He nodded in an absent-minded kind of way and just kept eating until he had finished his food. He took a large swig of coffee before taking a glance at my face. His eyes roamed from my hair down to my mouth and finally focused in on the crusty patch of skin at the corner of my mouth. He leaned in closer and studied the spot for a few minutes. It seemed to have gotten bigger during the day. He straightened up and looked over at Mom.

"How long has he had this?" he asked. Mom just shrugged.

"I only noticed it this morning," she said. "What do you think it is?" she asked with concern in her voice.

Dad leaned down and peered at it again. "I think it is impetigo. It is one of those things that you get when you are dirty and don't clean yourself." He leaned over and looked at it again. "It can be contagious. It can also be a booger to clear up." He looked up at the ceiling and rubbed his neck. "I think I will take him to the vet and see what she has to say about it. In the meantime we need to keep the other kids away from Dale. We certainly don't want all of them to come down with this at the same time."

The vet seemed to be a rough lady on the surface, but I found that she was really kind and understanding. I wasn't in any pain this time, and I looked forward to seeing her again.

She lived right there at the clinic, and it wasn't unusual for people to bring animals for her to work on at all hours of the day and night. Everyone respected her, and she knew just about everything about everybody in town. Dad had invited her to church several times. She always refused politely but firmly. She told Dad that she and God had reached an understanding, and she felt good about it. She certainly didn't want to mess it up by going to church.

Dad drove me over to her clinic and marched me inside. He rang the bell that she kept on a desk in her outer office. In a few minutes she appeared from the back and stood in the doorway with her hands on her hips.

"What's going on, Preacher Jim?" she asked Dad. "Has this young man been playing rough games again?"

Dad shook his head and kind of pushed me toward her. "Dale has a spot on his mouth that I want you to look at," he said.

She bent down and looked me over, paying special attention to the spot on my mouth. She studied the spot for a few minutes and then straightened back up. "Have you been swimming in horse watering tanks or in stock tanks where cattle have been wading?"

"No, ma'am," I said quietly.

She kind of made a sound like "hrumph" and then looked over at Dad.

"I thought for a minute there that he might have hoof and mouth disease, but I think this is just the old garden variety impetigo." She bent over and studied the spot again. "I think I have something in the back room that might just clear this thing up."

She disappeared into the back part of the clinic and soon reappeared holding a small tin in her hand. She held it out to Dad who took it and looked it over suspiciously. "I use that stuff for something similar that we see in horses. I make it up myself in the back room, and it seems to be pretty effective," she said proudly.

Dad unscrewed the lid and looked at it for a minute before holding it up to his nose to smell it. He wrinkled up his nose and said, "This stuff stinks!"

The vet chuckled. "Yes, I suppose it does. But there is no doubt about its effectiveness. I use it for several different skin problems, especially on horses, and it always clears things up." She held out her hand. "That'll be five dollars, Preacher Jim. Just apply it to that spot several times a day. Make sure that he doesn't share a bed with any of the other children. Make sure that you keep him out of school for a couple of days as well. Have Mrs. Sims wash all of his clothes and set aside a special plate, cup, and silverware for him to use all by himself until that is all cleared up."

Dad looked a little startled. "Five dollars?" he exclaimed. "All you did was look at him for a minute and then give me this stuff that you make up yourself. Five dollars is a lot of money for a little bit of nothing."

The vet looked at Dad as if he was some kind of vermin. "You came to me for help because you didn't know what to do. I run a business, not a charity. The boy needs that medicine in order to get well. You do want him to get well, don't you?"

Dad looked at me in a thoughtful way, and I could tell he was considering whether it was worth paying five dollars to get me better. He grumbled a little bit under his breath and dug out his wallet. He pulled out a five dollar bill and reluctantly handed it over to the vet.

Folding it up, she stuck it in her shirt pocket and waved as we turned to go.

Back at the house Dad shared all of the information with Mom. He showed her the tin and opened it up so that they could look at it together. Mom took it from dad and walked over to me. She showed it to me, holding it down on my eye level so that I could see it and smell it. It was black and gooey looking.

I sniffed at it and immediately pulled my head back. It smelled like a combination of old garbage and used match sticks.

"Put your finger in there and get a little bit on it. Then rub it on your sore," she said. I did as she instructed. I smeared the black goo on the spot and then wiped my hand on my pants. Dad swatted me on the rear.

"Don't do that," he bellowed. "Use a rag or toilet paper or something to wipe your finger. Don't just wipe it on your pants where it could get on anything you sit down on." He turned to Mom and pointed at me. "See? He is getting more like a savage every day. I just don't have much hope for that one."

Mom set aside a separate plate, cup, spoon, and fork for me to use. She also took an old blanket and set it on the floor next to the rollaway bed to serve as a kind of pallet for me to sleep on. Mom had me take off all my clothes, and she washed them in the bathtub, hanging them in the bathroom to dry.

That night I slept on the floor while Roger and Paul slept in the bed. I fell asleep quickly, but later I was awakened by something scurrying around on the floor.

As my eyes adjusted to the dark I focused in on the source of the sound. I heard it off to my left, and I turned my head slightly to see better. I saw a small movement, and the thought immediately ran through my head: *That is a mouse!*

It irked me that we still had mice in the house. Every morning for many months I had disposed of six little mouse bodies. Something was wrong, and I determined to figure out how the mice were getting into the house.

I watched the mouse scurry across the floor toward the kitchen. Silently I got up and followed the little critter, staying back far enough to not scare it. Once we were in the kitchen I saw the mouse make a beeline for a place along the back wall where there were some old cans of paint stored. The mouse quickly squeezed itself between two cans and disappeared. I waited to see if it would come back, but after about ten minutes I got tired and bored of waiting. I went back to my pallet on the floor and decided to check things out in the morning.

All night long I had strange dreams about mice running all over my body and licking my face. I even felt them grab my toes and pull on my foot. I jerked in my sleep, and my foot hit something very hard.

I opened my eyes to see Dad standing there kicking my foot.

"Get up," he commanded. "Go check the mouse traps and start doing your chores for the day. Did you remember to wake up Paul and take him to the bathroom?"

"No," I replied with a yawn. "I was down here on the floor, and I forgot all about it."

Dad reached over and pulled the covers away from Paul who was still asleep and all scrunched up in the bed. He leaned down and smelled the sheet. He gently moved Paul over to one side and studied the sheet where he had been lying.

He nodded to himself and looked down at me. "There doesn't appear to have been any accidents last night. Wake up your brother and take him to the bathroom now. When he finishes let him get back in bed."

I nodded to show that I understood. I threw off my blanket and leaned over the bed to pick up Paul. He grumbled a little in his sleep but allowed me to set him on his feet. I took his hand and guided him to the bathroom. He kept his head down the whole time, kind of like he was sleepwalking.

After he finished his business I led him back to the bed. I folded up my blanket and laid it on top of my pillow, pushing both of them out of sight under the rollaway bed. I went to the bathroom and found that my clothes had dried overnight. I dressed and began my daily chore of checking the mouse traps.

In the kitchen area Dad was pouring himself a cup of coffee. He turned to look at me with a critical gaze.

"You won't be going to school today," he said grimly. "That means that you must help your mother as much as possible. Wash your hands a lot. Use that black goo we got from the vet. Use it three times today. Maybe you will heal quickly."

He took another swig of coffee before heading out the door. I watched him through the window as he got into the car and drove off.

I wished more than anything that he liked me as much as he liked the other kids. I wanted to tell him that I was sorry for being a willful, stubborn, disobedient, bad, violent, and idiot son. I certainly didn't think of myself that way, but it sure seemed to be the way that Dad saw me. I began to think of ways in which I could prove to Dad that he was wrong. I looked around the kitchen for inspiration, and my eyes fell on the old paint cans at the back wall of the kitchen.

"That's it!" I thought to myself. "If I can figure out the mouse problem then maybe I can prove to him that I am useful."

I walked to the back wall and moved the paint cans. I got down on my hands and knees and saw that the floor was covered with little pellets of mouse manure. I moved a few more cans and saw a hole that was about the size of a silver dollar. I watched the hole for a minute or two, but I didn't see anything move.

I used the broom and dustpan to gather up all of the little pellets and throw them away. Then I went around the house and gathered up the mousetraps. As I was emptying them I was thinking about ways to plug up that hole. When I got back to the kitchen Mom was standing by the stove cracking eggs into a skillet. She studied my face as I walked by with the empty traps. I reset each trap and put it out for the next batch of furry rodents.

"What are you doing?" Mom asked me.

"I'm doing like I always do, Mom. I'm resetting the mousetraps."

"No, no," she said, moving closer to me. She bent down to look more closely at my face. "Why are you rubbing your nose?"

"Well, I'm thinking," I replied while rubbing the sides of my nose. "My nose has been itching, and I scratch it while I'm thinking."

"Well, don't scratch it," Mom said in a concerned tone of voice.

She straightened up and held me out at arms' length. "I think that spot on the corner of your mouth looks better today, but you won't get well if you keep scratching your face."

I saw concern in her eyes, but I shrugged. "Okay, Mom, if that is what you want."

She crossed her arms over her breasts and smiled down at me. "Now, tell me what you have been thinking about."

I pointed to the back wall. "I found a hole back there that the mice are using to get into the house. I am trying to figure out a way to plug up the hole."

I walked over to where the hole was and pointed. Mom got down and looked closely at the hole and then backed up a bit.

"I know just what to do about that," she said firmly. She quickly marched over to the kitchen sink and rustled around in the storage space under it. She made so much noise that the little kids came into the kitchen rubbing the sleep out of their eyes. Roger was holding one of Paul's hands. Linda was already dressed and ready to go to school.

Mom smiled at them before turning to me and holding out her hand. "Use this," she said. "Those little mice won't try to chew through this thing."

Mom had given me a large steel wool pad. I looked at her, and she made a small motion with her hand toward the back wall. "Kind of spread it out and then stuff it in the hole. Mice hate the way it feels in their mouth, and they won't chew on it."

I stuffed the steel wool into the hole and stepped back to look at my work.

Mom came to stand beside me and pointed at the hole.

"I am going to fill a pail with warm, soapy water, and I want you to use it to clean up that area. We can get rid of those old paint cans and keep that area open. That way we can watch to see if the mice keep showing up." She smiled down at me and put her hand on my shoulder. "You have done a fine job with the mousetraps. You are so smart to figure out how those mice got in and out of here. You are growing up to be quite a guy. I am really proud of you."

I smiled back at her and wiggled with pleasure, kind of like a dog does when you scratch his ears. It was so good to hear any kind of praise that I just felt good all over. I was hoping that Dad would have something good to say as well.

That evening over supper Mom shared with Dad about the mouse hole. He looked at me over his coffee mug as Mom explained about the steel wool. He got up from the table and walked over to look at the hole and the steel wool. He spent a few minutes squatting down to look at it before returning to sit with us. He took a bite of supper and chewed it thoughtfully for a minute.

"Dale, after you finish eating we will get some tools, and I will show you the real way to fix that problem," he said. "Hurry up eating, and we will get that taken care of."

I shoveled my food in quickly. Dad watched impatiently and finally stood up. He hitched up his pants and walked over to a cabinet where he stored an old toolbox. He rummaged around in it for a few minutes grumbling to himself. I ate my last bite and trotted over to see what he was doing.

When he straightened up I saw that he had a hammer and a few nails in one hand and a small wooden board in his other. He marched over to the mouse hole and quickly nailed the board over the hole.

"That's how you do it," he said decisively. "Forget about doing something stupid like plugging the hole with steel wool." He kneeled down and tested the board to see if it was nailed tight to the wall. The board didn't move, and he gave a satisfied grunt.

"You should have figured out where those mice were coming from a long time before now," he growled at me. He reached over and thumped me hard on the head. "You are as dumb as a stump." He stood up and walked over to the toolbox to put away the hammer.

After a few days went by I noticed three things. The first was that the number of mice I caught in the traps decreased to where there was finally a week in which none were trapped. I checked every day and rejoiced to see the empty traps.

The second thing I noticed was that the impetigo at the corner of my mouth rapidly disappeared. It became a small crusty area and then a very small red area before my skin finally cleared up. I was glad because I wanted to go back to school. I missed the lessons and my friends. I was also still worried about my sister. I was afraid that the Gray boys might try to hurt her again since I wasn't there to help her.

The third thing I noticed was that the skin of my face, especially around my nose, began to itch all the time. I couldn't help but scratch it. My skin began to flake off and long running sores began to appear on my face. Mom had me put some of the black goo that I had used for the impetigo on it, but that didn't help at all. I was kept out of school while Mom and Dad discussed the problem.

They sat at the kitchen table one evening to talk about me. I sat in the living area close to the door leading to the kitchen so that I could hear what they said.

"Jim, I just don't think that the thing going on with Dale's face is normal," Mom said in a worried tone of voice. "He says that the skin around his nose itches something terrible all of the time."

Dad took a sip of coffee and drummed his fingers on the table. "That boy has been nothing but trouble lately," he growled. "I think that all of this will clear up if we just give it some time."

"How much time do you think we need to give it?" Mom asked. "This has been going on for about a month. The impetigo cleared up just fine. This has got to be something very different."

"Look," Dad said sharply, "we have already spent some money on that black goo from the veterinarian. I am not going back to that woman. We don't have the money to take him to the doctor in Albuquerque."

"I know, I know," Mom sighed. "But we have to do **something**," she said.

I heard them sipping coffee as they silently considered their options. I heard Dad bang his coffee mug down on the table as if he had made a decision. I knew it was Dad's coffee mug because Mom always set her mug down lightly.

"There is a man down at the sawmill who seems to know a little bit about medicine. I think I will take Dale with me to have that guy look at him. Let's see what he says about it," Dad said it in a way that gave no room for argument.

Mom didn't say anything but her little "Hmmm" seemed to express some doubt.

Dad stood up and yelled, "Dale, come in here!"

I got up and quickly ran into the kitchen to stand in front of him. He reached down, grabbed my chin and tilted my face upwards so that he could study it. "Boy, you are as ugly as sin," Dad said quietly. "You are coming with me to see a man who might know how to treat your problem."

As we drove out to the man's house Dad told me some things about him. The man's name was Gary, and he had treated men who had been bitten by coyotes and snakes. He was real smart, and Dad was sure that he would know what to do.

It wasn't a far drive to his house, but we had to go slow because the roads there were more like rutted dirt paths than a regular road. We finally arrived at an old log cabin close to a little village named Galina. Dad honked the horn to alert Gary that we were there. We stayed by the car until the cabin door opened.

A large man exited the cabin. He was a little bent over, but I could tell that he was still strong. His shoulders were wide and his arms and legs were huge. He kind of straightened up when he saw us. His stride was strong and purposeful. He reached out a massive callused hand to shake hands with Dad.

"What brings you around here, Preacher Jim?" he asked with a smile. "I haven't had time or money enough to get into trouble lately so you can spare giving me a sermon." He and Dad laughed. They seemed comfortable around each other. "Come over to the side of the cabin where I have a sittin' place," the man said as he motioned toward the right side of the cabin.

We followed him around the corner where a bench and two old metal lawn chairs were pushed up against the wall. That side of the cabin was in the shade, and it was pleasant sitting there with him as he shared bits of gossip about the people in Galina.

When there was a suitable break in the conversation Dad cleared his throat.

"Gary, I came out here so that you would look at my son. I know that you are kind of an old timey medicine guy, and I thought that maybe you would have an idea about how to fix him up."

Gary leaned forward a bit to study my face. He didn't touch me, but he stared real hard at me until I got uncomfortable. He gave a nod and kind of sighed as if he had made up his mind about something. He tilted his head back and looked up into the sky. He scratched the beard stubble under his chin and muttered to himself for a minute.

"Well, Jim, I have only seen something like this twice." He stopped and passed a hand over his eyes as if he were blocking out the sunshine in order to see some picture in his mind more clearly. "I had a dog once that had something that looked just like this. Let me ask a question. Does the boy go around dirty and stinkin' most of the time?"

Dad nodded. "When he sweats he smells like roadkill. It is a real challenge to get him cleaned up once each week."

Gary looked off into the distance as if he was thinking very hard. "I think the boy is just plain dirty. Get some of the roughest soap you can find and scour his whole head and body down twice each day. It worked on the dog, and I figure it will work on a kid like him who is just a little shy of being an animal himself."

Dad looked at me and then back at Gary. "That sounds like good advice. Sound words, Gary. You have to be one of the smartest men I have ever met."

Gary didn't answer, but he cut his eyes over to me and studied me hard again. He clenched his teeth, squinting his eyes.

"Say, Gary," Dad said quietly. "What was the other time you saw something like this?"

Gary coughed and kind of hung his head. "The other time I saw something like this was in India while I was in the navy. There was this man who had something similar but not exactly. They told me he had leprosy, and you could tell it was eatin' away at his face." He looked at me and grinned. "You are ugly, boy, but I don't think you have leprosy. Otherwise I would make you wear a scarf over your face and go around yelling 'Unclean! Unclean!' so that regular folk wouldn't get your sickness."

Dad and Gary laughed long and hard at that. They said other witty things that set them to laughing again, but I wasn't listening. Leprosy didn't seem to me to be something to joke about.

After an hour we left Gary to drive back home. He stood outside the cabin waving until we couldn't see him anymore.

I turned my attention to the road ahead. I really hadn't realized that I stunk. I didn't think of myself as more unclean than anyone else. If that was the case I was kind of looking forward to getting cleaned up more often. On the way home Dad stopped at a grocery store where he bought four big blocks of Lava soap.

Back at the house Dad told Mom all about his conversation with Gary. When he mentioned what Gary said about leprosy Mom let out a little squeal and covered her mouth with her hand. Dad told her that everything would be just fine. He told her that I was to be separated from the other kids until things cleared up.

The funny thing was that Roger's crusty eyes were getting cleared up, and his snotty nose was no longer spouting a river of pouring snot. Now it was my turn to have a face that repulsed others.

Dad grabbed my arm and wheeled me to the bathroom. I took off my clothes, and Dad scrubbed me from head to toe with soap that felt like it was tearing off my hide. I tried not cry or wiggle, but it certainly was painful.

Mom and Dad instituted some quarantine type things. I was made to wait until everyone else finished eating before I could sit at the table to eat. Afterwards Mom wore gloves as she cleaned my plate and silverware. She cleaned everything in boiling water, twice, just in case. I couldn't play with Linda, Roger, or Paul. I slept on the floor every night. Roger took over the responsibility of getting Paul up at night to go to the bathroom.

The next morning, after my heavy duty scrub down, and after I got dressed for school, Dad gave me a letter to take to my teacher. I looked at it, and Dad said, "Open it up and read it out loud."

I unfolded the letter and read, "Dear Mrs. Garza, our son Dale has some kind of strange skin disease that looks like leprosy but isn't. Please set him back away from the other kids, and keep him in at recess time so that he won't infect everyone. Make him sit away at the back of the bus, and tell the lunch ladies to make him sit by himself at lunch. Call me if you have any trouble with him. Sincerely, James. E. Sims."

I knew that this was going to be a difficult time, but I certainly didn't want anyone to get what I had. I refolded the letter and put it in my pocket.

"I'll do everything you say, Dad," I told him.

He kind of huffed a little bit and plunked me on the head.

So that was the way things went for a miserable two long months. The kids at school made fun of me, and I didn't blame them. I felt lonely all the time. Sometimes my sister would sit about four feet away from me and talk to me, but the other kids stayed far away.

On top of that it appeared that I was getting worse. The deep sores on my face seemed to be clean, but they were not disappearing. They were actually spreading into my scalp and around my ears. When Dad poured Vitalis on it I felt as if my whole head was melting off. I tried not to cry, but it was just too much to take. Mom begged Dad to take me to the veterinarian, but he refused.

One day a door-to-door salesman came to the house. I was the closest to the door when he knocked on it so I opened it to see what he wanted. The man jumped back when he saw me and shouted "Good sweet Jesus! What is wrong with you, boy?"

Mom came up behind me before I could answer. "We don't approve of blasphemous people in this house, mister," she said coldly.

"I apologize," the man said quickly. "It's just that the boy looks like he was beat with an ugly stick, and he scared the living sh. . ." He coughed and kind of grinned. "He scared me so much that I just forgot myself."

Mom pointed at him. "You don't need to apologize to me. You need to apologize to the Almighty God Himself for using the name of Jesus in that way!"

The man bowed his head. "O God, please forgive this sinner. I am not worthy to be forgiven, but I ask it anyway." He looked up at Mom and grinned. "Do you think God forgave me?" he asked sweetly.

"That is not for me to decide," Mom said. "Stand away from the door, Dale," she commanded me. "I am going to shut the door on this poor excuse for a man."

I moved over to the side, and the man gasped as my face was illuminated by the sun. "Don't shut the door," he said in a pleading voice. "I think I might know what is wrong with the boy."

Mom looked at him suspiciously. "We have been treating him with all kinds of things, Mister, but nothing seems to work."

"I think I've seen this before," the man said thoughtfully. "His problem is his hair. If you cut off his hair the problem will go away."

Mom looked doubtful. "I have never heard of anything like that in my life," she said. "What would hair have to do with this?"

"I don't really know," said the man. "I just remember a guy that had a problem like your boy's, and it went away when he cut off all of his hair. He even shaved off his eyebrows."

Mom looked at him and then looked at me. "Well, I will have to talk to my husband about this. Now you just leave us alone, and go on to bother somebody else." She shut the door, and I heard the man clump down the stairs mumbling about a crazy woman and an ugly boy.

That night over supper Mom told Dad about the encounter with the salesman. Dad chewed his food mechanically like a cow chewing cud as he looked thoughtfully over Mom's shoulder. He took several more bites while he was deep in thought. Finally he swiveled around and looked at me.

"Well, I suppose we can't make him look any uglier," Dad said. "What could it hurt? That's the first time that anyone has given a good suggestion since this whole mess began."

I wanted to remind him that Mom had suggested they take me to the vet, and one old Navajo had suggested that I be dunked in a special healing pool that was located west of the reservation and smelled of sulfur. In the end I didn't say anything. I simply endured the indignity of having Dad shave off all of my hair, even my eyebrows.

I looked even uglier with my hair gone. The twice-daily soap scrubbings continued but, alas, the sores got larger and deeper and uglier. Dad bought me one of those winter coverings that you could put on your head and pull down over your face. It had holes in it for the eyes and the mouth, and it hid my face.

Mrs. Zonni took me to see the nurse one day. The nurse at school saw that my skin was flaky, and she began to put some lotion all over my head. She did that every day, but it didn't seem to help at all. I was just miserable, and so was Mom.

"Jim, I am begging you to take Dale to the doctor in Albuquerque. Please get some help for our boy!" she pleaded.

Dad looked over at me, and then he nodded. He had exhausted all of his ideas, and he was finally giving in.

The next day he kept me out of school, and he drove me into the big city. He didn't know much about the city, but he figured that someone could point us in the right direction. While we were driving to Albuquerque he began to talk to me about the Indians, especially Mrs. Zonni.

"You know that stupid woman who sang that blessing over you? Well, look at how that turned out! God is punishing you because you let that witch sing her magic over you," he said angrily. "God says that he hates sorcerers, liars, and adulterers. So, the way I figure it is that you are experiencing the wrath of God."

"But I didn't ask for the blessing," I protested. "I didn't even know what was happening until it was all over with."

"It doesn't matter," Dad said grimly. "Why, this is such a serious thing that I wouldn't be surprised if you won't have to carry this curse from God with you for your whole life."

I looked out of the car window as the sage brush and cactus flashed by. The desert seemed hot and impersonal. The desert didn't care about my problems. Dad didn't care what happened to me because of God's judgement. Maybe Mom cared a little bit. It seemed that God cared, but I wasn't sure why he would waste time and effort cursing a kid. In my mind I imagined myself being ugly for all the years of my life. When I died I was sure that someone would look down into the casket and say, "He was a good man, but there never lived an uglier person on the face of the earth." I hung my head and cried silent tears as Dad went on and on about God's judgement.

When we got to town Dad pulled up to a pharmacy. "Let's go in there and ask the pharmacist where we can find a good doctor. He should know something about that," Dad said as he slid out of the car. I followed him inside and kept my head down so I wouldn't scare people.

We found the pharmacist stocking shelves at the side of the store. He seemed to be a happy man because he was humming to himself as he worked. Dad walked up and shook the man's hand.

He pointed to me and explained that he was trying to find a doctor who would have a look at me. While Dad talked the pharmacist stared wide-eyed at me. He put up his hand like he was stopping traffic, and Dad stopped talking.

"I have some questions for you," he said to Dad. "I think I know what the problem is, but I need you to answer the questions first."

Dad shrugged. "Ask away," he said.

The pharmacist looked at me again. He began asking questions, and Dad gave short replies.

"How long has this been going on?"

Dad grimaced. "Five months."

"Did you shave off the hair or did it fall out?"

"Shaved it off," Dad said.

"Have you been treating it?"

"Sure," Dad replied with pride. "I soap him down with Lava soap twice every day."

"The nurse puts some skin cream on it too," I said, trying to be helpful.

The pharmacist clucked his tongue and wagged his head. "Everything you have told me you have done has made this boy's problem worse," he said sadly. "Your boy has a problem of aggravated seborrheic dermatitis. His hair produces way too much oil. It makes his skin itch which causes him to scratch it. Everybody thinks it looks dry or unclean. That is why they use soap and lotions. But that is exactly the kind of thing that makes it worse."

He stopped talking, and I could see compassion in his eyes. He snapped his fingers and cried, "I have just the thing to cure him. Follow me."

He led Dad and me to the very back of the pharmacy, the storeroom area. He went directly to a shelf that held a bunch of old bottles covered in a thick layer of dust. Picking up a bottle he blew away some of the dust before using a rag to wipe it clean. He held out the bottle so that we could see it clearly. The label read Doctor Eustace's Coal Tar Extract.

The pharmacist unscrewed the lid and let us have a smell. Dad recoiled, and I almost passed out when I smelled it.

"Yesiree!" the pharmacist exclaimed. "You pour this stuff on your son's head twice every day. Cover his head with an old rag or towel and just let it soak in for about thirty minutes. In about a week or two you will see that he is well on his way to getting better. Throw away the soap and the lotions. Just use regular water to clean him up."

Dad looked suspiciously at the bottle and then over at the pharmacist. "But I shaved off all of his hair. How can he still have a problem?"

The pharmacist smiled knowingly. "Under the skin of his head are these glands called sebaceous glands. They keep his hair oiled, but when there isn't any hair they release the oil onto his skin. But this stuff . . ." and he held a bottle of coal tar extract. "This stuff will control all of that."

Dad took the bottle and weighed it in his hand. "How much does this stuff cost?"

The pharmacist looked at me, and I could tell that he just wanted to help. "If you buy five bottles for 75 cents each then I will give you another five bottles for free."

Dad smiled and stuck out his hand. "That's a deal. This saves me the cost and the time to take the kid to the doctor." He dug out the money and paid the pharmacist, who carefully wrapped the bottles in thick paper and put them into gunny sacks.

"Make sure that you don't break any of these in the car," he warned. "You will never get the smell out if you do. Also make sure you keep them away from open flames."

We carried them carefully to the car and wedged them down on the floor in back so that they wouldn't roll around. Dad drove extra slow and careful all the way home.

When we got to the house Dad told Mom the whole story. He gloated about saving money and time. He wasted no time in trying out the repulsive-smelling liquid. He sat me on the front porch and used a rag to wipe the stuff all over my face and head. Then he wrapped the rag around my head and covered that with an old towel.

I could just barely breathe, but somehow endured the process for thirty minutes. After it was over I took in deep gulps of sweet, clear air.

That became our twice-daily routine for several weeks. The results were amazing, and the healing happened quickly. Day by day I could see my skin healing. The sores began to get smaller and shallower. My hair began to grow back in.

There were two side effects, though. One was that the smell stayed with me. I stunk of sulfur, and even though everyone quit making fun of me because I was ugly they stayed away from me because I stunk to high heaven.

The other side effect was that the liquid stained the skin of my face and head brown. I was as brown as tree bark. I was as brown as a nut. I was as brown as an Indian. Of course, the rest of my body was as white as a ghost, except that I had a few dark brown freckles.

Many years later, after I left home, I went to see a doctor about the problem. It would crop up every now and then, and I got tired of using the coal tar extract. The doctor gave me a steroid cream and good shampoo that didn't smell bad. The doctor's visit, the cream, and the shampoo cost me ten dollars.

I have thought about this many times over the years. I wonder if Mrs. Zonni really blessed me. I feel that I have been blessed in this life, and I am grateful. Did God really curse me? I don't think so. I think God has given me many blessings. I think that my body malfunctioned, probably because of our poor living conditions and unhealthy diet.

I wonder why I had to go through all of that. Although there are no lasting scars on my face or head, I still have a few on the inside of me from being bullied and from looking so ugly. I have spent my life trying to be a blessing to other people. I have spent my life accepting the way people look without using their appearance to judge their character. I have found that a person can be good looking on the outside and ugly on the inside.

All of those things that happened to me, and the things I learned during the ordeal, prepared me for the things that were soon to come.

I needed that preparation because quickly I would have to deal with something far more serious.

ELEVEN

LESSONS

MAY 1963

Spring came late to our area. When it finally put in an appearance it just seemed glorious! Flowers bloomed, and the hummingbirds came back in droves. Small showers caused the sagebrush to bloom and give out a wonderful smell. I felt alive and strong.

My skin problem was under control. My hair had grown back in. The Brave Family included me in projects and storytelling times as we continued to help the poor and needy. Although Dad tried to keep me away from the Indians, Mom would take me over to Yas and the boys of the Brave Family when they were trying to help the drunks in town. She would do as she normally did on those days, walking up and down the row of Indians lined up in front of the bars, handing out food and giving drinks of milk. Then she would walk me over to where Yas was setting up behind the bar building and leave me there with him.

I would help cover the drunks with blankets and keep them from being robbed or beaten while they were passed out on the ground. I figured it was my Christian duty and also part of my duty being a member of the Brave Family. I felt as if I had found a place and a people that accepted me and treated me with kindness and respect. I felt as if I had been adopted into the tribe, and I wanted to be a worthy member of the Brave Family.

I came home from school one afternoon to see Mr. Bernandez, Hutch's dad, sitting at our kitchen table with Dad drinking coffee. I heard snatches of the conversation before going into the other room to help Mom with the little kids. I heard the phrase "Dale can come with us."

As I kept Roger and Paul occupied by rolling a ball to them I thought about why Mr. Bernandez would ask for me to go with him anywhere.

His family was almost legendary in New Mexico. The original Bernandez had come to the New World as a conquistador. One of the old Spanish kings had given him a very large land grant for service to the crown—at least that is what Hutch told me. When the Americans took over the New Mexico area they started whit- tling away at the Bernandez land. Although the Bernandez family owned the land they didn't have the manpower to work it all or save it all. Most of it ended up being taken over by the U.S. government to be used as reservation land for the Indians. There had been some kind of compromise worked out. The Bernandez family had perpetual rights to go onto the reservations and harvest trees for lumber. The government, through the Bureau of Indian Affairs, sometimes hired the family to maintain roads on the reservation or help blast out rock to create new roads. The Bernandez family was one of the very few non-Indian families that could hunt and fish on the reservation without special permission. Every other non-Indian who hunted or fished on the reservation without tribal permission and an Indian guide was considered a poacher, and the Bureau of Indian Affairs, the Reservation Police, and the Tribal Elders went after them with a vengeance.

"Dale," I heard my dad shout. "Come in here. We need to talk."

Linda took over with Roger and Paul. I walked slowly to the kitchen trying hard to remember if I had done anything wrong. There was always the possibility that I had slipped up. Dad didn't sound particularly angry so I figured that I wasn't going to get a spanking. I kind of edged into the room and stood with my hands behind me to protect my butt. Dad looked at me and gave an exasperated sigh.

"Stand up straight! What is wrong with you? Say hello to Mr. Bernandez." He looked at me from under his bushy eyebrows as if I were an unwelcome pest.

"Hey, Mr. Bernandez," I said quietly. "It's good to see you, sir."

Mr. Bernandez had a tan from all of his time outdoors. He seemed large and tough to me. He did have a good face, though, and I knew right off that a person could trust him. He wore a cowboy hat and jeans.

Mr. Bernandez made a motion with his hand toward a chair, and I sat down. "Boy, I have heard that you have gotten into quite a bit of trouble lately. Is that true?"

I looked at Dad who squinted his eyes and drilled me with a look that would peel paint off a wall.

"Yes, sir," I replied in a quavering voice. "I suppose I have been in trouble a lot."

Mr. Bernandez nodded and kind of shrugged. "My son gets into trouble every now and then as well. I was talking with your dad about a plan to help the two of you."

I looked over at Dad who was studying the ground around his feet as if there was something very interesting down there. Mr. Bernandez was looking at me as if he were measuring me up for something. He cleared his throat and took a drink of coffee.

"Every Saturday, starting this coming Saturday, I am going to take Hutch with me out to the sawmill on the reservation. I have a couple of Indian guys who are going to help me out there. I figure that maybe Hutch can run around in the mountains and burn off some of that devilment he seems to have stored up inside of him. I am going to assign one of them Indians to kind of watch him and maybe teach him a few things. I was just suggesting to your dad that maybe you could come along with us." Mr. Bernandez took another drink of coffee and kind of settled back in his chair as if he was just going to wait for an answer.

I looked over at Dad to see if I could figure out which way he was leaning on the offer. I knew that he had some real problems with my relations to the Indians. He had accused them of turning me into a savage. He still talked about God's judgement on me for accepting a Navajo blessing from Mrs. Zonni. Dad was looking at me, but I couldn't read his look. I looked back at Mr. Bernandez and saw open honesty and encouragement.

"I think that it would be good," I stammered out. "If it is okay with Dad and Mom then I would like to do it."

Dad nodded his head. He turned to Mr. Bernandez with a tight smile. "You can see for yourself that he is not too bright. I don't know why he stutters like that. It doesn't happen all the time, just every now and then." Dad reached over and thumped me hard on the head. "He won't give you any trouble because he knows what will happen to him if he does, don't you boy?" Dad said with a growl. I nodded and kept my head bowed.

Mr. Bernandez chuckled. "That's settled then. I will send somebody over to bring Dale to my place early on Saturday morning." He looked at me and smiled. "We will go up to the sawmill, and you can run around to your heart's content."

Mr. Bernandez got up to leave, and Dad stood up to walk him to the door. When he left, Dad stood there for a few minutes watching him walk away. He turned to see me standing there gawking with my mouth open. He glowered at me. "Close your mouth, you idiot. You will at least look smarter if you close your mouth." He shook his head in an exasperated manner. "Mar," he yelled for Mom. "Come on in here. We need to talk."

Mom walked in with a smile on her face. She gave me a quick

hug before going to stand in front of Dad. "What is it? Did you finally find all of that gold that is buried in New Mexico?" she asked with a small laugh.

"Nothing that good," he replied. "I told Mr. Bernandez that Dale can spend Saturdays with him up in the mountains at his sawmill. His son Hutch will be there as well. He said that there will be some Indians along to help. They are starting this Saturday."

Mom looked at me, and I saw concern in her eyes. "I have heard that there are bears and wolves and mountain lions up in those mountains," Mom said, her voice quavering a little.

Dad gave a small shrug. "If a wild beast gets a hold of him then it means we would have one less mouth to feed and one less troublemaker to worry about."

Mom put a protective arm around me. "Don't say that, Jim. Down deep I know he is a good boy. I honestly don't know why he does some of the things that he does. I do think God has a plan for his life."

Dad looked at me over the rim of his coffee cup as he took a sip. He kind of gave out a "Humph" and turned his back on me. "I will be going to Albuquerque to get some things for the reservation on Saturday. When Mr. Bernandez comes by just let Dale go with him."

I looked up at Mom who tousled my hair and gave me a big smile. It was all the encouragement I needed.

Saturday morning couldn't come around fast enough for me. I didn't sleep much on Friday night because I was so excited. I didn't know what to expect, but the idea of running around in the mountains really appealed to me. I wanted to be a combination of Daniel Boone, Davy Crockett, and Kit Carson all wrapped up in one person. I could imagine myself roaming the mountains and fighting off bears and wolves. So, I was real eager to go when the knock on the door came about seven that morning.

Mom answered the door. She seemed to be surprised because I

heard her say, "Oh, it's you. Where is Mr. Bernandez?" I edged around until I could squirm under the arm that she was using to hold open the door. There stood Yas with a smile on his face.

"Morning, Mrs. Sims," he said politely. "Mr. Bernandez's truck broke down, and he will probably spend the whole day getting it fixed. He wants Hutch to stay by him today, but I thought maybe Dale and I could do a few things together."

Mom looked at me with an appraising glance. I smiled and nodded to show that it sounded good to me. Mom nodded back. "I think that is fine. Just have him back here before supper time."

I jumped past her and ran down the steps. I heard Yas tell Mom that he would make sure that I got a lunch. I turned and waved at Mom, who gave me a return wave and a smile before shutting the door.

Yas took off walking toward town. I trotted after him, trying to match his long even strides. "Where are we going?" I asked, just a little bit breathless from trying to keep up.

Yas stopped and looked back, waiting for me to catch up. "I have been giving a lot of thought to what to do with you, Young White." He looked up at the hills to the north of town and gave a slight nod, as if he was satisfied with his decision. "I am going to do my best to teach you and to help you to understand. I am going to give you as much knowledge as I think you can stand."

I smiled because that sounded great to me! I loved learning new things. "Will you teach me how to hunt and scalp things?" I asked excitedly.

Yas chuckled. "No," he said and began to walk into town again. I was very confused. What exactly was he going to teach me? He slowed down a little, and I tried to walk faster to stay up with him. Soon we were passing by the big Catholic church. Yas stopped at the gates to the courtyard, and I stood beside him. A man was walking across the courtyard, and Yas called out to him.

"Father," Yas yelled. "Do you have a minute to talk to us?" The man changed course and began to walk toward us. As he got closer

I recognized him as the priest who had been holding the cross in the parade when we first got to town. When he got to the gate he smiled at Yas and looked down at me.

"What can I do for you, my son?" he asked in a kind voice.

"Is this your dad?" I asked Yas in surprise.

"No, no," Yas said with amusement in his voice. "I call him 'father' out of respect. He is the priest, kind of the preacher for this church."

Yas turned to the man and held out his hand. The priest reached through the gate to shake hands with Yas and again asked what he could do. Yas cleared his throat and looked a little uncomfortable. "I was wondering if I could ask you a question."

"What kind of question?" the priest asked. He looked at Yas suspiciously.

"Well, the first question I would like to ask is if you would explain to Dale and I," and he motioned to me, "why you decided to become a priest."

A slow smile spread over the priest's face. "I became a priest so that I could serve God. I love God. I rejoice in the redeeming work of Jesus. I want others to know him and follow him."

I was shocked. That sounded exactly like the way my dad explained his calling. I was very confused. Mom and Dad said that the Catholics weren't Christians, but this man sure sounded like one to me.

Yas nodded as the priest gave his short testimony of his time of searching for God and his training at the seminary. "Is that enough of an answer for you?" the priest asked.

"Yes, thank you," Yas replied. "I think that is all the questions I have for you now. Perhaps I will have more later."

The priest lifted his hand and made the sign of the cross in the air. "Come by any time to confess and be forgiven. If you wish to talk I am always here."

Yas nodded and, placing a hand on my shoulder, propelled me

away from the gates. He set out again toward the other end of town. That short conversation left me with many questions.

"Why did you ask the priest that question?" I said. "What was the point?"

Yas answered as we walked. "I know your mom and dad. They tell us all the time that the Catholics aren't Christians. I wanted you to hear from a Catholic about their Christianity. I wanted you to have a fuller perspective on things than your parents have."

I thought about that in silence as we walked through town. I was stunned to hear a man like the priest say what he did. My mother and father felt the same things about God and Jesus that the Catholics did. I kept thinking to myself, *Who is right?* And I carried confusion in my soul as we walked.

Yas stopped walking, and I almost ran into the back of him. We had stopped on the far side of town where there was a large corral fashioned out of pinion pine logs. He stepped up to the corral and leaned on the top log, putting his right foot up on the lowest log. I tried to imitate him, but the logs were spaced too far apart for me. I finally kind of hung my body over the middle log.

"What are we doing here?" I asked him. He looked down at me and motioned with his chin toward the other side of the corral.

"This morning we will watch two men break a horse to saddle so that it is useful to ride." He shaded his eyes and looked at a small group of men leading a horse toward the corral. "There are several ways to do this. Today we will watch two men use two different ways to break a horse."

I looked across the corral as three Indian men walked into the corral with a horse. One man stayed behind to shut the gate. The man with the rope led the horse over to a place by the side and tied him up to one of the posts of the corral. Then he put a blindfold over the horse's eyes. He threw a saddle blanket on the horse's back. The horse was kind of skittish and pulled back on the rope. After a few minutes he walked forward a little bit, lessening the tension on the rope. The two other men sidled up beside the horse, one on either side. One of the men whistled, and the two men each grabbed one of the horse's ears in unison, stuffed it into their mouths, bit down hard and just kind of hung there. The horse snorted and whinnied, but it didn't move. It just stood there shuddering. It looked to me like it was afraid to move. The third man grabbed a hunk of the horse's mane and leaped onto the horse's back. He began to yell at the horse. He had a quirt in his hand that he slashed back and forth on both sides of the horse's flanks. Great long ropes of slobber began to flow out of the horse's mouth. Blood began to appear on the flanks. The man on the horse dug his heels into the horse's sides again and again as he continued yelling. One of the men hanging on the horse's ears reached over and deftly undid the rope from the corral post. He passed the end of it to the man on the horse's back. The other man quickly untied the blindfold. The horse whinnied, but it still just stood there shuddering and slobbering. The man on top of the horse whistled, and the other two men opened their mouths and released their bite on the horse's ears. They quickly ran to the side of the corral and climbed the logs to sit on the top rail. The horse stood still for a couple of seconds as the man on its back screamed and slashed it. Suddenly the horse reared up and began to buck around the corral. The two men sitting on the top rails shouted encouragement. The man on the horse continued to slash it with the quirt and kick it with his heels. The horse continued to squeal and buck wildly for ten or fifteen minutes until finally it just sort of gave up. It came to a shuddering stop. Its head was lowered and its ears were laid back. The horse was really lathered up with sweat, and it just kind of huffed and snorted. It stood there as if it just didn't have any more energy. The horse was kind of gnashing its teeth and slobber fell to the ground. The men sitting on the top rail jumped down and one of them took the rope from the man who had been riding the horse. That man slid off the horse's back. Together they led the horse back to the side of the corral and tied it once again to the corral post. One brought the horse a bucket of water, and they let it drink its fill in peace.

I was glad that was over. It had hurt to see a fine animal treated so badly. I tried not to judge those men breaking the horse. For all I knew they were doing it the right way. I sure was surprised though when they put the blindfold back on the horse and went through the same process all over again with another man sitting on the horse this time. The first rider became one of the men biting down hard on one of the horse's ears. Everything they did the first time was repeated, but this time the horse didn't buck as long or jump as high as it did before.

"Make them stop," I shouted to Yas. He just looked stonily ahead, watching as the whole thing played out again. "Make them stop," I shouted again, almost in tears. Yas reached down and put his hand on my arm.

"Not yet," he replied. "Just watch."

Once more they led the shaking horse over to the side of the corral. They tied it up and gave it water to drink. They repeated everything exactly as before, only this time the third man jumped up on the horse's back. This third time, though, things played out differently. When the horse was let loose it did not jump or buck. The man on the horse's back used the rope and his knees to make the horse go where he wanted. The horse tamely and shakily walked around the corral. The men gave the horse some hay and water and dried off the sweat with some old gunny sacks. They tied the horse up and sloshed water over it to wash off the sweat and dirt. One man picked up each of the horse's hoofs and cleaned them with a curved knife. Another man used a brush to curry the horse. It simply stood there shaking as the men worked on it. They laughed and pushed on the horse with their hands. It seemed to be as docile as a pet dog. The men finally untied it and led it away with a man riding on its back. That horse was broke for sure. The whole thing had taken an hour and a half.

Yas watched them go, and then he spit on the ground. He didn't seem to be too perturbed, but he also didn't seem to like it much. He looked down at me in a thoughtful way. "Now I want you to watch this other man break a horse. He will use a different method."

Looking past the corral I saw an Indian man calmly and slowly walk into the corral leading a large brown horse by a rope. He tied the horse to a corral post. While he was doing all of this he was calmly and quietly talking and singing to the horse. He scratched the horse's fetlock and rubbed its nose. He blew into its nostrils. He ran his hands confidently and gently over the horse's flanks and withers, up and down its legs, and across its back. The horse quivered, but it stood still, and its ears swiveled to follow the man wherever he was walking. There was a sense of quiet and peace in the corral that had not existed while the first group was breaking their horse.

The man left the horse tied to the post as he walked back out of the corral. He continued to speak to the horse until he was out of sight. I saw him walk around the edge of a building, and I looked inquiringly at Yas. He simply smiled and nodded, making a motion with his hand as if to say, "Wait." A few minutes later I saw the man come back around the building pushing a wheelbarrow with what appeared to be a saddle on top of some other things. The man walked the wheelbarrow over to a place close to the horse's head where it could see him as he worked. The man was continually talking, humming, or singing to the horse in a soft and low voice. Slowly he lifted up the saddle and brought it over to the horse. He let the horse smell it and he rubbed it gently up and down the horse's neck on both sides. He laid it down on the ground in front of the horse and went to pick up some other things. I noticed that the horse smelled it and kind of pushed it a bit with its nose.

I watched as the man lifted a full and heavy burlap bag out of the wheelbarrow. "What's in the bag?" I whispered to Yas.

"Sand," Yas answered quietly. "He will have three bags with

him. One is very light. One is medium heavy. One will be very heavy. Watch him as he works."

The man lifted out two more bags just as Yas described. As the man lifted out the bags he showed them to the horse. He walked calmly up to the horse with each bag and let the horse smell it. He gently rubbed each bag along the horse's neck on both sides, just like he had done with the saddle. He lifted out an old shirt and showed it to the horse. He let the horse smell it. He leaned in and blew his breath into the horse's nostrils. He lifted out a saddle blanket and slowly and calmly put it on the horse's back while singing a quiet song to the horse. Finally he took a curry brush from the wheelbarrow and carefully, gently, slowly began to curry the horse. He went under the horse's neck and walked around the horse quietly talking as he brushed the horse. He gently lifted each hoof of the horse and cleaned it.

I was waiting for the horse to kick or squeal or bite him, but it simply watched curiously as the man walked around it.

"Why does the horse seem so relaxed around that man?" I asked Yas. "The other horse was real nervous and seemed angry."

Yas nodded. He continued to stare at the horse as he answered me.

"That man in there has been working with that horse since it was very young. He has built up a relationship with the horse. The horse trusts him. You will see how he breaks the horse to the saddle if you will be patient and will watch."

I turned my attention back to the corral just as the man lifted up the saddle and slowly placed it on the back of the horse. He cinched it up under the horse and let the stirrups gently slide down to hang at the sides. While he was doing that he sang or hummed or talked to the horse. He took a stirrup in his hand and let it gently bump the horse's side. He walked around to the other side of the horse and did the same thing. The horse turned its head and watched him, but it didn't move. The man picked up the smallest of the three bags of sand. He let the horse smell it. With casual, slow steps he carried the sack back and gently placed it in the saddle. The horse shook its mane but otherwise seemed to be calm. The man grabbed a stirrup in both hands and pulled down on it until he was kind leaning on it. He stood that way for about a minute before gradually straightening up. He slowly walked to where the rope was tied to the fence post. He untied it, gently clucking to the horse. The rope was wrapped around the horse's nose and allowed the man to lead the horse.

"That kind of setup is called a hackamore," Yas told me. "It is sometimes used to train horses. It doesn't have a bit so it is less irritating to the horse."

The man led the horse in a slow figure eight around the corral. He hummed as he walked, the horse following after him like a giant dog. The horse seemed to be calm. After ten or fifteen minutes of walking the man led the horse back to the fence post and tied him to it. He scratched the horse's head while talking in its ear. He reached into his pocket and pulled out something which he fed to the horse and which the horse greedily gobbled up.

"Did you see the man give his horse some apple bits to eat?" Yas asked. "He is rewarding the horse a little bit, a very little bit, for doing a good job."

The man sat in front of the horse and talked to it in a low and quiet voice. The horse lowered its head as if it wanted to hear better. They stayed that way for a few minutes until the man reached out and stroked the horse's nose. He slowly rose to his feet, still stroking the horse's nose and jaw. Slowly he reached behind him and grabbed the medium size bag which he carried back to the saddle. Cautiously he removed the small bag from the saddle and set it on the ground. Slowly and gently he placed the medium size bag up in the saddle. The horse's ears swiveled toward the back, but the horse continued to face forward. The man leaned on the stirrup again this time he patted the horse's neck while he was doing that. He quit leaning on the stirrup and walked to the post to untie the horse. He hung onto the horse's mane and slowly untied the hackamore. With one hand he deftly readjusted the rope around the horse's nose and jaw so that the ends of the rope hung down on both sides rather than just on one side. Grabbing both ends of the rope he clucked at the horse and began to urge it to move forward. The man pulled, and the horse followed. He walked over to one side, guiding the horse to walk in a large figure eight around and around the corral. Whenever the man wanted the horse to make a turn he would gently lay one end of the rope across the horse's neck and gently pull on the other end. After about fifteen minutes of walking the man led the horse back to the post and tied the horse back up to it. He reached into his pocket and pulled out some apple bits, offering them to the horse with the palm of his hand. As the horse chewed on the morsels the man scratched its neck and spoke softly in its ear. He blew in the horse's nostrils and stroked its nose gently. I saw the man look over at the large bag of sand as if he were considering something. After a few moments he gave a slight shrug and picked up the curry brush. Once again he walked all around the horse gently brushing every part of the horse, who seemed to enjoy the attention.

When the man finished he walked over to the large bag of sand. He lifted it and placed it into the wheelbarrow. He put in the other bags of sand as well. He pushed the wheelbarrow out of the corral before walking back to the horse. He was quietly singing as he untied the horse from the post. He kept ahold of both ends of the hackamore as he walked to the horse's side. Gently and cautiously he reached up and grabbed the saddle horn. He put one foot in a stirrup and leaned his weight on it. The horse did not move, although its head came up a bit, and its ears swiveled toward the back. Slowly the man lifted himself up and into the saddle. He sat on the saddle as if it would break, his rump just barely touching it. He continued to speak softly to the horse as he cautiously lowered himself into the saddle. He moved around a bit to get himself situated. He leaned forward and patted the horse on the neck. Using his knees and the hackamore he guided the horse to the gate of the corral. Gently dismounting he opened the gate and led the horse out of the corral, tying it to a post on the outside of the corral. He took off the saddle blanket and saddle, placing them into the wheelbarrow. He walked the wheelbarrow around to the other side of the building and a few minutes later reappeared. He carried with him a curry brush and a pail of water. He curried the horse once more, singing softly as it drank the water. He gave it a few more bits of apple before untying it and leading it off down the street. We watched until he reached a bend in the road and disappeared from our view.

Yas looked down at me and smiled. "We have been here all morning, Young White," he said with a smile. "It is time for lunch."

I had been so absorbed in watching the men work on the horses that I had lost all track of time. The sun was shining directly overhead. My stomach rumbled as if to confirm Yas's remark about lunchtime. Yas eased away from the corral and began to walk back into town. I trotted beside him as he veered off the main road onto a dirt path that led to a small adobe building. When it appeared that the building was going to be our destination I stopped dead in my tracks. Yas noticed and turned around.

"What is wrong, Young White?" he asked.

I pointed with my chin toward the building. "My dad said that I wasn't ever to go to that building. He said that sin walks in and out of that door. He said that I should stay away from that sinful place."

Yas smiled and nodded. "Your dad has the right idea when he warns you to stay away from bad places. This place, though, is not a bad place. Your father is mistaken. You are with me, and you will be safe here."

Yas turned and walked right through the door without any hesitation. I trusted Yas, but I didn't know what was inside of that building. After a moment of thought I cautiously approached and walked inside. Imagine my surprise when I found that it was a small store. There were canned goods on shelves. Coats, hats, and gloves hung from pegs on the walls. Sacks of brown beans and pinion nuts were stacked on the floor. A large, older Indian woman was standing behind a counter talking to Yas. They seemed to know each other. The woman looked at me as if she could see right through me. After a minute her broad face split into a smile.

"Hey, Young White. I thought your dad told you to never come in here." She chuckled and said something to Yas which made him laugh. I was surprised that she knew about my dad's warning.

"I'm with Yas today, ma'am," I said politely. "Wherever he goes, that is where I will go."

She nodded and moved her hand across the top of the counter as if she were brushing away from dust. She had large turquoise and silver jewelry on her hands and arms that clunked on the counter as she moved.

"Do you have any fry bread and chili in your back room, Auntie?" Yas asked her.

She arched an eyebrow and half-turned, as if to look around to see if anybody else was listening in on the conversation. Directly behind her were two large blankets hanging from a wire stretched across a large opening. The colors on the blankets were faded, and it seemed as if they were covered in dust. I got the impression that they had been hanging there for a long time. The woman turned back to look at Yas.

"I have food and some clean bowls back there. You are in luck because the food is free today," she said as she lifted one of the blankets and disappeared into the space behind it. Yas motioned with his hand for me to follow as he lifted the blanket. I followed hard on his heels, unsure of what I would find in the back of the store.

My first impression was of a long and dark hallway. There were blankets and animal skins hanging on the walls. The walls had large timbers which held up the ceiling. The ceiling itself was made up of many sticks. The hall wasn't quite as long as I thought it was because a large blanket at the end covered the opening to another room. Yas lifted the blanket and held it up so that I could go ahead of him. On the other side of the blanket was a kitchen. There was a gas stove, a small sink, and a large standalone cupboard. Auntie was spooning food into two bowls on the counter beside the stove. In the middle of the room was a table that was so old the wood had faded to a gray color and had twisted a bit. There were four chairs around the table that looked very old but still seemed to be sturdy. Yas pulled out a chair and sat in it. He seemed to be very familiar with the place. It was as if he fit there, as if the place had been expecting him and had accepted him as a natural part of it. I pulled out a chair on the other side of the table and sat gingerly on the edge of it. I watched as Auntie used a large knife to saw off two chunks of bread from a fry bread loaf. She deftly balanced the bowls and fry bread as she walked over to the table. Yas took a bowl and a piece of fry bread. I followed his lead, and Auntie smiled at me. She half-turned around and hollered something in Navajo toward one of the walls covered in a beautiful gray, red, and black blanket. I noticed that Yas began to eat immediately. Either he was very hungry, or the food was very good, or perhaps it was both, because he ate noisily. I looked at my bowl, and it had a few things in it that I could identify. There were some brown beans, a few chunks of meat, and some charred chili peppers that were all floating in kind of a stew. While I was contemplating the food Auntie set a glass of cold milk down beside my plate.

"That is goat's milk," she said with a smile. "It will be good for you." She walked over to the beautiful blanket and lifted it, yelling at someone or something on the other side.

I began by eating some of the stew. At first it just seemed a little spicy hot, but as I swallowed it liquid fire began to melt my throat and stomach. Yas saw the look on my face and smiled.

"Eat some fry bread, and then drink a little milk. It will help. Soon you will find that you enjoy it so much that you will want more," he told me through a mouthful of bread.

Quickly I tore off some fry bread and stuffed it in my mouth. I chewed as if my life depended on it, which at that time I was convinced that it did. I washed that bite down with a gulp of milk. It didn't take long, and the molten river of fire began to subside to a more manageable level. I watched as Yas spooned some of the stew onto the fry bread and took a bite. I followed his example and found that it helped dampen the pain. As I slowly worked my way through the delicious fiery food, Auntie plopped herself down in one of the chairs with a sigh. Yas smiled at her, looking at her as if he was trying to figure something out.

"How old are you now, Auntie?" he asked taking a last mouthful of food. He swallowed and gave a light belch. "I figure that you and Uncle might be the two oldest people in the tribe."

Auntie waved a turquoise-laden hand at him. "I am not so old, but Uncle. . .now he is an old one. He is so old that he was able to talk to people who had made the long walk."

As if on cue the beautiful blanket was moved aside, and an old man walked out into the room from under it. He had long white hair. His face was covered in wrinkles. He was bent over, walking with a cane that was carved in a way that made it look like it was covered in rattlesnake skin. He wore an old pair of jeans and a very faded blue shirt. He had a red bandana tied around his head to hold back his long, snowy white hair. He had leather moccasins on his feet, and he shuffled as he tottered into the room. He gave out a small groan as he eased his back and straightened up as much as he could. He hobbled over to the table and after a few paces suddenly stopped as if he had run into a wall. He bent down, staring at me from under his white, bushy eyebrows. His eyes were watering, and he seemed to have trouble focusing.

"Hi, my name is Young White," I said politely. He leaned back away from me as if he had seen a ghost. He groped for a chair and, pulling it away from the table, he lowered himself into it with a grunt.

"Why are you here?" he asked in a cracked voice. Yas swallowed a bite of fry bread and answered before I could figure out what to say.

"He is with me today, Uncle. I am trying to teach him some things, if he is not too stupid to learn." Yas looked over at Auntie. "Is that old truck still running? I was wondering if I could borrow it to drive out to the mesa. I will only use it for a little while, and then I will bring it back." Auntie shot him a skeptical look. "I have money," he added hopefully. "I can fill it up with gas before I bring it back."

Uncle coughed and raised a hand while he was trying to clear his throat. His eyes watered even more until he finally quit coughing. "The truck belongs to me," he said. "You can only use it if you take me along with you."

"You are too old for that kind of trip," Auntie protested. "Surely you are not thinking of climbing the mesa," she said forcefully.

"I am going, and I will climb the mesa a last time," Uncle said in a high-pitched quiet voice. "These two young ones will help me." He sighed heavily. "This may be the last time that I will have the chance to look out from the mesa. If I do not do it now then I am afraid that I will never again see into the distance or smell the sage and cedars or commune with the ghosts of our people." Spittle had formed on his lips, and he used his left hand to wipe it away. He turned to Yas. "The truck belongs to me. If you want to use the truck you will have to take me to the mesa." He took a deep breath and blew it out noisily. He nodded to himself. "I have spoken. . . and that is what I want."

Yas chewed thoughtfully on a small chunk of fry bread. He looked at me appraisingly before casting a thoughtful eye on old Uncle. He looked at Auntie out of the corner of his eye as he sopped up some chili with another piece of fry bread. "It is a lot of responsibility. I understand why Uncle wants to do this. I think that Dale and I can get him there and home safely."

Auntie shook her head in exasperation. "Stupid men!" she said angrily. "I will have nothing to do with this. Take him if you want to, but don't come crying to me if you all die up there." She got up from the table and prepared a bowl and some fry bread for Uncle.

She set it on the table with just enough force to show her anger but not enough to show disrespect. She helped Uncle move his chair up to the table and stood beside him as he ate his meal. She wiped his lips and rubbed his back. Uncle groaned with pleasure. When he finished eating he gave his bowl to Auntie.

"Help me to stand up," he commanded. Yas and I quickly went to his aid, one of us on each side of him. I noticed that he wasn't very heavy as we gently helped him to stand. Auntie came over and gave some keys to Yas.

"If anything happens to Uncle I will make you eat these keys," she said vehemently. "Then I will kill you and rip out your guts with a deer antler. Then I will feed what is left of you to the dogs."

Yas laughed and kissed her on the cheek. "I don't want any of those things to happen," he said lightly. "I have no doubt that you will do them if I am not careful. Believe me, I will bring Uncle back in one piece. I will give him the chance to climb the mesa. We will take the easy trail that loops around to the west. It takes longer, but it is not as steep."

Yas walked out a back door, and I followed. Auntie walked with Uncle as he slowly made his way out. She spoke to him quietly and gently in Navajo. He replied in a reassuring manner.

The truck was old and rusty. In different places there were patches of the original green paint left on it. The fenders had places that had rusted through. When I opened the passenger side door I noticed that there was a hole in the floorboard through which I could see the ground. Yas and I each took one of Uncle's arms and kind of hoisted him up while Auntie pushed on his rear end. He slid over to about the middle of the seat, and I climbed in to sit beside him. Yas jumped into the truck and swiftly fired up the old engine. It was loud, backfiring a few times as it warmed up. Yas waved out the window as he pulled away from the building and bounced onto the road. Looking in the rearview mirror I saw Auntie standing there watching us. She did not wave, but I thought I saw her shoulders slump.

Yas drove fast in the truck. Dust from the road came up from the holes in the floorboard. We drove with the windows down. It was so noisy that there was no reason to talk. Occasionally I would glance down to see the road flashing by through the hole in the floor. The day was warm, and the cab of the truck was spacious. I felt safe and comfortable sitting with the adults. It was as if we were setting out on a grand adventure. We all bounced around as the truck hit potholes and ruts. It got worse when we turned off the blacktop onto a narrow dirt road. After about twenty minutes I saw the mesa. As we got closer it appeared to rise majestically out of the dusty countryside. It was red and tan in color with green on top where plants grew. Yas left the road and bumped us across the ground until we were close to the base. I saw that there were large boulders that had broken free and rolled down the side of the mesa. I opened my door and jumped out. Yas came around to my side, and together we kind of lifted Uncle out of the truck. He groaned as he moved his arms and legs to try to limber up. Yas helped him to straighten his back. He stood there rubbing Uncle's back muscle until the old man signaled for him to stop.

"Wait right here for a minute while I check the trail ahead," Yas said as he jogged off to our left. Uncle looked around, took a deep breath, and threw his head back so that the sun fell directly upon it. He stood that way until Yas jogged back into view.

"The trail is in good shape, Uncle. If we take it easy I am sure that you can make it," Yas said with a smile. He took one of Uncle's arms, and I took the other. Slowly, step by step, we guided Uncle to the trail that led up to the top of the mesa. We did not go quickly, but we made steady progress.

It seemed to me that the trail had been made many years ago. The ground was beaten hard by the passing of many feet over many centuries. There were places where small trees grew close to the path. I saw that the bark had been worn away in smooth and shiny spots by hands that had instinctively grabbed a branch to keep a person steady and propel them up the trail. Uncle used his cane and seemed to breathe easier the farther up the trail we walked. We finally came to a spot where there were about ten steps that had been hacked out of the side of the mesa. The steps were a little steeper than the trail, but it was obvious that they ended at the top of the mesa. Next to each step was a series of handholds that could be used. Yas went up a few steps and then reached back for Uncle. I pushed and Yas pulled until we all reached the top of the mesa. Uncle was breathing hard, and I was concerned.

"Why don't you sit down and rest, Uncle?" Yas said with concern in his voice. The old man coughed a few times and pointed with his rattlesnake cane.

"Take me over to the edge so that I can see," he commanded. Yas and I helped him hobble over to a large rocky ledge that stuck out over the lip of the mesa. The sun had warmed its surface, and Uncle groaned with pleasure as he sat down. He pointed with his cane toward the other side of the mesa. "Yas, take Young White over to the ruins. Show him what to look for, and teach him about our ways."

Yas nodded and motioned for me to follow him. After a short walk we came upon a pile of old logs. "There was a hogan right here," Yas told me. "Look at the ground and tell me what you see."

I bent down to look and immediately saw that the ground was littered with pieces of pottery. "I see lots of broken pottery pieces," I told him with a smile. He came and knelt beside me. Reverently he picked up a large pottery shard.

"This is a really old style of pottery. The people who lived here made some really beautiful things." Yas scouted the ground around him. "If you are good at it you might be able to find all of the pieces for a pottery jar. You can kind of put it together to see how it looked."

He and I worked on that for ten minutes until we almost had a complete jar. We didn't have any glue with us to hold the pieces together so they kept falling apart. Still, we could get a good idea of what the jar looked like when it was whole. One piece had a lot of red and black on it. I started to put it into my pocket, but Yas put out a hand to stop me.

"Do not take anything away from here unless Uncle gives it to you," Yas said quietly and earnestly. "The things we see up here belong to this place and to the people who lived in this place so long ago. Let their spirits rest peaceful, and do not disturb them by taking their things."

I wasn't sure that I really understood, but I nodded and dropped the pottery piece back onto the ground. Yas smiled and patted my shoulder. He looked around as if he were searching specifically for something. He got up and walked over to a pile of dirt and small rocks. I followed him, wondering why he was interested in something so uninteresting. He knelt beside the pile and carefully brushed away some of the dirt. I knelt beside him to see what he was doing. He dug a finger into the pile, and soon he grasped something between his thumb and forefinger. He held it up for me to see. He turned it this way and that so that I could see it from several different angles. It was a piece of white rock that was small and pointed on one end. He held it out to me, and I took it.

"What is it?" I asked as I examined it.

Yas looked at me in a questioning way. "What do you think it is?" he asked.

"I think it is a pointy little rock," I said. "That seems kind of obvious, don't you think?" I said sarcastically.

"Give me that!" Yas said in an exasperated tone of voice. He snatched the rock out of my hand and held it up again for me to look at. "This is an arrowhead," he said proudly. "Sometimes we just call them points. This pile of chips is where an arrowhead maker used to work. Maybe two hundred years ago a man hunkered down right here and carefully chipped away at some rock until he fashioned some arrowheads. He was a craftsman who was highly valued by the people."

I eyed the pointy rock with skepticism. "That isn't an arrowhead," I argued. "Arrowheads are big and black. This thing is small and white."

Yas chuckled and shook his head. "I don't know where you kids learn this stuff, but I do know that you need to learn the truth." He held up the pointy rock. "Arrowheads were very practical things. A plain old pointy stick might work to bring down an animal, but it also might just bounce off the prey. Add a pointy rock, and your chances of success went up. Those people didn't just hunt for sport. They were hunting for food, and it was important that they were successful."

He gave the arrowhead back to me to hold. "Most of the things the people hunted were small. They hunted rabbits and birds mainly. If you used a big arrowhead on a rabbit or bird it might tear up too much of the hide and meat. So, the point maker made little arrowheads as well as big arrowheads." He reached over and reverently took the arrowhead from me. "It actually takes more time and skill to chip out a small point than it does to create a large arrowhead."

Yas carefully replaced the small point in the pile. He picked up some dust in his hand and poured it over the pile. He patted it into place and then bowed his head for a minute. When he looked up he seemed to be at peace.

"Why did you do that?" I asked him. "Why did you put the point back in there, cover it with dust and then bow your head?"

"I put it back where it belongs," he said quietly. "I covered it up so it would not be easy to find by others who might come to rob this ground. I bowed my head because I was praying to God to thank him for letting me see the skill of my ancestors."

He stood up and looked down on me with a smile. "Remember, Young White, to make your tools match the job. Use the right tool for the job, and things will go easier for you." He looked behind him and studied the old hogan ruin. "We are going to walk back over there, and I will show you something else."

I followed him to the ruins, all the while wondering what he was thinking about. Yas stopped and stood quietly looking at the ruins. I noticed that he was silently crying. He turned away and walked around the site, always looking at the ground and giving an occasional small grunt. He walked in a circle around the whole site. He stopped circling at some point and then walked straight to a grove of pinion trees. He saw something among the trees that held his attention. He would look at something about eye-level and walk a few paces then stop. He did this several times and then disappeared behind a large rock. I wasn't too concerned, but I kept watching to see when he would reappear. Soon I saw him emerge from the grove. "Come over here," he shouted. I obediently hurried over to where he stood. He motioned for me to sit down. He lowered himself to sit with me. He was quiet for a few moments, and then he began to speak to me about what we saw on the mesa.

"Many years ago some people lived up here. There are several old hogan ruins on this mesa so I know that there were several families that lived up here. If you look over there," and he pointed with his chin toward a large gray rock, "you will see a cougar carved on that rock. Go look and come back."

I ran over there and found a large cougar etched into the rock. I looked at it carefully. It could have been mistaken for the action of water and wind on the rock, but seen from a certain angle it was obvious that it had been carved on the surface of the rock. I thoughtfully walked back and sat down to hear some more. Yas pointed with his chin. "There is a small pool of water on the other side of those trees. In those trees is an old dead tree. In the old dead tree there is a hive of bees. Go over there and look."

Sure enough, when I got to the trees I heard and then saw the bees. They were making trips from the hive to a small of pool of water. By the pool I found grinding stones. I began to get a mental picture of a whole group of families that had made this mesa their home. I went back to sit again by Yas. He explained how the little village had been laid out, how the people lived, why they chose certain spots for hogans, and why grinding stones are found in particular places. He explained that the ruins told a story of a peaceful life that had been shattered. A group of people had attacked the village, killed the people, and destroyed the village. He didn't know if they were white army soldiers or another tribe. He showed me how the things scattered on the ground and the location of things left behind gave clues. The answers were there for anyone who knew what to look for.

He finished talking, and we sat silently for many minutes. Finally, he gave a great sigh and stood up. "Let us go check on Uncle," he said with a slight smile.

We walked to the edge of the mesa and sat next to Uncle. He had not moved. He seemed to be at peace, and I enjoyed resting beside him. As we were resting, I watched Uncle. He lifted his eyes to the sky, and it was obvious to me that he was looking for something. I finally asked him what he was looking for. He was silent for a long time after I asked. I almost repeated myself because I was convinced that he had not heard me. Something in the way he held his head warned me to be patient, so I kept silent. Finally, he cleared his throat and said in his high-pitched, cracked voice, "I am trying to imagine what the people who used to live here saw when they were alive. I imagine that every morning they would come here to see if God was riding on the clouds to come see them."

Yas nodded as if he could also see what Uncle saw. "Is that why you wanted to come here?" Yas asked. Uncle looked over at Yas, and then he turned to look at me. He nodded slightly and motioned toward the ground with his head.

"Young White, look on the ground," he commanded me. "There are many rocks. I want you to pick up one of those rocks and give it to me. It doesn't have to be a particular rock. Just pick up the first one that catches your eye, pick it up, and hand it to me."

I thought that was really a strange request. I wasn't sure what the rocks had to do with anything, but I figured that it wouldn't hurt to do what he told me to do. I looked around me. There were red rocks, black rocks, and brown rocks. One black rock was kind of shiny and just a bit larger than the other rocks. I picked it up and lifted it up for Uncle to see. His bony hand reached out and took it from my palm. He grunted and hefted the rock. He transferred it to his other hand, tossing it up and catching it. His eyes gleamed and he looked at me with new interest.

"I asked to come here because of a dream that I had," he told Yas. "It was a dream about a white boy. I wondered in my soul why I would be dreaming about a white boy, and when I came out of my room there was a white boy sitting at my table."

Yas scratched his head. "Do you think your dream was about Young White?"

Uncle held the rock out in front of himself. "Who else would it be about? I don't know any white boys. I haven't even seen any white boys for many years. Last night I had a dream about a white boy, and today here is one. . .in my house, at my table, with us at the mesa. Also, he chose a black rock. The dream was about Young White!"

I was shocked. Why would an old Indian man have a dream about me? "What was the dream about?" I asked Uncle.

The old man put the rock in his lap. He put his hands on his knees and stared out at the sky.

"In my dream. . ." he began. "In my dream I saw many people of all different colors running on a large road. At one point another smaller road branched off the large road, and some people began to run on the smaller road while the others kept running on the large road. Along the way there were other roads that branched off the smaller road. Each road got narrower and narrower. There were people who took off on each smaller road. Soon there was just a trail that branched off the small road. It went into the forest, and I could not see where it would go. A white boy left the other people and took that trail. He did not run fast and he did not run slow, but he ran strong and steady. He jumped over trees and rocks. He ran through mud and water. He ran with purpose. He ran with joy. Nothing kept him from his pace. Every now and then he would look behind him. What he saw was the form of a man who was all black. He had no eyes, no ears, no mouth, no arms, and no legs. He was not a shadow, but he always followed the white boy. He did not gain on the boy. He always stayed the same distance away. The longer the boy ran on the road the larger he grew and the smaller the black man got. The boy ran alone, always alone except for the black man who was always behind him. The boy grew very large, and the man became very small." Uncle picked up the black rock and gave it to Yas. "When Young White picked the black rock I knew that the dream was about him."

I was excited about the dream. "What does it mean, Uncle? Who is the black man? Is he good or bad? Did you see the end of the boy's running? Where did he go?"

Uncle shook his head sadly. "I do not know those things, Young White. I only tell you what I saw. I do know that the black man said nothing good or bad. He did not slow the white boy down, stop him, or speed him up. He was just there, and he never left."

Uncle licked his lips. "Talking has dried me out. Young White, run to the truck and bring me the water jug."

I got up and did as I was told. I climbed down the steps and ran down the trail to the truck. I found the jug on the floorboard and lifted it out. I ran as fast as I could back up the trail and carefully climbed the steps. When I got back to Uncle I helped him to take a drink. I steadied the jug and watched as he drank his fill. Yas reached over and took the jug next. He took a long drink, let out an "ahhhh," and took another long drink. I didn't need much water, but I also drank from the jug. The water wasn't cold, but it had not gotten hot while it was in the truck. I plopped down next to Uncle, staring out at the blue sky and white clouds.

Uncle looked at me. "Yas just told me that Mrs. Zonni gave you a blessing. How did she do it?"

I held my hands like she had held her hands and then kind of chanted what I remembered of the tune of the song. Uncle looked at Yas and shrugged. "I do not know the words that she used, but the Zonni clan is known for giving powerful blessings. I hope it takes. You are white, and I don't know if the blessing will stay with you."

We sat there quietly for a few minutes. Yas was deep in thought, and he seemed to be concentrating on something in the far distance. He started to hum a song but stopped suddenly.

"Young White," he said quietly without looking at me. "Let me explain about the horses and the men we saw this morning." I looked at him and nodded. I certainly wanted to know why we had to watch all of that. "Young White, you are like those horses. Your father is like those men. Your father thinks he must break you so that you can grow up to be useful. He is using the method of the three men that we saw first. He will make your life miserable. He will ride you hard. He wants to break your spirit. He will keep on trying to break you down until you submit."

"But why doesn't my dad use the other method?" I cried out. "Why doesn't he use the kinder method?"

Yas shrugged and rubbed his chin. "Maybe your dad is using the only method he knows. Maybe he has only been taught one way. Maybe he is trying to toughen you up. I don't know the real answer."

"So this is what I am to expect for my whole life?" I asked close to tears. "Will my dad be this way with me my whole life?"

Yas shook his head. "No, no, no. There will come a time when you can leave home. You will be your own person then. Until that day, who knows? *Quien sabe?* But you have choices, Young White. You can choose to be broken or to be stronger than those who wish to break you. Use your mind. Use your spirit to bear up under the pressure."

Yas spoke quietly to Uncle in the Navajo language for a few minutes. I was saddened by the prospect of long years ahead, trying not to be broken, and trying to be a good son under those circumstances.

"Young White!" Uncle said quietly. "I will tell you two things.

You must listen closely. These two things will help your spirit if you will accept them. The first is a saying that the People, our warriors, have used for centuries. In English, you would say 'Eat the pain.'"

Uncle turned his body so that he was looking directly at me. It hurt his joints, and he bit back a groan. "Every day the great God gives us something to drink and something to eat. Sometimes we must drink from the glass of sorrow. Sometimes we must eat the meal of pain. You must drink and eat what God puts in front of you each day. God always gives beauty, and joy, happiness, and strength along with pain and sorrow. We must take what we get. We must not complain or reject the day. We must accept it and live with it."

I nodded to show that I had heard. I wasn't sure that I really understood, but I knew that I would remember what he said, and perhaps I would understand it later on. "What is the other thing you must tell me?" I asked. No adult had ever spoken to me as these Indian men were doing now. I felt that they were trying to help me, and I was grateful for the help.

Uncle straightened up his back and eased his right shoulder a little bit. He took a drink from the jug. He licked his lips and moved his rattlesnake cane. He seemed to be weighing his next words carefully before he spoke them.

"Young White, you must have a vision of the kind of man you will become," he said, looking me right in the eye. "You must decide whether you will be strong and brave or weak and cowardly. You must decide how you will deal with problems that come up in life. You must decide how you will live your life into the future." Uncle picked up the cane and touched me on the shoulder with it. "You do not have to be like your father. You can decide to be a different man. You can decide to see the world in a different way. You can decide to see people differently than your father sees people." He moved the cane and touched me on the other shoulder. "You can decide to use your life to make things better for others. Ask God for a vision of what that looks like. Perhaps that is the very narrow trail that you will take. You must run your own race."

I didn't know what to say, so I said nothing. I was stunned by what Uncle told me. Nobody had ever told me that I could decide for myself. I just figured that life forced you into being one way or another. I respected Uncle for talking to me. I wanted in that moment to be someone who would make Uncle and Yas proud of me.

Uncle turned himself around again with an effort. He groaned a little from the pain. "My joints hurt today, but the warmth here on the mesa has helped." He coughed a little bit and adjusted the can beside him. "Yas, soon I will die. I will sing my death song. Promise me that you will have my body taken care of in the old way. Promise me that!"

Yas nodded and put his hand on the old man's shoulder. "I will do what you ask, Uncle. I promise. What will be your death song?"

Uncle stared up into the blue sky. "I will sing the journey song. Whether I am with others or by myself when I die, I will sing the song with my last breath."

We all sat for a few more minutes in quiet until Yas broke out into song. "This is my father's world. And to my listening ears, all nature sings, and round me rings the music of the spheres. This is my father's world, I rest me in the thought of rocks and trees, of skies and seas, his hand the wonders wrought."

Yas sighed heavily and sat back in a satisfied way. "When I am here on this mesa I think of all those of our people who have been here before us. I look out, and I see the world of my fathers, the rocks and trees and all nature. Of course, I know the song is about Father God, but it also reminds me of our fathers who helped to shape this land. I wish that I could have been here back in those days when we were free. Our lives belonged to us. It was a simpler, better time. Uncle, like you, when I die, I want my body handled in the old way."

"Is that your death song?" I asked Yas. He smiled and shook his head.

"My death song will be 'Higher Ground,'" Yas said. "That is the song that made me want to get well from the alcohol drink and come back home." He tilted his head back and sang softly. "I'm pressing on the upward way, new heights I'm gaining every day; still praying as I onward bound, Lord, plant my feet on higher ground. Lord, lift me up and help me stand, by faith, on heaven's table land. A higher plane than I have found; Lord, plant my feet on higher ground."

Uncle nodded. "It is a good song. I like it. I have never heard it before, but it makes sense to have such a song for the soul's journey."

Yas smiled. "I have always thought of the mesa as heaven's table land. I want my soul to journey to the Great Mesa where I can see my fathers and where I can see out into eternity."

I wasn't sure that I understood any of that, but I kept quiet and was glad to be with those men. I don't know how much time we sat there enjoying each other's company. It seemed so short, and yet it seemed to stretch into eternity.

"Yas," Uncle said. "Take me home. My bones are tired, and Auntie will be worried."

Yas laughed and hopped up. I did the same, dusting off my rear end. Yas and I helped Uncle to slowly rise to his feet. His bones creaked and snapped. He swayed a little as he leaned on the rattlesnake cane. Slowly and cautiously we led him to the steps and just as cautiously helped him down, one step at a time. We helped him to the truck and lifted his light frame into the seat. He sat back with a sigh of relief.

Yas dropped me by my house first. I waved as the men drove off. When I got inside I saw that Mom was cooking supper. Dad wasn't home yet. I went to the bathroom to clean up a bit. Linda, Roger, and Paul asked me about my day, and I told them about the horses, the arrowheads, the pottery, and the mesa. At supper I kept quiet as Dad talked to us about his day. He didn't ask about mine, and I didn't tell him.

That night I had a dream. In my dream I was standing on a high mesa looking out into the distance. A man and a woman came to stand beside me. Others joined us until there was a great crowd of people around me. I felt their presence and their warmth. I was not alone, and I was comforted.

TWELVE

MY FATHER'S WORLD

EARLY AUGUST 1963

Saturdays in the spring, summer, and early fall of 1963 became my days of escape. On those days I could walk out the door of our small apartment and travel to a wild and free place. Every Saturday brought the opportunity to ride out to the Bernandez sawmill on the reservation. Although I think it was on the Pueblo reservation named the Jemez Pueblo there was usually a Navajo and a Pueblo man who worked together for Mr. Bernandez. The Navajo man was always Yas. The Pueblo man was usually Joe, although sometimes another man took his place. I kind of got the impression that Joe was related to Mary, and maybe that is why Yas was with him.

Hutch and I were becoming good friends because of our Saturday adventures. Sometimes my friend Jerry was able to join us. I would walk over to the Bernandez compound early on Saturday morning. I would hear the roar of the old diesel engine on the big logging truck and follow the sound to where it was parked. Mr. Bernandez would be leaning against the truck drinking coffee from a thermos. Hutch and Jerry would already be in the cab staking out their spot on the long bench seat.

I always stopped to give my respects to Mr. Bernandez. He usually told me a little bit about what he was going to be working on at the sawmill. He also explained to me who would be going with us or working with us. I liked those few moments when it seemed like I was just one of the guys on the crew. I liked the way that Mr. Bernandez would sip his coffee as we talked. Dad did the same thing. One Saturday morning I begged Mom to make me a cup of coffee.

"Mom, can I have a cup of coffee to take with me over to the Bernandez place?" I asked earnestly. Mom's mouth widened into a smile.

"What do you want coffee for? You know it could stunt your growth," she said bending down to look me in the face as if she were emphasizing the point that I had more growing to do.

"Well. . .whenever I go over there Mr. Bernandez is drinking coffee and leaning against the truck. I figured it might make me seem more like one of the guys rather than just a kid. When I go over there with coffee in a mug I could lean against the truck like Mr. Bernandez and just talk. I think it might be cool," I said with a grin. I pantomimed holding a mug in my hand and leaning against a truck, taking a sip every now and then.

Mom laughed out loud. She turned and began to search through the cupboard until she pulled out an old cracked mug. She filled it up with some hot coffee and blew on it before handing it to me.

"Do you want sugar and cream in that?" she asked.

"Nope. Black is just fine," I said. I had heard Dad say that about a thousand times so I figured that would be good enough for me.

I grabbed my sack lunch in one hand and held my coffee mug in the other. I marched straight-backed over to the compound and followed the sound of the truck engine over to where Mr. Bernandez was leaning against the truck, sipping from his thermos. I casually sidled up to the truck and leaned against it like I imagined a cool adult would do.

"Morning, Mr. Bernandez," I said.

He acknowledged me with a lifting of his chin and a sip from his thermos. I took a gulp from my mug, holding the coffee in my mouth and letting some trickle down my throat. The coffee had cooled on the walk over, for which I was thankful, but something was very wrong. The coffee was extremely bitter. It tasted like burnt plastic and old paint. My body rebelled against any more of that making its way down my throat. I looked down into the mug, and all I saw was brown liquid that looked harmless. It looked fine, but it tasted like something that could poison a person and kill them dead. I was in a wretched way because I still held a bunch of the vile stuff in my mouth. I found that I either had to spit it out or swallow it down. I turned my head and spit it out.

Mr. Bernandez chuckled. "What's wrong?" he asked in an amused voice.

I coughed and spit until I could answer. "I think Mom put the wrong stuff in this mug. I asked her for black coffee, not poisoned crud."

Mr. Bernandez stuck out his hand, and I gave him my cup. He smelled the coffee and then took a big swig of it. He shrugged as if it tasted like he expected it to taste. "I think it might be older coffee that has been brewed twice. A lot of military guys like it that way. They figure that it concentrates the caffeine in it so that it has more of a kick to it." He handed the cup back to me.

I thoughtfully took the cup and peered once more at the placid brown liquid. I looked up at Mr. Bernandez and down at the coffee a few times before making up my mind. I tossed out the rest of the coffee and spit a few times on the ground. I guessed that I wasn't going to be one of the guys. I swore off coffee for the rest of my life.

Usually on Saturday mornings we would wait a bit at the compound. Sometimes Joe or Yas would show up all by their lonesome. Sometimes they would show up together. Sometimes they just wouldn't show up at all. After a decent amount of time waiting Mr. Bernandez would haul himself up into the cab. "You boys hang on now," he would holler. He would shift the truck into gear and slowly let up on the clutch so that we rolled forward. Once the truck got going the whine of its engine drowned out all opportunity for talking. If we wanted to say anything to each other we had to shout directly into an ear. Mr. Bernandez would drive out of town, navigating all of the road's many curves with an athletic confidence. I swear that once I saw him swerve to miss a sheep that had wandered out onto the road, shift gears, take a sip of coffee, check his mirrors, tweak Hutch back into his place on the seat, and wave at a passing Indian all at the same time without breaking a sweat. It was like he had six hands and two heads!

When we got to the reservation Mr. Bernandez would drive over to the pueblo. Whichever men were missing would normally be there beside the road waiting for us. Mr. Bernandez would slow the truck down to a crawl, and the guys would hop on. He would look in the mirror, and when he was convinced that the men were safely on the truck he would speed up. The truck bounced through the ruts and potholes throwing up rocks and dust. Sometimes we would hit a deeper rut, and all of us boys would be thrown up into the air where we would stay for just a split second before we came crashing back down on the seat in a tangled heap, grasping for something to hang on to that might stabilize us. We would catch our breath, look over at each other, and bust out laughing. There were no seatbelts in those days, and the danger of getting thrown around just increased the joy of the experience. I could smell sagebrush and pine as we rocked along. It was a glorious ride, and I always enjoyed it immensely.

Once we got to the sawmill Mr. Bernandez would turn off the engine, and we would coast a ways down a little hill to a spot close to the operations. The truck had been so noisy that the silence was weird. He would set the brake and look in the mirror to see if Yas and Joe were still there. After he saw them jump down off the back of the truck he would sit up straight, kind of stretching his back. He would look at us with a grin and say, "End of the line. Everybody hop out." We would eagerly throw open the big creaky door and pile out. We left our sack lunches behind in the truck, taking only our energy and enthusiasm with us.

Yas had been appointed as our tutor, but there was work to be done at the mill. In order to fulfill both responsibilities he had adopted an approach that worked quite well. We would gather around him at the mill and squat on our haunches. He would give us a piece of paper with instructions and a map drawn on it.

"If you follow this map correctly you will eventually make it to an interesting site. On your way there you must find these things," he would say quietly. He would point to a list of about two dozen things we were to find on our walk. They would be such things as "a blaze on a large pine," or "a crow's nest," or "a deer trail." His routes would start off at the mill and head out in a compass direction. Hutch had an old pocket compass which we used to navigate by. Yas would point out which direction to start on, and we would use the compass to stay true to the direction. The goal was to make it to the destination by noon. We knew when it was noon because Mr. Bernandez would blow a big steam whistle which was there at the mill. We would wait until Yas would show up with our sack lunches. I don't know how he did it, but even if we were not at the exact right destination he would find us. We would all eat together, and Yas would quiz us about what we had seen. He would explain why he had wanted us to find those things, and he would teach us the importance of each one. After we finished our food he would continue our lessons.

"Stand together over there shoulder to shoulder," he would say and patiently wait while we got into position. "Now close your eyes, and become very quiet." When we had been still for a couple of minutes he would say, "Hutch, what do you hear? Listen closely, and tell us everything you hear."

Up in those mountains there were no airplanes or cars making noise. The only sounds that we could hear were made by the nature that surrounded us. We strained our ears to hear. Hutch would start to list the things he was hearing, and Yas would stop him.

"English is a good language, but it is a listing language," Yas would tell us. "Navajo is a better language because it is a describing language. Try to think about describing what you hear. You heard a bird. That is good. What kind of bird? Is it a small sound or a shrill sound? Is it one bird or many birds? Can you tell from the sound if it is a large bird or a small bird?"

We all had to go through the same exercise. After listening and describing what we heard Yas would ask us what we smelled or what we felt. We went through these exercises so many times that we began to incorporate them into everything we did. Regardless of whether Yas was with us or not, when we were walking along in the forest we would stop and hear and smell and observe.

After we completed our exercises Yas would explain to us why he wanted us to see the place to which he had sent us. Sometimes there had been a famous battle at the site, and Yas would describe it to us. Sometimes he sent us to a place simply because the view was outstanding.

One day he sent us to the edge of a cliff overhang. It was a very large rock that didn't have anything growing on it, the surface swept clean by wind and rain. We met Yas there at noon and ate our lunches while looking at a horizon that disappeared way out in the distance. Because of places like that I am convinced to this day that there is something pure and good and almost mystic about the mountains on the Jemez reservation.

When lunch had been eaten and we were sitting quietly looking out over the wonderful scene before us, Jerry turned to me and asked a question.

"Dale, all white people have a middle name," he said as if it was a known fact. "I don't know why they have middle names, but I have noticed it. So, what is your middle name?"

"My middle name is Benjamin," I replied with a smile. "My

Grandpa Sims's first name was Benjamin, and I have that as my middle name."

"How ironic," Yas said, shaking his head. "Do you know what the word Benjamin means?" he asked me. I shook my head in the negative, and Yas gave out a little sigh. "It literally means 'son of the right hand,' or you can think of it meaning 'favorite son.'"

"What does ironic mean?" I asked him.

He studied me for bit and then reached down and picked up a small rock. He closed his fist around it and shook it while he was talking. "It means that something is the opposite of what it says." He opened his fist and gave me the rock. It was warm from being in his hand. "I do not think that you are your father's favorite son."

"I don't understand," I said, almost in tears. "I try to always obey. I try to help around the house. I look after the little kids and help them." I threw the rock as far as I could and watched it disappear over the edge of the cliff. "Why doesn't my dad treat me like the other kids?"

Hutch and Jerry reached over and touched me lightly on my arm and shoulder to show that they cared. I appreciated the small gesture and took comfort from it.

"I don't know the answer, Young White," Yas said quietly. "What I do know is that you have a Heavenly Father. God is our father, and we can trust that He loves us and cares for us. It does not matter about your earthly father. Remember that you have a Heavenly Father who will teach you and watch over you."

Yas got up and helped us to our feet. "I have to go back to work now. You can roam around all you want this afternoon. When the shadows lengthen you must start making your way to the mill. When the whistle blows you must be there quickly. I will see you there." He smiled and shook each of our hands. If I had known what was to happen that afternoon I would have taken his hand and never let him go. Instead I simply waved at his retreating back.

We stayed at the cliff overhang for another hour just looking and listening. We talked about school and our families. We talked about hunting and fishing and camping. When we got tired of talking we decided to go exploring. We set off in the general direction of the sawmill and then followed a deer trail that led off to our right. We were not paying much attention to where we were going or what we were doing. The weather was great, we were enjoying each other's company, and the whole afternoon stretched out before us as if time was suspended forever. We were walking single-file, Jerry in the lead, when suddenly he stopped and held up his hand.

"I smell smoke," he said. "Do you smell it?"

I tried to pay more attention to my surroundings, standing still with my face tilted up, taking in big deep breaths through my nostrils. Hutch was doing the same thing.

"I smell it, too," I told Jerry. I pointed to my left. "I think it is coming from over there. Let's go see what is going on."

Jerry nodded and veered off toward the smell, Hutch and I following close behind. We didn't walk far, just a few more minutes, when Jerry stopped again. He turned to us and hissed in a whispery voice, "Get down!"

We immediately dropped down on all fours and followed Jerry as he crept up to a stand of bushes. Jerry stopped, and Hutch and I crawled up next to him. We cautiously lifted our heads to have a look. Ahead of us was a clearing with a small campfire going. There was a table set up by the fire. I saw tin cans of food on the table along with plates and forks and knives. There were two tents set up on the other side of the clearing, one small and one large. Then I saw something that caught and held my attention. Hanging from trees on the other side of the fire were the carcasses of three large bucks. They had been strung up by their antlers. I could see that their bellies had been slit and all their innards taken out of them. A small puddle of blood lay in the dirt under each carcass.

"Wow," I said loudly, standing up for a better look. Hutch did the same thing, but Jerry remained on all fours. "Let's go look," I said and Hutch smiled in agreement.

"No," Jerry said in a loud whisper. "Don't go over there. Something doesn't feel right to me. I think these are poachers."

"What's a poacher?" I asked.

Jerry looked around before answering, as if he were afraid of something. "Poachers kill animals in places they are not supposed to go. They don't have permission to hunt, but they do it anyway."

I looked back at the peaceful campground. It looked safe to me. "How do you know these are poachers?" I asked.

Jerry just shrugged. "It doesn't feel right," he said, screwing up his face.

I looked again and then made up my mind. "I am going to have a look at those deer," I said. I pushed past Jerry and walked into the clearing. Hutch followed, and we grinned at each other. We walked over to the deer and looked up at the bodies. I reached out to touch their hides and hooves. Hutch did the same and he commented in a loud voice about the size of the antlers on his deer. Before I could reply I heard a noise behind me and turned to see what it was.

A man came stumbling out of the small tent. He was a short, wiry man who looked like he needed a shave. He was wearing blue jeans, boots, and a red and black flannel shirt. He had a baseball cap on his head. He stood still for a minute looking at us in a shocked manner. He shook his head and then his whole body. "Good sweet Jesus!" he said loudly. "Where did you boys come from?"

"Hey, mister," I said with a smile. "My friend and I saw the deer hanging here, and we just wanted to get a better look. Did you shoot them?"

He took off his hat and threw it on the ground. Then he stomped around a little bit and picked up the hat again. He came toward us kind of waving the hat. "You kids have to get out of here, do you understand me? You have to leave right now. For your own sake I am telling you to get the hell out of here!" I looked behind him in time to see Jerry take off running in the direction of the sawmill.

"I'm sorry, mister," I said. "We didn't mean anything by coming here."

Then a man came out of the big tent. He was a large man with a black beard and shaggy hair. He was wearing blue jeans, boots, and a tee shirt with a hole in it. I also noticed that he was wearing a holster and gun on his belt. He stood looking at us, scratching his head. I saw another man almost as large as him lumber out of the big tent. The second man was dressed just like the first man. His tee shirt rode up on his large stomach, and I could see his belly button. The shaggy man walked forward a few steps and seemed to be studying Hutch and me. The short, wiry guy just groaned and kept running his hand over his face as if to wipe something away. He came over to stand by the shaggy man.

"Listen, Greg," he said in a pleading voice. "These here boys are just leaving right now, ain't ya, boys," he said with an attempt at a smile. He nodded his head up and down like it was on a string.

The shaggy man looked at him as if he were an insect. "Shut up, Dan. These boys just dropped into our lap, and I intend to keep them there," he said in a determined tone of voice.

The fat guy laughed and said, "That's a good one, Greg. Yeah, we do intend to keep them there."

Dan went to stand in front of the other two. "Listen, just listen to me for a minute," he pleaded. "These are white boys. They are not like them Mexican kids you had at other times. White kids are looked after. Their parents have to be around here somewhere." Dan looked at us and then back at Greg. "We don't want the authorities combing these hills looking for lost white boys. People care about what happens to white kids. Now, if they was Mexican or Indian we might be all right, but white kids. . ..Jeez, I don't know."

Greg used a massive arm to push Dan over to the side as he walked around him. He pointed at the fat man. "Stan, you help with that other kid, okay?" Stan nodded and went to stand by Hutch. Dan stood there biting his lip and wringing his hands.

Greg stopped a little bit in front of me and kind of bent down. "Do you like to look at the deer, kid? They are awful purty, ain't they?"

I turned and stroked the hide again. The buck was majestic even in death. I saw Hutch just staring at the man they called Stan. I started to turn around and say something when I saw Greg's fist coming at my face. I moved my head just a bit, and the fist hit me in the left eye rather than the right. The force of the blow lifted me off my feet, and I fell flat on my back. I looked over and saw the same thing happening to Hutch. My mind was having a hard time comprehending what was happening. I figured that the men were angry because we had been messing around with their deer carcasses. But all they would have had to say was that we had to go, and Hutch and I would have politely left.

My eye was almost swelled shut, but I could see some through it. I looked over at Hutch who had also been knocked on the ground. The fat man walked over and hit him right in the mouth. Blood spurted out, and Hutch started to cry. The fat man straightened up and laughed. I felt fingers grabbing my hair, pulling me off my back to my knees. I was so stunned that I didn't cry. I knew what pain was. I had felt worse pain before. I was quickly becoming angry, outraged at the way we were being treated. Greg bent down and looked in my face. I spit in his eye and immediately felt better. Greg pulled back his hand and slapped me hard across the face. My head swiveled, and my body followed. I was wallowing in the dust when I felt fingers in my hair again. This time I was lifted to my feet, but my knees were so weak I could hardly stand.

I heard Hutch crying, giving out great heaving sobs of pain and fear. Greg pulled back his hand and made a fist. This time he hit me right in the stomach. I doubled over and fell to the ground. Once more he grabbed my hair and set me on my knees. I was gasping for breath. Anger had left me and a cold hard knot of fear began to take its place.

Dan ran over to stand in front of me. "Okay, Greg, now that you and Stan have had your fun you should just let these kids go. There is no reason to continue beating them."

Greg stood up and moved forward until he was nose to nose with Dan. "I have only begun to have my fun. That boy is not going anywhere until I am satisfied. You know those Mexican kids we used last year? Well, nobody has asked us about them. Their death never even made it into the newspaper. We used 'em up and threw them over a cliff. By the time their bodies were found they had decomposed, and everybody thought that they had died in a tragic accident." Greg laughed and stuck his huge fist under Dan's nose.

I noticed that Greg had a forehead that stuck out and kind of hung over his eyes. Even though he was a large man his eyes looked small and had an evil glint to them. Dan kind of shrunk down and just slinked away. "That's what I thought!" Greg yelled after him. "That's what I thought!"

While Greg and Dan were talking I heard Hutch crying inconsolably. His sobs were deep and painful. I was still trying to catch my breath while I kneeled there in the dirt. I looked up at the deer carcass as Greg and Dan argued, and I suddenly knew that I was going to die. I wasn't sure what the large man would do to me before I died, but that paled compared to the idea of death. My legs had no strength to carry me away. I looked around for an avenue of escape, and I knew that there was no way out. I began to shake uncontrollably. Fear sat on me, and I stared death right in the face.

Suddenly in the midst of all of that I remembered Uncle. He had told me that I must drink what God gives me to drink each day. I figured that God had given me pain, sorrow, and death for the day, and I must accept it. I also remembered distinctly, just as if Uncle were there with me, how he touched me with his cane and said, "You can decide to be strong and brave or weak and cowardly." A great peace came over me as I made my decision. I straightened up, and my breathing became more measured. I had decided a few months ago that my death song would be "This is My Father's

World." After I heard Yas sing one verse I looked it up in our hymnbook and memorized the whole thing. I wasn't sure that I had time to sing the whole song so I chose to sing the last verse. I opened my mouth and sang as loud as I could.

"This is my Father's world, O let me ne'er forget, that though the wrong seems oft so strong, God is the ruler yet. This is my Father's world, the battle is not done; Jesus who died shall be satisfied, and earth and heaven be one."

Hutch had stopped crying.

"Stay strong, Hutch. Stay strong, and be brave," I shouted to him.

Stan slapped him hard in the face, and Hutch sprawled in the dirt. He slowly picked himself up, and even though he was bleeding he didn't cry.

Dan and Greg had frozen in their tracks. Dan turned back to look at me with his mouth hanging open. Greg hooked his thumbs into his belt and stared at me with his small evil eyes.

"What was that?" Greg yelled at me. When I didn't answer he yelled again even louder. "WHAT WAS THAT?"

"That was my death song," I said as I lifted my chin in defiance. "Every brave has a death song, and that is mine. God holds me in his hand."

Greg stomped over until he was right in front of me. He leaned down until he could look me right in the eye. "Listen up, pretty boy," he growled at me. "There has never been a God. There is no God now, and there never will be a God. You want to know why I am so sure of that fact? Because I was in the war. I saw thousands and thousands of dead bodies. I saw bombs rain down on us as we sat helpless in fox holes. Men cried out for God to save them and guess what? The bombs fell on them anyway and obliterated any evidence that they ever existed." He stood up tall and swung his arms wide, swiveling to look from Dan to Stan and back. "Where was God when we needed him? Have you two ever seen God? No, of course not. That is. . ." and he bent down again to look me in the face ". . . because there IS NO GOD, YOU STINKING MAGGOT!"

He slowly reached down and unzipped his pants. He looked over at Stan who did the same thing. He laughed and put his hands on his hips. "I am going to do whatever I want to do with you, and you cannot do anything about it. Then I am going to do your friend over there, and Stan is going to do you. We are going to take turns until we are just too tired to do anything else. Then I am going to take you to a cliff and end your miserable life. When you die you will know the truth. There is no God to complain to. You are born, and then you die. That's it! God does not exist, and he will not save you."

Then I heard God call my name. At first I thought it was my imagination, but then I saw Stan and Dan and Greg kind of turn their heads toward the sound. I heard it again.

"Dale Benjamin," God called louder and closer than last time. It was weird, but God sure sounded like a Navajo to me. I thought that maybe it was because I was in the Brave Family and had sung my death song.

Just then I saw Yas and Joe burst through the bushes and jump into the clearing. Yas ran around Greg and knelt right in front of me, shielding me from the large man. Joe did the same, running around Stan and kneeling down to grab Hutch by the shoulders. Yas looked me over, and I saw anger flash in his eyes. Greg, Stan, and Dan stood frozen as if they were unsure of what was happening.

"Are you okay, Dale Benjamin?" Yas asked. I nodded in stunned silence. Yas put his hands on both sides of my head. "Listen quickly, Young White," he said urgently. "Look behind me at the bushes. Do you see Jerry?" I looked and saw Jerry's face poking up above the bushes. I nodded to show that I had seen him. "Good," Yas said. "Now I want you to stand up, go over and take Hutch by the hand, run to Jerry and then keep running all the way to the mill. Don't stop, do you hear me?" He lifted me to my feet, and I ran over to Hutch. Joe lifted him to his feet, and I took him by the hand.

Greg came alive with a roar. "Ain't no stupid idiot Indian going to take away my pleasure toy," he yelled loudly.

I saw Yas go to stand in front of him, talking quietly and making motions with his hands as if to calm the man down. Joe was doing the same thing with Stan. I pulled hard on Hutch's hand, and together we ran over to Jerry. He took off running, and we followed close behind, running as fast as we could for our very lives. I heard several gunshots behind us, and yelling and screaming. I just ran faster and urged Hutch to do the same. He was having trouble breathing because of his busted nose and lip but he somehow was able to keep up.

We ran and ran, the sweat just pouring off of us. We finally came in sight of the mill, and I tried to pick up speed, but my legs were turning to jelly. When we got to the mill we just collapsed on the ground. I heard sirens and rolled over to see two police cars driving up to the mill. Mr. Bernandez went over to talk to the policemen. He came back and lifted up Jerry in his arms.

"You boys stay here," he commanded. "Jerry is going with me to show us the way. That other policeman will stay with you to keep you safe until we get back." He ran with Jerry over to one of the police cars. He quickly settled himself and Jerry in the car, which took off before he had even closed the door. The other officer came over to help us to our feet so that we could walk to his car. He helped us into the back seat. He squatted down outside the open door to talk with us. We told him everything that happened, taking turns to tell the story, me talking more than Hutch because of his busted lip and nose. The officer hung his head and spit on the ground.

"How did you guys know to come out here?" I asked him.

He pointed his chin toward the mill. "Mr. Bernandez has a short wave radio over there in case of emergencies. He fired it up and told us to come out, so here I am."

The officer got up and opened the trunk of his car. He came back with a canteen of water and an old rag. He wet the rag and used it to wipe the blood off our faces. He pressed the rag gently against my swollen eye, and the cool water felt good. He walked over to the mill and came back with a couple of plastic cups and a gallon jug of drinking water. He poured water and handed it to us. I drank thirstily, but Hutch just held his cup. I noticed that he was shaking. The officer poked around in the trunk again and found an old blanket that he wrapped around Hutch. Soon Hutch was asleep in the back of the car. We waited for what seemed like a long time before we saw the other police car coming back to the mill from the forest. The car drove fast and skidded to a stop. Mr. Bernandez and Jerry got out. I heard Mr. Bernandez talk to the officer through the driver's side window of the car.

"Do you think you can get those men to the hospital in Albuquerque before they die?" he asked.

"I don't know," the officer shouted. "They were shot, cut up, and beat mighty bad. Those dudes left them for dead, that's for sure. I will drive as fast as I can, and we will do everything we can to save them." He gunned the engine, turned the car in a tight circle and drove as fast as possible over the bumpy road out of the reservation.

Mr. Bernandez walked slowly over to our car. He looked inside and saw that Hutch was fast asleep on the back seat. He gently picked up his son and carried him over to the logging truck. On his way back he stopped and spoke quietly to Jerry, who hopped into the logging truck to sit beside the sleeping Hutch.

"I am going to take Jerry to his house and my son back to his mom. Would you mind taking Dale home? He lives close to my place there in town. He can show you the way," Mr. Bernandez said.

The officer nodded and watched as Mr. Bernandez got in his truck and drove off. The officer told me to crawl up into the front seat. He fired up the engine and drove us slowly out of the reservation and back toward town. I fell asleep and only woke up when the car stopped over by my house. "This is your place isn't it, kid?" the officer asked. I nodded, and he nodded back at me. "Well," he said with a sigh, "Let's go in and talk with your parents."

Together we walked to the kitchen door. I opened it up, and we walked in to see Mom cooking supper over the stove. She turned away from the stove, and all color left her face as she looked at me and then the officer. The policeman had taken off his hat and was turning it nervously in his hand.

"Hello, Mrs. Sims," he said quietly. "Is your husband at home?"

Mom didn't even reply. She ran quickly out of the room, and soon she and Dad were hurrying back in with worried looks on their faces.

The officer shook Dad's hand and motioned to the table. "Perhaps we should sit down," he said.

Dad helped Mom sit shakily in a chair and he kind of plopped himself into one as he scanned my face. The officer and I sat in chairs across the table from them. We looked at each other for a second, and I saw great huge tears start to flow down Mom's face. The officer cleared his throat and then began to fill them in on what he knew about the incident in the mountains. As he spoke Mom would give out little wailing sounds and cover her mouth with her hand. When he finished Mom came over and held me close, her tears falling like a stream on my shirt. Dad had listened with his chin in his hand and had gradually sunk down in his chair as the officer wrapped up his report.

"Those Indian guys did the bravest thing I have ever heard of," he said with admiration in his voice. "They risked their lives to save your son and the Bernandez kid."

Dad walked him to the door and shook his hand. Mom just held me tight, sobbing and making small wailing sounds. Dad came back to us and pried me out of her arms. He knelt down and examined my eye. He looked me up and down without saying a word. He gently guided me so that I sat again in a chair. Mom sat next to me and held my hand. Dad sat across the table staring at me. "Tell me in your own words about what happened," he commanded.

I started slowly but talked faster as I got into the story. I told him everything and then just kind of ran out of words.

"Did that man touch you?" Dad asked.

"Sure," I said. "Just look at my eye. He hit me and slapped me," I told him.

"No," Dad said quietly. "Did he touch you in any other way, such as touching your privates?"

I wasn't sure what Dad was getting at, so I said, "No, he just beat me."

Mom got up and made me a plate of food. The little kids came in, and she began to serve them as well. Dad got a plate of food, but he didn't eat. After I finished eating Mom led me over to the roll-away bed where she undressed me. I had scratches on my knees and elbows. My chin had a large welt on it. My left eye was almost swollen shut. Mom kissed the top of my head and helped me get under the covers. I fell asleep almost immediately.

I was awakened later that night when I heard Mom and Dad talking quietly in the other room. It was dark in the house, and I noticed that Roger and Paul were in bed with me, fast asleep.

Dad was talking in a kind of hissing whisper. "Those men were queers. We had them in the Navy. I hate queers. Now our son has been turned into one."

"No, Jim," Mom replied. "He said that the men didn't touch him other than to beat him."

"That is a lie," Dad replied with an angry hiss. "He just doesn't understand what all of that was about so he doesn't know how to explain it. Our son is a queer."

"Don't say that!" Mom wailed quietly. "I refuse to believe that."

There was silence for a little bit, and Dad spoke up again. "I forbid him from going to the sawmill ever again. I don't even want him going to the reservation. He has been ruined by the Indians. We will never get him back. Once a queer, always a queer."

I heard Mom sobbing again.

I wasn't sure what a queer was, but it didn't sound good. I knew that the Greg guy had beat me up good, but I was sure that he had not done anything else. I was also sure that God had used Yas and Joe to save Hutch and me from death. That evil man with the shaggy hair was wrong. God existed, and He saved me. He heard my cry, and he called my name. He held me in his hands.

I felt someone crawl into bed beside me. I rolled over to see Linda looking at me with concern. We looked at other for minute before she spoke.

"Your eye looks bad," she said in a concerned voice. "Does it hurt?" I nodded, and she reached out to gently touch it. "I heard the policeman tell Mom and Dad and then I heard what you said to them. You were brave. I think God saved your life."

I nodded again, not sure of what to say. Linda reached over and put her arms around me. It was so comforting that I began to cry. She just continued to hold me until my crying stopped.

"I am glad that God kept you from dying," she said. "You are a good big brother. Maybe God knew that I needed you to help me." She smiled in the dark, and I smiled back at her. We looked at each for a few more minutes. I was very tired, and my eyelids grew heavy. I fell asleep in my sister's arms, and we stayed that way until morning.

THIRTEEN

THE UPWARD WAY

LATE AUGUST 1963

M y mother kept me home from church and school for many days while I healed up. Hutch and Jerry came by for a few minutes each day after school to hand over some homework assignments. Hutch had some bruises and scabs on his face. It was good to see him, but I worried about him. One evening he laughed at a small joke that Jerry made. After that I figured that he would come out all right, and I could stop worrying about him. They also shared any news they had of Yas and Joe. They were both still in the hospital. Their beatings had been terrible. Yas had been shot in the leg and one arm. Joe had been stabbed and slashed with a knife. Both men had been beaten with fists, stones, and clubs. They had broken bones and internal injuries. They had almost died, but the doctors were able to save them, and they seemed to be on the mend. Jerry said that Yas had requested that pain-killing medicine not be used, but sometimes the pain was too much, and the doctors gave it to him anyway.

Dad was very strange during those days. I caught him looking at me as if he was trying to decide something. He didn't badger me about chores or correct me for anything. He and Mom continued to have whispered conversations that sometimes got a little heated, and their voices would be raised. Dad would look over at me and kind of clear his throat. Mom would blush a little bit and then come over to talk with me. She would smile and hug me, tousling my hair and rubbing my back a little bit. Sometimes she asked me what I was thinking about. Although the attack in the forest occupied most of my thoughts I usually lied and told her that I was thinking about a book I was reading. That seemed to satisfy her, and she would go about her household chores humming a little tune.

I was still sore when I finally went back to school. The bruises and welts were changing colors to green and brown. As I walked past the office Mrs. Zonni came out and stood in front of me. She leaned down and studied my face.

"Are you okay?" she asked with concern in her voice. I nodded without saying anything. She put her arm around me and guided me into the quiet office area. "Everyone has heard about. . ." She hesitated and shook her head. "We all heard about what happened in the Jemez. Was it very bad?"

"I spit in his eye," I said. "Then I sang my death song. I thought I was going to die."

Mrs. Zonni blinked and leaned down to get on my level. "Good for you!" she said forcefully. "If I had been there I would have killed that man. Well. . .he really wasn't a man. A real man doesn't beat up kids." She stood up tall and looked at me thoughtfully. "You have a death song?"

I nodded and sang it for her. Her lips quivered, and she put a hand over her eyes for a minute. She reached out and grabbed me, pressing me to her. "I am so proud of you, Young White," she said in a shaky voice. That was really strange because she had told me early on not to use that name at school. She released me and kind of waved at the door with one hand while she wiped tears from her eyes with the other. "You go on to class now. I will see you later."

I walked out of the office and down the hall to my classroom. Mrs. Garza was at her desk. The room was empty because all the kids were still out on the playground trying to burn off some energy before settling into their seats. I said, "Good morning," to Mrs. Garza and handed her my homework assignments. She didn't even look at the papers. She gazed at my face for a minute. Slowly and gently she reached out and touched the bruises and welts.

"I am sorry, Dale, that you were hurt. I am glad that you are here today." She opened the top desk drawer and pulled out a chocolate candy bar. She held it up so that I could see it. "You must stay inside during recess for the next week. I want those hurt places to heal up. You may eat this at recess, but only when everyone is gone." I took the bar and went to my seat, waiting quietly for all of the other children to come inside. Mrs. Garza regarded me thoughtfully and then dropped her gaze to her desk and shuffled papers around.

I heard the tromp of shoes and the excited voices coming down the hall before the kids even made it to the room. Jerry and Reuben were the first two through the door. When they saw me they just stopped in their tracks, which prevented the other kids from coming in. I heard shouts of "What's going on?" and "Hey, move already."

Reuben shouted back behind him, "Dale is in the room."

The hallway got quiet. Jerry came forward and shook my hand before sliding into his desk seat. Reuben did the same. So did all the other kids. One at a time they came quietly to my desk and shook my hand before going to sit down. Mrs. Garza stepped out of the room for a minute, and when she returned she was wiping her eyes with a paper hanky. I was a white kid surrounded by a crowd of Indian and Mexican kids, but that morning I felt that I was part of something bigger than myself. I heard Mrs. Garza sigh, and I saw her standing in front of the class as if she were collecting herself. She forced a smile onto her face.

"Good morning, class," she said, and our day began. We recited the pledge. Mrs. Garza began our lessons, and the day began to flow in its normal way.

That morning, during recess, I took out the chocolate bar and slowly nibbled away at it. I heard a noise at the door, and when I looked over I saw Mary standing there.

"Is it okay if I talk with Dale for a few minutes?" she asked my teacher. Mrs. Garza smiled and nodded. There was a big smile on Mary's face as she came over to see me.

"How are you, Young White?" she asked.

I held up the candy bar. "Mrs. Garza gave me some candy, so I think I am doing fine." I broke off a piece for Mary and gave it to her. She pulled a desk around so that we could sit face to face and kind of squirmed her way into it. We ate the chocolate together and smiled at each other.

"Yas sent me to check on you," she said. "He has been worried about you."

"How is he?" I asked. "I heard that he was beat up and shot and stabbed."

"Yes," Mary said sadly. "That is true, but he is getting much better. He is back on the reservation now, and he is recovering." She cleared her throat and ducked her head for a second before raising it to look at me. "What happened in the Jemez?" she asked. "I know what happened to Yas, but I don't know what happened to you."

I gave her a brief account. She sat up straight with one hand over her mouth and the other clutching at her throat. Tears welled up in her eyes. When I finished she let out a deep breath as if she had been holding it in.

"You have a death song? Can I hear it?" she asked.

I sang the song, and she began to sob. When I finished she wiped her eyes. "I am so sorry, Young White, but I am glad that God heard your song and sent Yas."

"Did Yas get to sing his death song?" I asked her.

She blinked her eyes as if surprised to hear that he had one. "What is Yas's song?" she asked. "Do you know it? Can you sing it for me?"

I thought for a minute. My mind went back to that afternoon with Uncle, and I heard Yas sing the song clearly in my memory. I sang it to my best of my ability.

"I'm pressing on the upward way, new heights I'm gaining every day; still praying as I onward bound, Lord, plant my feet on higher ground. Lord, lift me up and let me stand, by faith, on heaven's table land. A higher plane than I have found, Lord, plant my feet on higher ground."

"It is a hymn," I told her. "I saw it in our hymnbook at church."

She hung her head and stretched out her hands in front of her on the desktop. "Thank you," she said. "That is good to know." She had a small leather pouch hanging from her shoulder, kind of like a purse. She folded back the flap, reached in, and pulled something out. She held it out for me and dropped it into my open palm. It was a polished black rock. "Yas told me to give this to you. He said that you should keep this to remind you of Uncle's vision."

I closed my fist around the rock and shook it just like I had seen Yas do. "I wish I could go see him," I said. "Dad has forbidden me from going back to the reservation."

Mary chuckled and shook her head. "Your dad. . ." she said ruefully. She did not finish that thought, but she did not have to. I understood. She squirmed out of the desk and stood up. "Yas said that he is praying for you. Perhaps when he is fully recovered he will come and see you." She turned with a smile and left the room.

That day finished just like every other school day. Linda and I rode the bus home together. She talked non-stop about her day while we rode. I tried to listen, but my mind was on the black rock that I held in my hand. It was a message from Yas that said, "All will be well." I stuffed the rock into my pocket and have kept it over all of these years to remind me of the vision.

The days, weeks, and months rolled by with a return to some kind of normalcy. My bruises and welts disappeared. Hutch gradually quit coming by for visits. I think he was haunted by what happened, and every time he saw me it reminded him of the event.

Jerry continued to feed me news about Yas and his recovery. He had started to drink again, and sometimes he passed out. Mary and Yas's mother looked after him. There were some old Marine buddies of his that had showed up on the reservation, Navajo men who had served alongside Yas in Korea. They encouraged Yas to drink, and Jerry said that everyone was worried. The men seemed to be worthless good-for-nothings who lived to create trouble. I prayed for my friend. I asked God to give him peace and help him to get well in mind, body, and spirit.

Sometimes in the dark, still hours of the night I would think about Yas's problems. I began to consider that perhaps I was somehow to blame for his problems. If I had not gone to look at those stupid deer carcasses none of what followed would have happened. Yas would not have had to come rescue a stupid white boy. He would never have been badly hurt and gone to the hospital. He would never have had to spend time in recovery, and he would not be drinking again. Hutch would not have been beaten badly. All of that was because of me. I despised myself for not being smarter and for making such a poor decision. I despised myself so much that sometimes I wished that the shaggy large man had actually thrown me over the cliff. In the night I cried bitter tears of regret. I was not sure how anyone could ever respect me or trust me.

One evening there was a knock at the kitchen door. It was right after supper and the table was cleared off, the dishes cleaned up. Dad opened the door cautiously and then wider. He had a whispered conversation with someone outside and then stood aside to let them come in. I watched as Mary and Andy slowly walked into the room. Their heads were bowed, and I sensed that something was wrong. Dad motioned to the table and pulled out chairs for them to sit down. Mom and Dad sat across the table from them. I stood in the doorway between the kitchen and living room. Andy was the first to speak.

"Something happened today, and Yas has died," he said

abruptly. "I don't know if there is really an easy way to break the news." He looked at me with a bleak expression on his face. He was usually inscrutable and to see him this way was as shocking as the news. "I am sorry, Young White."

"No!" I shouted. "It is not possible. How, how could he have died?"

Mary got up and walked over to me. Taking me by the hand she led me over to the table. She sat while I just stood there in disbelief at what I heard.

"Yas died trying to stop some people from doing something wrong," she said while looking intently into my eyes. "You need to know that he died doing something good." She cleared her throat and told all of us about what had happened.

Yas was getting restless just sitting around. He was starting to walk well again. He had also begun to gradually give up alcohol. About noon he had asked Mary to take him to one of the trading posts that ringed the reservation. He said he wanted to buy a few little things, but he really just wanted to go somewhere different and move around a bit. They went in Mary's old car, and when they got to the trading post, they saw that two of Yas's Marine friends were there. They were standing outside of the building yelling and throwing rocks. Mary stayed by the car while Yas went to see what was wrong. The men were angry because Mr. Compton, the white man who owned the trading post, would not sell them liquor. He told them to leave. He said he didn't have any alcohol in the place, but the men thought he was lying. While Yas was talking to them one of the men went to their truck and got a pistol out of it. The other man went over to a new station wagon that was owned by Mr. Compton and began to use large stones to bust out the windows. Mr. Compton came to the door of the trading post with a rifle, and Yas's friend raised his pistol to shoot him. Yas jumped in front of his friend and tried to wrestle the pistol away from him. The pistol went off, and Yas was shot. Mr.

Compton shot his rifle off into the air, and the men got into their truck and drove off.

"I ran over to Yas to help him," Mary said through her tears. "There was a tremendous amount of blood. I held Yas as the blood drained from his body. I saw the light dim in his eyes. He said, "Heaven's tableland," then he took a deep breath and died. I could not save him." Mary looked around the table at all of us. "I could not save him," she said again. Her tears fell like rain, and she put her hand on her head as she cried. I began to cry as well, and I hugged her. We stayed that way for a long time. Finally Mom came over and took me away from Mary. She brought me to her chair and set me in her lap. I clung to her neck and just sobbed.

I heard Andy ask Dad to preach Yas's funeral, and Dad said he would do it. Andy said that the funeral would be the next day about noon.

"We want to know if Dale can go back with us to the reservation," Mary asked through her tears. I quit sobbing so that I could hear better. Snot was running from my nose, and I wiped it away with my shirt sleeve. "We are going to handle Yas's body in the old way, and we want Dale to see how it is done. Yas always said that he wanted Dale to be a different white, one who knew how the People did things. He felt that it was important for some reason."

Mom looked at Dad, and it was like they had a silent conversation. Mom nodded, and Dad nodded. I don't know why they agreed to let me go with them. Perhaps it was because I had already been through so much, or maybe it was because Yas had saved my life. I was just grateful to be able to go. Mary reached across the table and patted Mom on the arm. "We will take care of him," she assured Mom. "Mrs. Roberts said that she will help as well. He can sit with you at the service tomorrow."

Dad looked at Andy. "My son is different, and I don't know yet if it is a good different or a bad different. I only ask that you keep him safe with you. Don't let anything happen to him."

Andy nodded and stood up. Mary stood and followed him as he

walked to the door. I gave Mom a last hug and started to walk around the table, but Dad grabbed my arm. "Son, do as they tell you, but keep a sharp lookout for trouble." He let go of my arm and made a motion as if he were shooing me away. I hesitated just a second and then rushed over and hugged Dad. He didn't hug back, but he didn't stop me from hugging him. He finally pushed me away, and I walked out the door behind Andy and Mary. We got into Andy's old truck and drove away.

I was wedged in the seat between Andy and Mary. Andy drove hunched over the steering wheel and stared straight ahead. Mary's head was bowed and an occasional sniffle escaped from her. I put my hand in my pocket and felt the rock that Yas had given me. He had touched the rock. He had chosen it specifically for me. He told Mary that he gave it to me so that I would remember the vision of Uncle. I thought and thought about that afternoon with Yas and Uncle. I tried to understand, but I could not make much sense of it.

We finally drove up to the village, and Andy drove around until he found a good spot to park the truck. We piled out and looked around a little bit. It was getting dark, the sun setting in a red haze.

Mary pointed with her chin in a direction off to our right. "I see the glow from a fire over there. I think that is where they are gathered."

We walked together in the direction of the fire's glow. I heard the people before I saw them. There was a great murmuring of voices and shuffling of feet. We rounded the corner of a hogan, and suddenly I saw many people gathered around a fire. They were all talking quietly among themselves, some standing together in small knots of people and others sitting on logs or chairs set around the fire. Mary and Andy walked over to talk with some of them. I sat on the end of a log and just stared at the fire. A woman came by and gave me a bowl with beans in it and some fry bread. I didn't think I was hungry, but I ended up eating the whole thing. The woman came back by and collected the bowl without saying anything. I felt a hand on my shoulder, and I looked around to see Mary standing there.

"Come with me, Young White. There is something I want you to see." She helped me stand up and grabbed my hand. She led over to a hogan that was surrounded by men. The men had on what looked like war paint. None of them wore shirts even though the evening was cool. Mary approached the door of the hogan, and I noticed that there was not a blanket hanging over the door. A light shone from inside the building. A painted man stood in front of the door, and Mary approached him.

"This is Young White," she told the man. "I want to show him what we are doing and explain to him what it means."

The man grunted and stepped aside. Mary pushed past him and stopped at the threshold. She pulled me over to stand beside her. I saw a hogan that was empty except for something in the middle of the floor. Small fires were burning around the inside circle of the building. The medicine man was chanting and dancing around whatever was in the middle of the room. I looked closely to see what was on the floor. At first I thought it was simply a blanket thrown down on the dirt floor. I looked closer and saw that a man was under the blanket. I saw his face, and it was Yas.

Mary leaned down and spoke softly to me as I watched the medicine man take some powder and throw it on the blanket. "This hogan belonged to Yas. You see that we brought him home. His body is resting on a blanket, and his body is covered by a blanket. Notice that there are tassels on the corners of the blankets. We believe that a man's spirit will leave his body and go into the blankets. The medicine man is praying that God will allow Yas's spirit to inhabit the blankets. He will pray and dance all night. In the morning we will take Yas's body away from here, but we will leave the blankets on the floor. We will knot up the tassels to keep Yas's spirit in them. We will put Yas's body in a casket. Then we will burn down this hogan so that Yas's spirit will be released to start the upward journey on the trail to the afterlife."

I looked at Yas's face flickering in the light of the fires. He seemed at peace to me. The medicine man danced over our way, and Mary kind of bowed to him as she backed us away from the building. "We have to go now," she told me. "I have some things to do to help the people prepare for tomorrow. You sit on that log. People know about you, Young White. They know of your bravery. They know of your strength. They know about the Zonni blessing. They will keep you safe, and they will look after you."

I watched Mary's retreating back before turning to look into the fire. I felt many eyes on me, but nobody spoke to me. I was surrounded by people, but I was not one of them. I would never be one of them. I was alone, and I felt the lonesome right down into my soul. I reached into my pocket and pulled out the black rock. What did it mean? Why was I here with these people? I did not have answers. I grew tired from the grief and stress of the evening. The fire held my eyes, but soon they fluttered closed, and I fell asleep.

The next morning I woke up in the mission building. I was lying on two blankets, and I was covered by a coat that I was sure belonged to Amos. I didn't know how I got there, but I was glad to be in someplace familiar. Mrs. Roberts came in carrying a plate of bacon, eggs, and toast.

"Get up, sleepy head," she said cheerfully. "It is almost 11:30. Your family will be here soon, and the service will begin about noon. You have to clean up and get ready."

I gratefully ate my food and submitted to Mrs. Roberts' attentions as she brushed my hair and tweaked my clothes into some semblance of shape. She took me by the hand and we walked over to the large square where the chairs were set up. Everything was set up just like the last time when we had the big funeral for the chief's daughter. Mrs. Roberts left me, and I sat in a folding chair under a canvas canopy and waited for everything to start. In the front, men were putting together a large platform. They worked silently and efficiently as if they had done this together many times before.

My eyes roamed over the area around and down toward the end of the village. In the distance I saw a large group making their way slowly toward me. I watched with interest as they drew closer. They were walking with a measured tread, and it was not obvious to me who they were or what they were doing. I waited patiently until I could see what was going on. One man stumbled slightly, and the whole group turned a bit, just enough for me to suddenly realize that they were carrying a coffin. I heard the men chanting something in a language I could not understand as they walked. I looked back at the stage and saw that some men were setting up a kind of table. I figured that the coffin would be set on that. As the men carrying the coffin got closer I recognized that Andy and Amos were helping to carry it. The men made their way to the platform and shoved the coffin up onto it. They each clambered up a short ladder so that they were soon standing on the platform. They took their places and picked up the coffin, grunting as they did so. They carefully edged up to the table and set the coffin on it, fiddling around with it until they were convinced that it was square and secure on the table. When everything seemed to be just right Amos lifted the coffin lid. All of the men looked into the coffin before turning away to climb back down. Amos and Andy stayed on the platform standing by the coffin. Men and women began to come by in a silent and steady stream. They each had something in their hands to put into the coffin. They handed their death gifts up to Amos and Andy who threw them into the coffin. I noticed that it didn't take long for the gifts to start overflowing the coffin.

My family showed up and came to sit by me. Paul was on one side of me, and Roger sat on the other. Dad climbed the ladder up to the platform. He spoke to Amos and Andy for a few minutes. A chair was passed up to the platform, and Dad sat in the chair. We all waited patiently as more people filed in, and the medicine man made his way among them. He chanted softly and threw some kind of powder over the people. I had heard that he had danced all night, and I wasn't sure how he had the strength to keep going.

Finally Dad stood up to speak. Andy acted as the interpreter. Dad talked about Yas and his military service. He talked about how Yas had tried to break the hold that alcohol had on him. Then Dad read a scripture, John 15:13. I remember it to this day.

"Greater love hath no man than this, that a man lay down his life for his friends," Dad said loudly. "That is what Yas did. He is a hero. He saved my son's life, and he saved the life of Mr. Compton at the trading post. Yas gave up his life so that others might live."

The people in the crowd began to make noises like grunts and yips and something that sounded like "haehae." I liked what Dad said because I regarded Yas as a hero. It was nice to hear Dad say it as well.

I looked over to the side of the square. There was a huge old cottonwood tree there. In the shade of that tree sat a small group of people. Looking closer I saw that Uncle was sitting in a chair, and behind him was Auntie with Mary beside her. I got up and walked over to them.

Uncle saw me first and waved his cane at me. I came up to them and said, "Hey." Auntie gave me a hug.

"How are you, Young White?" she asked me.

"I miss Yas," I said as I hung my head.

Uncle chuckled. "Yas is now on the upward way to heaven's table land. He is happy now and at peace. He is not there in the coffin, Young White."

"I know, I know," I said quickly. "That is only his body. I know that the real Yas is with Jesus."

"No," Uncle said, and Auntie chuckled. "I mean his body is not up there. He is not there in that coffin."

I looked at Uncle and thought that perhaps he was crazy. "Uncle," I began, "I saw the men carry his coffin to the platform. If he is not there then where is he?"

Uncle laughed a kind of creaking laugh, and it caused him to cough. Auntie rubbed his back until he could breathe better. "Look out there, Young White," he said. He pointed with his cane out to our right. I looked and saw something in the distance. I shaded my eyes to see better.

"What do you see?" Uncle asked.

"I think I see two men leading a horse that is hitched to a flatbed wagon. There is something on the wagon, but I can't see what it is because they are so far away."

Uncle nodded. "Those men are handling Yas's body in the old way, just as he asked to be handled. Mary and Andy and Amos helped me to set it up." I looked over at Mary, and she smiled at me.

"Those men will take Yas's body to a distant mesa," Uncle said. "They will find a place for his body and put him there. Eventually his body will turn to dust, and the dust will become part of the mesa. Whenever the wind blows over the mesa and dust comes off of the mesa a little bit of Yas will travel with the wind. Whenever you see dust you will see Yas. He will ride the wind and be free. He will always travel the upward way."

I looked out at the small group traveling in the distance. I watched until my eyes watered with the strain as they grew smaller and smaller. A bit of dust was stirred up and hid them from my sight. When the dust was gone I could no longer see them.

Mary came over to hug me. "We cannot tell people because it is not legal to do things like this in the old way. Just keep it to yourself. Do remember Yas, though, because he was a good man."

I reached into my pocket and pulled out the black rock. I held it up, and we all looked at it. "He gave his life for his friends," I said, fighting back the tears. "I hope that I can be that kind of friend to people someday."

Uncle nodded. "In my vision I saw that you ran well on the path. Trust God. Run strong. Be good."

That night when my family got home and we kids were all in bed, I lay there thinking about Uncle. I decided to trust God and be good. I just hoped that God would point out the path for me.

FOURTEEN

DUST CLOUDS

PRESENT DAY

W e left the area soon after the funeral and never went back to New Mexico. As I was growing up I longed to see the mountains and once again eat fry bread and beans. I wanted to see the way that the setting sun changed the colors of the trees from a greenish yellow to a deep green and finally to a dark blue that faded into black as night fell. I wanted to drink from the Jemez springs and roam the mountains once more. But, more than anything, I missed the wonderful people. They had been kind to me, a white kid in a brown world. They had taught me about kindness, integrity, compassion, and charity. For all of my days I will consider myself part of the Brave Family, a tribe that is fearless and strong, with the charge to help others.

Sometimes I take my black rock out of the box I have kept it in all of these years. I remember the message that the rock was meant to send. I remember the sender. I still miss Yas. He took a personal interest in me, and he taught me to be a better person. The things that I learned are things that still help me today.

I am very different from the rest of my family. My brothers, who were so very young when we lived among the Indians, do not remember that time. They do not know about the experiences or people who shaped my view of the world and my way of living in it.

I have gone through life feeling different from those around me because of my experiences. Sometimes I sit quietly and reflect on those far off days among the tribes. I try to bring the sights, sounds, and smells into sharp focus, but the dust of time and space obscures my vision. Yet, even then, I hear the voice of my friend Yas at those times when I am most alone. I remember his advice and his lessons. I remember his wisdom and his kindness. I remember his pain and his very hard fight against his demons. I want to be worthy of the effort he put into making me a better person. I have tried to understand the world in a bigger sense. I have determined to love people. I will give my life, to my dying breath, trying to teach and to help. I want to be worthy of the Zonni blessing. I want to be worthy of Uncle's vision.

Sometimes when I am out hunting or hiking or fishing the wind kicks up dust. I always figure that some of that dust has to be from my friend Yas. I welcome it because I know that someday I too will go from dust to dust. I will travel the upward way. In the meantime I will enjoy my Father's world. I say "Thank you!" to God every day for my life and the people who come out of the dust to cross my very narrow trail.

ABOUT THE AUTHOR

Dr. Sims has served as Associate Dean and Dean for the College of Business at Dallas Baptist University and is currently Senior Professor of Systems Technology and Information Management. He is a Fulbright Scholar and has been named outstanding professor of the year for the university (Piper Scholar) and the college of business. Dr. Sims has been married to the wonderful Debbie Sims, a retired Principal, for 43 years. They have a grown son and daughter and three grandsons. In his spare time Dr. Sims enjoys woodworking, writing, hunting, fishing, gardening, and spending time with his family.